A
CICERO
Workbook

Latin Literature Workbook Series

A Series Edited by LeaAnn A. Osburn

A Horace Workbook (2005)

A Horace Workbook Teacher's Manual (2006)

A Vergil Workbook (2006)

An Ovid Workbook (2006)

An Ovid Workbook Teacher's Manual (2007)

A Catullus Workbook (2006)

A
CICERO
Workbook

Jane W. Crawford
& Judith A. Hayes

With a Vocabulary by
Steven M. Cerutti, Patsy Rodden Ricks
& Sheila K. Dickison

Bolchazy-Carducci Publishers, Inc.
Wauconda, Illinois USA

Series Editor
LeaAnn A. Osburn

Volume General Editor
Donald E. Sprague

Volume Contributing Editor
Karen Singh

Cover Design
Adam Phillip Velez

A Cicero Workbook

by Jane W. Crawford and Judith A. Hayes

Bolchazy-Carducci Publishers, Inc.
1000 Brown Street
Wauconda, IL 60084 USA
www.bolchazy.com

Printed in the United States of America
2006
by United Graphics

ISBN-13: 978-0-86516-643-1
ISBN-10: 0-86516-643-9

The vocabulary of the present work is a compilation with some slight variations
of the glossaries published in *Cicero De Amicitia Selections,* by Patsy Rodden Ricks
and Sheila K. Dickison, Bolchazy-Carducci Publishers (2006): 65–73
© 2006 Bolchazy-Carducci Publishers and *M. Tulli Ciceronis Pro Archia Poeta Oratio*
2nd Edition by Steven M. Cerutti, Bolchazy-Carducci Publishers (2006): 105–128.
© 2006 Bolchazy-Carducci Publishers.

CONTENTS

FOREWORD

All Latin teachers want their students to read ancient authors in the original. Yet to study the authentic Latin of an ancient Roman author is a complex task. It requires comprehension of the text and its grammatical underpinnings; an understanding of the world events and the culture in which the work of literature was produced; an ability to recognize the figures of speech the author uses and to grasp the impact they have on the text; sensitivity to the way sound effects, including meter if a passage is poetry, interact with the meaning of the text; and the ability to probe whatever thoughts and ideas the author may be expressing. To be successful in this multifaceted task, students need not only a comprehensive textbook but also exercises of different kinds, in which to practice their newly developing literary and critical skills.

Students often need extensive drill and practice material—something not available in the traditional Latin author textbook—to help them master the grammar and syntax of the Latin text as well as the literary skills that the text demands of its readers. Teachers, too, no matter how many questions they ask in class to help their students analyze the syntax and the literary qualities of the text, often need and want more questions to be available. Realizing this need on the part of both students and teachers, Bolchazy-Carducci Publishers has begun to develop a series of workbooks to accompany Advanced Placement textbooks. There will be five workbooks in the series, one for each advanced placement author: Catullus, Cicero, Horace, Ovid, and Vergil. A team of authors—one, a university scholar with special expertise in the Latin literary text and the other, a high school Advanced Placement Latin teacher—will write each workbook.

Workbooks in this series will contain the Latin text as delineated on the Advanced Placement Syllabus and exercises that drill grammar, syntax, and figures of speech. In addition, multiple choice questions will be included and will focus on the student's comprehension of the passage and on items of literary analysis. The workbooks will also feature scansion practice, essays to write, and other short analysis questions in each section. By reading and answering these types of questions, students will gain experience with the types of questions that are found on the Advanced Placement Examinations. Students at the college level will also benefit from the additional practice offered in the workbooks.

These workbooks contain neither textual notes nor vocabulary on the page with the text nor on the facing page. The absence of these traditional features of textbooks will allow students, after reading the Latin passage in the textbook, to practice in the workbook what they have learned and to assess how much they have mastered already and what needs more study. The workbooks will, however, contain a Latin to English Vocabulary at the back of the book.

We are confident that this series of workbooks has a unique role to play in fostering students' understanding of authentic Latin text and will be a significant addition to the Advanced Placement and college materials that already exist.

LeaAnn A. Osburn
Series Editor

PREFACE

This book is intended to assist students who are reading Cicero's *Pro Archia* and *De Amicitia*, whether in an Advanced Placement course or not. Cicero's prose is challenging, and it is our hope that this book will enhance the students' reading ability, from the incipient stages of working out the translation, word by word, through to the literary analysis of the work. To this end we have provided several types of questions, some of which parallel the AP* test format, and others which we have designed to facilitate the students' progress through the text.

Each work is divided into manageable chapters or sections. At the beginning of each, the text under consideration is provided. For the *Pro Archia*, the text is that of Steven M. Cerutti, *Cicero Pro Archia Poeta Oratio* (Wauconda, IL: Bolchazy-Carducci Publishers, 1998, Second Edition 2006). For the *De Amicitia*, the text is that of Patsy Rodden Ricks and Sheila K. Dickison, *Cicero De Amicitia Selections* (Wauconda, IL: Bolchazy-Carducci Publishers 2006). Line numbering and spacing follow that presented in these texts.

I. Preparatory Questions

Following the text we present preparatory questions. These are prompts that guide students through the text line by line, asking them to identify syntactical constructions and their components, in order to understand the relationships among them that are critical to the translation. In some instances, a question involving several lines will appear before those questions involving a single word in a given line. This arrangement is designed to prompt recognition of the major clauses and facilitate a student's seeing the big picture. Not every student will feel the need to write down answers for every prompt; lines are provided in the text for written answers.

II. Multiple Choice Questions

Next come multiple choice questions, which are meant to be done after the student has completed the translation. These questions cover a variety of topics, including agreement, reference, translation, syntax, comprehension, and figures of speech. As these, for the most part, replicate the multiple choice sections on the AP* exam, time limits are suggested for each. Teachers may want to break the lengthier multiple choice sections into two assignments.

III. Translation

A passage for translation follows, approximately the same length as those found on the AP* exams. Students should provide as literal a translation as possible, paying particular attention to maintaining the original voice and tense of verbs.

---

* AP is a registered trademark of the College Entrance Examination Board, which was not involved in the production of, and does not endorse, this product.

IV. Short Analysis Questions

Short analysis questions are designed to help the students focus on key ideas in the passage. They often ask students to quote and translate accurately specific words or phrases in support of their answer. Insight and brevity are essential elements here. Similar questions appear on Advanced Placement exams.

V. Essay Questions

Finally, for each chapter or section, an essay question is provided, in which students will gain valuable experience with in-depth literary analysis. Consistent with AP* expectations for short essays, students should formulate cogent arguments with appropriate support from the Latin text, to demonstrate their understanding of the passage.

* * * * * * * *

We hope that this approach will be valuable for students and teachers alike.

We would like to thank LeaAnn Osburn and Donald Sprague of Bolchazy-Carducci for encouraging us to undertake this project together and for continuing to support our efforts. We thank Gary Varney for his proofreading assistance. We very much appreciate the work of our predecessors on these texts, especially Steven Cerutti, whose excellent edition of the *Pro Archia* has been invaluable. The opportunity to collaborate on the *De Amicitia* has taught us the truth of Cicero's statement in chapter 6: "Nam et secundas res splendidiores facit amicitia, et adversas partiens communicansque leviores."

JANE CRAWFORD
University of Virginia
Charlottesville, Virginia

JUDITH HAYES
New Trier High School
Winnetka, IL

---

* AP is a registered trademark of the College Entrance Examination Board, which was not involved in the production of, and does not endorse, this product.

TEXT SELECTIONS FROM THE *PRO ARCHIA POETA ORATIO* WITH EXERCISES

M. TULLI CICERONIS
PRO ARCHIA POETA ORATIO
CHAPTER 1: LINES 1–22

1 Si quid est in me ingeni, iudices, quod sentio
quam sit exiguum, aut si qua exercitatio dicendi, in qua
me non infitior mediocriter esse versatum, aut si huiusce
rei ratio aliqua ab optimarum artium studiis ac disciplina
5 profecta, a qua ego nullum confiteor aetatis meae tempus
abhorruisse, earum rerum omnium vel in primis hic A. Licinius fructum a me repetere prope suo iure debet. Nam
quoad longissime potest mens mea respicere spatium
praeteriti temporis et pueritiae memoriam recordari
10 ultimam, inde usque repetens hunc video mihi principem
et ad suscipiendam et ad ingrediendam rationem horum
studiorum exstitisse. Quod si haec vox huius hortatu
praeceptisque conformata non nullis aliquando saluti fuit,
a quo id accepimus quo ceteris opitulari et alios servare
15 possemus, huic profecto ipsi, quantum est situm in nobis,
et opem et salutem ferre debemus. 2 Ac ne quis a nobis hoc
ita dici forte miretur, quod alia quaedam in hoc facultas
sit ingeni neque haec dicendi ratio aut disciplina, ne nos
quidem huic uni studio penitus umquam dediti fuimus.
20 Etenim omnes artes quae ad humanitatem pertinent habent
quoddam commune vinculum et quasi cognatione quadam
inter se continentur.

Preparatory Questions

Line 1   What is the dictionary form of *quid*? _____

Identify the case and use of *ingeni*. _____

What is the antecedent of *quod*? _____

Line 2   Identify the form and syntax of *sit*. _____

What word does *exiguum* modify? _____

What is the dictionary form of *qua*? _____

Identify the form and the case of *dicendi*. _____

What is the antecedent of the <u>second</u> *qua*? _____

Lines 2–3	Find an indirect statement._____
	What verb must be supplied with *si . . .* and *si . . .*? _____
Line 3	Identify the case and use of *me*. _____
	What is the subject of *esse versatum?* _____
Line 4	Identify the case and use of *ratio*. _____
	What word does *aliqua* modify?_____
	What words are determined (governed) by *ab?* _____
Lines 1–4	Identify the three protases ("if" clauses) in the sentence. _____
	_____
Line 5	What form is *profecta?* _____
	What word does *profecta* modify? _____
	To what word does *qua* refer? _____
	Identify the case and use of *tempus*. _____
	What word does *nullum* modify? _____
	Identify the case and use of *aetatis meae*._____
Line 6	Identify the form and use of *abhorruisse*. _____
	What words does *hic* modify? _____
Line 7	What is the subject of *debet?* _____
	Identify the case and use of *fructum*._____
	Identify the form and use of *repetere*. _____
	What does *prope* modify? _____
	To whom does *suo* refer?_____
Lines 6–7	Identify the apodosis ("then" clause) of the sentence._____
Lines 1–7	Identify the type of condition. _____
Lines 7–12	Find the main verb of this sentence. _____
Line 8	What form is *longissime?* _____
	What word does it modify? _____
	What is the subject of *potest?* _____
	Identify the form and syntax of *respicere*. _____
	What is the case and use of *spatium?*_____

Lines 8–9   Find two infinitives that are dependent on *potest*. _____

Line 9   Identify the case and use of *memoriam*._____

Line 10   Identify the form of *repetens*. _____

   Identify the case and use of *repetens*._____

   Identify the case and use of *hunc*. _____

   Identify the case and use of *mihi*._____

   What does *principem* modify?_____

Line 11   What is the syntax of *ad suscipiendam* and *ad ingrediendam?* _____

   _____

Line 12   Identify the form and syntax of *exstitisse*._____

   What part of speech is *quod?* _____

   To whom does *huius* refer? _____

Lines 12–16   Find the verbs that make up the condition in this sentence._____

   _____

   What kind of condition is it? _____

Line 13   Identify the case and use of *praeceptis*. _____

   Identify the form of *conformata*. _____

   What word does it modify? _____

   Identify the case and use of *non nullis . . . saluti*. _____

Line 14   To whom does the phrase *a quo* refer? _____

   Identify the case and use of *id*._____

   Identify the form and use of *opitulari*._____

   What is the object of *opitulari?* _____

Line 15   Identify the case and use of *huic ipsi*. _____

   To whom does the phrase *huic ipsi* refer? _____

   What is the subject of *est?* _____

   Who is meant by *nobis?* _____

Lines 16–17   Find a negative purpose clause._____

Line 16   Identify the dictionary form of *quis*. _____

   Identify the case and use of *nobis*. _____

Find the subject of an indirect statement._____

Line 17   What word does *quaedam* modify? _____

To whom does *hoc* refer?_____

Line 18   Identify the tense and mood of *sit*. _____

What words does *haec* modify? _____

What words does *neque* connect?_____

Identify the form and case of *dicendi*. _____

Identify the case and use of *nos*. _____

Line 19   Identify the case and use of *studio*. _____

What words modify it? _____

Identify the tense and voice of *dediti fuimus*. _____

Line 20   Find a relative clause. _____

What is the antecedent of *quae*? _____

What is the subject of *habent*? _____

Line 21   Identify the case and use of *vinculum*. _____

Identify the case and use of *cognatione*._____

Line 22   To what or whom does *se* refer? _____

What is the subject of *continentur*? _____

Multiple Choice Questions *Suggested time: 37 minutes*

1.   The case and number of *iudices* (line 1) is
    a. nominative plural
    c. vocative plural
    b. nominative singular
    d. accusative plural

2.   *mediocriter* (line 3) is
    a. a noun
    c. an adjective
    b. an adverb
    d. a verb

3.   The subject of *abhorruisse* (line 6) is
    a. *ego* (line 5)
    c. *tempus* (line 5)
    b. *aetatis* (line 5)
    d. *hic* (line 6)

4. The phrase *earum rerum omnium* (line 6) refers to

   a. *sentio* (line 1), *infitior* (line 3), and *confiteor* (line 5)

   b. *ingeni* (line 1), *exercitatio* (line 2), and *ratio* (line 4)

   c. *huiusce rei* (lines 3–4), *tempus* (line 5), and *fructum* (line 7)

   d. Cicero (understood), *iudices* (line 1), and *Licinius* (lines 6–7)

5. In lines 1–6 (*Si quid . . . abhorruisse*), we learn that Cicero

   a. thinks that he has great talent

   b. practices speaking every day

   c. has studied all the liberal arts

   d. says that he has always liked studying

6. In lines 6–7 (*earum rerum . . . iure debet*), we learn that

   a. Licinius owes Cicero money

   b. Cicero owes Licinius something

   c. Licinius is among the leading men

   d. Cicero is acting in his own right

7. Lines 7–10 (*Nam . . . ultimam*) tell us that

   a. Cicero is remembering his past

   b. the mind is a wonderful thing

   c. a great deal of time has passed by

   d. Cicero cannot recall his youth

8. The case of *praeteriti* (line 9)

   a. nominative

   b. genitive

   c. dative

   d. ablative

9. The word *ultimam* (line 10) is translated

   a. latest

   b. best

   c. earliest

   d. clearest

10. The words *inde usque repetens* (line 10) are translated

    a. looking from here to there

    b. searching from that point on

    c. asking where and when

    d. repeating continuously ever since

11. In line 11, the phrase *ad suscipiendam . . . rationem* expresses

    a. purpose

    b. result

    c. condition

    d. obligation

12. From lines 10–12 (*inde . . . exstitisse*), we learn that

    a. Cicero and Archias were longtime friends

    b. Archias had a plan for studying the arts

    c. Archias was an important influence on Cicero

    d. Cicero and Archias took walks together

13. The enclitic *–que* in line 13 connects
    a. *vox* (line 12) and *conformata* (line 13)
    b. *hortatu* (line 12) and *saluti* (line 13)
    c. *hortatu* (line 12) and *praeceptis* (line 13)
    d. *Quod* (line 12) and *quo* (line 14)

14. In line 13, *non nullis* is an example of
    a. anaphora
    b. hyperbole
    c. litotes
    d. hysteron proteron

15. In line 14, *a quo* is translated
    a. by whom
    b. by which
    c. from whom
    d. from which

16. In line 14, *id* refers to
    a. Cicero's plan of study
    b. Archias's encouragement of Cicero
    c. Cicero's oratorical skill
    d. Archias's citizenship

17. The antecedent of the <u>second</u> *quo* in line 14 is
    a. *hortatu* (line 12)
    b. *aliquando* (line 13)
    c. *quo* (the first one in line 14)
    d. *id* (line 14)

18. The word *quantum* (line 15) refers to
    a. *id* (line 14)
    b. *huic* (line 15)
    c. *ipsi* (line 15)
    d. *opem* (line 16)

19. In line 17, *dici* is
    a. an imperative
    b. an infinitive
    c. a participle
    d. a main verb

20. In line 17, *forte* is translated
    a. outdoors
    b. strongly
    c. by chance
    d. with bravery

21. The word *alia* (line 17) modifies
    a. *hoc* (line 16)
    b. *quaedam* (line 17)
    c. *facultas* (line 17)
    d. *ratio* (line 18)

22. In line 17, *quod* is translated
    a. because
    b. which
    c. but
    d. what

23. The case of *ingeni* (line 18) is
    a. nominative
    b. genitive
    c. dative
    d. ablative

24. A figure of speech found in lines 17–18 (*quod alia . . . ratio aut disciplina*) is
    a. asyndeton
    b. alliteration
    c. chiasmus
    d. zeugma

25. In line 18, *nos* refers to
    a. Cicero and Archias
    b. Archias
    c. Cicero
    d. Cicero and the jurors

26. The word *huic* (line 19) modifies
    a. *quidem* (line 19)
    b. *uni* (line 19)
    c. *studio* (line 19)
    d. *dediti* (line 19)

27. The case of *uni* (line 19) is
    a. nominative
    b. genitive
    c. dative
    d. ablative

28. From lines 20–22 (*Etenim . . . se continentur*), we learn that
    a. all humans enjoy the arts
    b. there is a relationship among the arts
    c. only humans can be true artists
    d. the arts must be controlled and contained

29. In line 21, *quoddam* is translated
    a. certain
    b. formerly
    c. whatever
    d. especially

30. The case of *commune* (line 21) is
    a. nominative
    b. dative
    c. accusative
    d. ablative

31. The case and number of *quadam* (line 21) is
    a. nominative singular
    b. nominative plural
    c. accusative plural
    d. ablative singular

Translation *Suggested time: 15 minutes*

Nam
quoad longissime potest mens mea respicere spatium
praeteriti temporis et pueritiae memoriam recordari
ultimam, inde usque repetens hunc video mihi principem
5   et ad suscipiendam et ad ingrediendam rationem horum
studiorum exstitisse.

_____

_____

_____

_____

_____

_____

_____

Short Analysis Questions

Si quid est in me ingeni, iudices, quod sentio
quam sit exiguum, aut si qua exercitatio dicendi, in qua
me non infitior mediocriter esse versatum, aut si huiusce
rei ratio aliqua ab optimarum artium studiis ac disciplina
5   profecta, a qua ego nullum confiteor aetatis meae tempus
abhorruisse, earum rerum omnium vel in primis hic A. Licinius fructum a me repetere prope suo iure debet. Nam
quoad longissime potest mens mea respicere spatium
praeteriti temporis et pueritiae memoriam recordari
10 ultimam, inde usque repetens hunc video mihi principem
et ad suscipiendam et ad ingrediendam rationem horum
studiorum exstitisse.

1.   In lines 1–5 (*Si quid . . . profecta*), Cicero identifies three attributes which qualify him to
     undertake the defense of Archias. Cite and translate or accurately paraphrase one Latin
     phrase for each of those three qualities.

_____

_____

_____

2. Identify a figure of speech contained in line 3. Write out the Latin words that illustrate it.

   _____

3. To what does the phrase, *earum rerum omnium* (line 6) refer?

   _____

4. What is the *praenomen* of Archias? What is his *nomen*? Why does Cicero make a point of using these two names to refer to his client?

   _____

   _____

5. In what specific respects has Archias been *"principem"*, i.e., most important, to Cicero? Cite the Latin that answers the question and translate it.

   _____

   _____

   _____

> **Quod si haec vox huius hortatu**
> **praeceptisque conformata non nullis aliquando saluti fuit,**
> **a quo id accepimus quo ceteris opitulari et alios servare**
> **possemus, huic profecto ipsi, quantum est situm in nobis,**
> 5 **et opem et salutem ferre debemus. Ac ne quis a nobis hoc**
> **ita dici forte miretur, quod alia quaedam in hoc facultas**
> **sit ingeni neque haec dicendi ratio aut disciplina, ne nos**
> **quidem huic uni studio penitus umquam dediti fuimus.**
> **Etenim omnes artes quae ad humanitatem pertinent habent**
> 10 **quoddam commune vinculum et quasi cognatione quadam**
> **inter se continentur.**

6. Identify a figure of speech found in lines 1–2. Write out the Latin words that illustrate it.

   _____

7. According to lines 1–5, why does Archias deserve Cicero's assistance?

   _____

   _____

8. Cicero observes in lines 6–7 that Archias does not possess all the same skills that he has. What skills does Cicero possess that Archias lacks? Cite the Latin that supports your answer and translate or accurately paraphrase it.

   _____

   _____

Essay *Suggested time: 20 minutes*

> Si quid est in me ingeni, iudices, quod sentio
> quam sit exiguum, aut si qua exercitatio dicendi, in qua
> me non infitior mediocriter esse versatum, aut si huiusce
> rei ratio aliqua ab optimarum artium studiis ac disciplina
> 5   profecta, a qua ego nullum confiteor aetatis meae tempus
> abhorruisse, earum rerum omnium vel in primis hic A. Li-
> cinius fructum a me repetere prope suo iure debet.

In the opening of the *Pro Archia Poeta,* Cicero establishes for the jurors his qualifications as a trial lawyer but is also very careful to put on a show of humility. In a short essay, discuss how he balances these two approaches.

Support your assertions with references to the Latin text throughout the passage above. All Latin words must be copied or their line numbers provided, AND they must be translated or paraphrased closely enough that it is clear you understand the Latin. It is your responsibility to convince the reader that you are basing your conclusions on the Latin text and not merely on a general recollection of the passage. Direct your answer to the question; do not merely summarize the passage. Please write your essay on a separate piece of paper.

CHAPTER 2: LINES 22–41

Sed ne cui vestrum mirum esse
videatur, me in quaestione legitima et in iudicio publico,
cum res agatur apud praetorem populi Romani, lectissimum
25   virum, et apud severissimos iudices, tanto conventu hominum ac frequentia, hoc uti genere dicendi, quod non
modo a consuetudine iudiciorum, verum etiam a forensi sermone abhorreat, quaeso a vobis ut in hac causa
mihi detis hanc veniam accommodatam huic reo, vobis,
30   quemadmodum spero, non molestam, ut me pro summo
poeta atque eruditissimo homine dicentem hoc concursu
hominum litteratissimorum, hac vestra humanitate, hoc
denique praetore exercente iudicium, patiamini de studiis
humanitatis ac litterarum paulo loqui liberius, et in eius
35   modi persona quae propter otium ac studium minime
in iudiciis periculisque tractata est uti prope novo quodam et inusitato genere dicendi. 4 Quod si mihi a vobis
tribui concedique sentiam, perficiam profecto ut hunc A.
Licinium non modo non segregandum, cum sit civis, a
40   numero civium verum etiam, si non esset, putetis asciscendum fuisse.

Preparatory Questions

Lines 22–23   Find a negative purpose clause._____

Line 22   What is the case of *cui*? _____

What is the case and use of *vestrum*? _____

Line 23   Of which infinitive is *me* the subject? _____

Line 24   Find a *cum* clause. _____

What kind of *cum* clause is it? _____

Lines 24–25   Identify the case and use of *lectissimum virum*. _____

Line 25   Identify the case and use of *tanto conventu*. _____

Line 26   Identify the case and use of *genere*. _____

What is the antecedent of *quod*?_____

Line 27   What is the case and use of *consuetudine*? _____

Line 28   Find the main verb of the sentence. _____

Line 29   Identify the form and syntax of *detis*. _____

             What is the direct object of *detis?* _____

             Identify the case of *reo*. _____

             What word determines its case? _____

Line 30   What does *molestam* modify? _____

             Identify the case and use of *me*. _____

Lines 30–34 Find a subordinate clause expanding on *veniam* (line 29). _____

             _____

Line 31   Identify the form of *dicentem*. _____

Line 32   To whom does *vestra* refer? _____

             What does *hoc* modify? _____

Line 33   Identify the form and syntax of *patiamini*. _____

             Who is the subject of *patiamini?* _____

Lines 33–36 Find two infinitives that depend on *patiamini*. _____

             _____

Line 34   What is the case and use of *paulo?* _____

             Identify the form and use of *liberius*. _____

Line 35   What is the antecedent of *quae?* _____

Line 36   What is the subject of *tractata est?* _____

             On what word does *uti* depend? _____

Line 37   What is the case and use of *genere?* _____

Line 38   Identify the form and syntax of *tribui*. _____

             What is the tense and mood of *sentiam?* _____

             What type of condition does *sentiam* illustrate? _____

             What is the main verb of the apodosis? _____

Lines 38–40 Find a result clause. _____

Lines 38–41 Find an indirect statement. _____

Line 39   What word must be understood with *segregandum?* _____

             Find a *cum* clause. _____

Line 40   What type of condition is illustrated in the clause, *si non esset?* _____

_____

Lines 40–41   Identify the form and syntax of *asciscendum fuisse.*_____

Multiple Choice Questions *Suggested time: 42 minutes*

1. In line 22, *cui* is translated
    a. anyone
    c. everyone
    b. whom
    d. each

2. The mood and tense of *videatur* (line 23) is
    a. present subjunctive
    c. future indicative
    b. present indicative
    d. perfect subjunctive

3. In lines 22–25 (*Sed ne . . . iudices*), we learn that
    a. the trial is taking place in Herclea
    c. there is a question about propriety
    b. a praetor is in charge of the court
    d. the judges are very lax

4. In line 25, *apud* is translated
    a. near
    c. after
    b. before
    d. at

5. In lines 25–27 (*tanto conventu . . . iudiciorum*), we learn that
    a. many men were attending the trial
    c. Cicero is speaking generally
    b. trials like this were frequent
    d. the jury has been seated

6. In line 26, *dicendi* is translated
    a. about to speak
    c. for the speaker
    b. of speaking
    d. to be spoken

7. In line 26, *quod* is translated
    a. which
    c. because
    b. where
    d. what

8. The case of *forensi* (lines 27–28) is
    a. nominative
    c. dative
    b. genitive
    d. ablative

9. The tense and mood of *abhorreat* (line 28) is

   a. present indicative

   b. present subjunctive

   c. future indicative

   d. imperfect subjunctive

10. In line 28, *causa* is translated

    a. reason

    b. cause

    c. accident

    d. case

11. The case of *mihi* (line 29) is determined by

    a. *quaeso* (line 28)

    b. *vobis* (line 28)

    c. *detis* (line 29)

    d. *accommodatum* (line 29)

12. The case of *vobis* (line 29) is determined by

    a. *detis* (line 29)

    b. *quemadmodum* (line 30)

    c. *spero* (line 30)

    d. *molestam* (line 30)

13. What figure of speech is found in lines 29–30 (*accommodatam . . . molestam*)?

    a. anaphora

    b. anacoluthon

    c. chiasmus

    d. hendiadys

14. In lines 26–30 (*hoc uti . . . non molestam*), Cicero tells us that he

    a. speaks in a manner customary to jurors

    b. disapproves of conversing in court

    c. will use an unusual type of speaking

    d. thinks that his speaking style is not annoying

15. The word *dicentem* (line 31) modifies

    a. *accommodatam* (line 29)

    b. *me* (line 30)

    c. *poeta* (line 31)

    d. *hominum* (line 32)

16. In lines 31–32 (*hoc . . . iudicium*), we find an example of

    a. chiasmus

    b. anaphora

    c. assonance

    d. hyperbole

17. *exercente* (line 33) modifies

    a. *homine* (line 31)

    b. *concursu* (line 31)

    c. *humanitate* (line 32)

    d. *praetore* (line 33)

18. The word *iudicium* (line 33) is the object of

    a. *dicentem* (line 31)

    b. *exercente* (line 33)

    c. *patiamini* (line 33)

    d. *loqui* (line 34)

19. The case and number of *humanitatis* (line 34) is

   a. nominative singular

   b. genitive singular

   c. dative plural

   d. ablative plural

20. The word *loqui* (line 34) depends on

   a. *spero* (line 30)

   b. *exercente* (line 33)

   c. *patiamini* (line 33)

   d. *tractata est* (line 36)

21. In line 34, *paulo . . . liberius* is translated

   a. a little more freely

   b. with a little bit of freedom

   c. like a small child

   d. with few liberties

22. In line 35, *modi* is translated

   a. now

   b. sort

   c. measure

   d. limit

23. In line 36, *in iudiciis periculisque* is an example of

   a. asyndeton

   b. hyperbole

   c. chiasmus

   d. hendiadys

24. In lines 36–37, *quodam* is translated

   a. formerly

   b. certain

   c. since

   d. indeed

25. In lines 30–37 (*ut me pro summo . . . genere dicendi*), Cicero asks the jurors to

   a. show their humanity

   b. listen to the greatest poet speaking

   c. pursue the study of literature

   d. allow him to speak more freely

26. The antecedent of *quod* (line 37) is

   a. *otium et studium* (line 35)

   b. *quodam* (lines 36–37)

   c. *genere* (line 37)

   d. *hunc A. Licinium* (lines 38–39)

27. The subject of *tribui* (line 38) is

   a. *quod* (line 37)

   b. *hunc A. Licinium* (lines 38–39)

   c. *civis* (line 39)

   d. *verum* (line 40)

28. The word *concedique* (line 38) depends on

   a. *tribui* (line 38)

   b. *sentiam* (line 38)

   c. *perficiam* (line 38)

   d. *profecto* (line 38)

29. The mood of *sentiam* (line 38) is determined by
    a. *quod* (line 37)
    b. *si* (line 37)
    c. *a* (line 37)
    d. *ut* (line 38)

30. The word *ut* (line 38) governs
    a. *sit* (line 39)
    b. *esset* (line 40)
    c. *putetis* (line 40)
    d. *fuisse* (line 41)

31. The phrase *non modo* (line 39) is paired with
    a. *cum sit* (line 39)
    b. *a numero* (lines 39–40)
    c. *verum etiam* (line 40)
    d. *si non* (line 40)

32. In line 39, *cum* is translated
    a. since
    b. when
    c. with
    d. although

33. The tense and mood of *putetis* (line 40) is
    a. present indicative
    b. present subjunctive
    c. perfect subjunctive
    d. future indicative

34. The subject of *asciscendum* (lines 40–41) is
    a. *quod* (line 37)
    b. *Licinium* (line 39)
    c. *civium* (line 40)
    d. *verum* (line 40)

35. In lines 37–41 (*Quod si mihi . . . asciscendum fuisse*), we learn that
    a. Cicero is willing to make concessions
    b. Licinius must prove his citizenship
    c. Licinius is already a citizen
    d. the number of citizens is accurate

Translation *Suggested time: 10 minutes*

Quod si mihi a vobis
tribui concedique sentiam, perficiam profecto ut hunc A.
Licinium non modo non segregandum, cum sit civis, a
numero civium verum etiam, si non esset, putetis asciscen-
5 dum fuisse.

_____

_____

_____

_____

_____

_____

Short Analysis Questions

Sed ne cui vestrum mirum esse
videatur, me in quaestione legitima et in iudicio publico,
cum res agatur apud praetorem populi Romani, lectissimum
virum, et apud severissimos iudices, tanto conventu ho-
5 minum ac frequentia, hoc uti genere dicendi, quod non
modo a consuetudine iudiciorum, verum etiam a forensi sermone abhorreat, quaeso a vobis ut in hac causa
mihi detis hanc veniam accommodatam huic reo, vobis,
quemadmodum spero, non molestam, ut me pro summo
10 poeta atque eruditissimo homine dicentem hoc concursu
hominum litteratissimorum, hac vestra humanitate, hoc
denique praetore exercente iudicium, patiamini de studiis
humanitatis ac litterarum paulo loqui liberius, et in eius
modi persona quae propter otium ac studium minime
15 in iudiciis periculisque tractata est uti prope novo quodam et inusitato genere dicendi.

1. According to lines 3–4, before whom is Cicero arguing this case?

_____

2. Identify the figure of speech used in lines 4–5. Write out the Latin that illustrates this figure of speech. Comment on its effectiveness.

_____

_____

_____

_____

3. What do we learn from lines 5–6 about the kind of speech Cicero wishes to deliver? Cite the Latin that supports your answer and translate or accurately paraphrase it.

_____

_____

_____

_____

4. In lines 13–17, what does Cicero wish to be allowed to do during this trial? Cite the Latin that supports your answer and translate or accurately paraphrase it.

_____

_____

_____

_____

> **Quod si mihi a vobis
> tribui concedique sentiam, perficiam profecto ut hunc A.
> Licinium non modo non segregandum, cum sit civis, a
> numero civium verum etiam, si non esset, putetis asciscen-
> 5 dum fuisse.**

5. At the conclusion of the *exordium* (lines 4–5) Cicero states his intention to go a step further than proving that Archias is a citizen. What does he wish his audience to believe about Archias? Cite the Latin that supports your answer and translate or accurately paraphrase it.

_____

_____

_____

Essay *Suggested time: 20 minutes*

Sed ne cui vestrum mirum esse
videatur, me in quaestione legitima et in iudicio publico,
cum res agatur apud praetorem populi Romani, lectissimum
virum, et apud severissimos iudices, tanto conventu hominum ac frequentia, hoc uti genere dicendi, quod non
modo a consuetudine iudiciorum, verum etiam a forensi sermone abhorreat, quaeso a vobis ut in hac causa
mihi detis hanc veniam accommodatam huic reo, vobis,
quemadmodum spero, non molestam, ut me pro summo
poeta atque eruditissimo homine dicentem hoc concursu
hominum litteratissimorum, hac vestra humanitate, hoc
denique praetore exercente iudicium, patiamini de studiis
humanitatis ac litterarum paulo loqui liberius, et in eius
modi persona quae propter otium ac studium minime
in iudiciis periculisque tractata est uti prope novo quodam et inusitato genere dicendi.

5

10

15

Cicero asks the forbearance of the jury while he adopts a different style of speaking on behalf of Archias, his client. In a short essay, discuss some of the techniques he uses to enlist the support of the jury.

Support your assertions with references to the Latin text throughout the passage above. All Latin words must be copied or their line numbers provided, AND they must be translated or paraphrased closely enough that it is clear you understand the Latin. It is your responsibility to convince the reader that you are basing your conclusions on the Latin text and not merely on a general recollection of the passage. Direct your answer to the question; do not merely summarize the passage. Please write your essay on a separate piece of paper.

CHAPTER 3: LINES 42–68

Nam ut primum ex pueris excessit Archias atque ab eis artibus quibus aetas puerilis ad humanitatem informari solet, se ad scribendi studium contulit. Primum Antiochiae
45 —nam ibi natus est loco nobili—celebri quondam urbe et copiosa atque eruditissimis hominibus liberalissimisque studiis adfluenti, celeriter antecellere omnibus ingeni gloria coepit. Post in ceteris Asiae partibus cunctaque Graecia sic eius adventus celebrabantur ut famam ingeni exspectatio
50 hominis, exspectationem ipsius adventus admiratioque superaret.

5 Erat Italia tum plena Graecarum artium ac disciplinarum, studiaque haec et in Latio vehementius tum colebantur quam nunc isdem in oppidis, et hic Romae
55 propter tranquillitatem rei publicae non neglegebantur. Itaque hunc et Tarentini et Locrenses et Regini et Neapolitani civitate ceterisque praemiis donarunt, et omnes qui aliquid de ingeniis poterant iudicare cognitione atque hospitio dignum existimarunt. Hac tanta celebritate
60 famae cum esset iam absentibus notus, Romam venit Mario consule et Catulo. Nactus est primum consules eos quorum alter res ad scribendum maximas, alter cum res gestas tum etiam studium atque auris adhibere posset. Statim Luculli, cum praetextatus etiam tum Archias esset,
65 eum domum suam receperunt. Dedit etiam hoc non solum lumen ingeni ac litterarum, verum etiam naturae atque virtutis ut domus, quae huius adulescentiae prima favit, eadem esset familiarissima senectuti.

Preparatory Questions

Line 42   What is the subject of *excessit*? _____

Line 43   What is the antecedent of *quibus*? _____

                Identify the case and use of *quibus*. _____

                What word does *puerilis* modify? _____

                Identify the form and use of *informari*. _____

Line 44   What is the subject of *solet?* _____

To whom does *se* refer? _____

Identify the form and case of *scribendi.* _____

Identify the case and use of *studium.* _____

What is the case of *Antiochiae?* _____

Line 45   What is the tense and voice of *natus est?* _____

Identify the case and use of *loco nobili.* _____

What part of speech is *quondam?* _____

Lines 45–47   Find three adjectives that modify *urbe.* _____

Line 46   What does *–que* connect? _____

Line 47   What does *celeriter* modify? _____

Identify the case and use of *omnibus.* _____

Identify the case and use of *ingeni.* _____

Identify the case and use of *gloria.* _____

Line 48   What is the subject of *coepit?* _____

What part of speech is *post?* _____

Line 49   Identify the case and use of *adventus.* _____

Identify the case and use of *ingeni.* _____

Lines 49–51   Find a result clause. _____

What are the subjects of *superaret?* _____

Find two objects of *superaret.* _____

Line 50   Identify the case and use of *ipsius.* _____

What does *-que* connect? _____

Line 52   What word does *plena* modify? _____

Identify the case and use of *artium.* _____

Line 53   What does *haec* modify? _____

What part of speech is *vehementius?* _____

Line 54 What is the subject of *colebantur?*_____

    Identify the case and use of *oppidis.*_____

    What part of speech is *hic?*_____

    What is the case of *Romae?*_____

Line 55 Identify the case and use of *tranquillitatem.*_____

    What is the subject of *neglegebantur?*_____

Line 56 To whom does *hunc* refer?_____

Lines 56–57 Of what verb is *hunc* the object?_____

    Find the four subjects of *donarunt.*_____

Line 57 What is the unsyncopated form of *donarunt?*_____

    Identify the case and use of *omnes.*_____

Line 58 What is the antecedent of *qui?*_____

    Identify the case and use of *aliquid.*_____

    Identify the form and use of *iudicare.*_____

Lines 58–59 Identify the case and use of *cognitione* and *hospitio.*_____

Line 59 What is the tense and voice of *existimarunt?*_____

    What is the case and use of *celebritate?*_____

Line 60 Find a *cum* clause._____

    What kind of *cum* clause is it?_____

    Identify the case and use of *absentibus.*_____

    What does *notus* modify?_____

    What is the case and use of *Romam?*_____

    Who/what is the subject of *venit?*_____

Line 61 Identify the case and use of *Mario consule et Catulo.*_____

    What is the subject of *nactus est?*_____

    What is its object?_____

    What part of speech is *primum?*_____

    What word does *eos* modify?_____

Line 62   To whom does *alter . . . alter* refer?_____

      What construction is *ad scribendum*? _____

      What word does *maximas* modify? _____

Lines 62–63 Find a correlative clause. _____

      Find all the objects of *adhibere*. _____

Line 63   What is the subject of *posset?* _____

      What word does *statim* modify? _____

Line 64   Find a *cum* clause. _____

      What kind of *cum* clause is it? _____

      Identify the case and use of *praetextatus.* _____

Line 65   Identify the case and use of *eum.* _____

      Identify the case and use of *domum suam.* _____

      To whom does *suam* refer? _____

      What is the case and use of *hoc?* _____

Lines 65–66 Find a correlative clause. _____

      Find four genitives that are dependent on *lumen.*_____

Lines 66–68 Find an *ut* clause. _____

Line 67   Find a relative clause. _____

      What is the antecedent of *quae?* _____

      What is the case and use of *huius?* _____

      To whom does *huius* refer? _____

      Identify the case and use of *adulescentiae.*_____

      What word does *eadem* modify? _____

Line 68   What is the tense and mood of *esset?* _____

      What does *familiarissima* modify? _____

      Identify the case and use of *senectuti.* _____

Lines 67–68 Identify a figure of speech in these lines and write out the Latin words that illustrate it.

      _____

Multiple Choice Questions *Suggested time: 42 minutes*

1. In line 42, *ut primum* is translated
   a. in order to be first
   b. first of all
   c. as soon as
   d. sooner than

2. In line 43, *quibus* is translated
   a. from which
   b. by which
   c. to which
   d. which

3. The word *se* in line 44 refers to
   a. *pueris* (line 42)
   b. *Archias* (line 42)
   c. *aetas* (line 43)
   d. *humanitatem* (line 43)

4. In line 44, *scribendi* is a(n)
   a. gerund
   b. gerundive
   c. infinitive
   d. perfect indicative

5. The subject of *contulit* (line 44) is
   a. *Archias* (line 42)
   b. *aetas* (line 43)
   c. *se* (line 44)
   d. *studium* (line 44)

6. Line 44 contains an example of
   a. asyndeton
   b. hyperbole
   c. alliteration
   d. anaphora

7. In lines 42–44 (*Nam ut primum . . . studium contulit*), we learn that Archias
   a. was separated from his boyhood friends
   b. was an artist when he was a boy
   c. used to inform against people
   d. studied writing as a young man

8. In line 44, *Antiochiae* is translated
   a. of Antioch
   b. the Antiochians
   c. at Antioch
   d. for Antioch

9. In line 45, *celebri* is translated
   a. populous
   b. celebrated
   c. famous
   d. frequent

10. The word *adfluenti* (line 47) modifies
    a. *Antiochiae* (line 44)
    b. *loco* (line 45)
    c. *urbe* (line 45)
    d. *copiosa* (line 46)

11. In line 47, *adfluenti* is translated
    a. flowing to
    c. abounding in
    b. arising from
    d. influenced by

12. *antecellere* (line 47) depends on
    a. *natus est* (line 45)
    c. *celeriter* (line 47)
    b. *celebri* (line 45)
    d. *coepit* (line 48)

13. In lines 44–48 (*Primum . . . coepit*), Cicero tells us that
    a. Antioch was overcrowded
    c. learned men hurried to hear Archias
    b. noblemen lived in that place
    d. Archias had great natural ability

14. The case of *Asiae* in line 48 is
    a. nominative
    c. dative
    b. genitive
    d. locative

15. In line 48, *–que* connects
    a. *post* (line 48) and *sic* (line 48)
    c. *Asiae* (line 48) and *Graecia* (line 48)
    b. *ceteris* (line 48) and *partibus* (line 48)
    d. *partibus* (line 48) and *Graecia* (line 48)

16. In line 48, *sic* is translated
    a. such
    c. thus
    b. so
    d. if

17. In line 49, *adventus* is translated
    a. arrivals
    c. adventures
    b. appearances
    d. advantages

18. In line 50, *hominis* refers to
    a. Cicero
    c. a member of the jury
    b. Archias
    d. a citizen of Greece

19. Lines 48–51 (*Post in ceteris . . . superaret*) tells us that in Asia and Greece, Archias
    a. had many friends
    c. had a reputation for natural talent
    b. visited various cities frequently
    d. always kept people waiting

20. The conjunction *-que* in line 53 connects
    a. *erat* (line 52) and *colebantur* (line 54)
    c. *tum* (line 52) and *tum* (line 53)
    b. *Italia* (line 52) and *Latio* (line 53)
    d. *artium ac disciplinarum* (lines 52–53) and *studia* (line 53)

21. In line 53, *vehementius* is translated
    a. enthusiasm
    b. more enthusiastically
    c. very enthusiastically
    d. with enthusiasm

22. In line 54, *quam* is translated
    a. when
    b. that
    c. which
    d. than

23. In line 54, *isdem* is translated
    a. the same
    b. these
    c. theirs
    d. the others

24. In lines 52–55 (*Erat Italia . . . non neglegebantur*), Cicero tells us that
    a. many Greeks lived in Italy at one time
    b. studies are more important nowadays than before
    c. peace in Rome allowed studies to be cultivated
    d. people studied in towns but not in the city

25. Line 56 (*itaque . . . Nea-*) contains an example of
    a. asyndeton
    b. hyperbole
    c. polysyndeton
    d. anaphora

26. The adjective *dignum* in line 59 modifies
    a. *hunc* (line 56)
    b. *qui* (line 58)
    c. *aliquid* (line 58)
    d. *hospitio* (line 59)

27. From lines 56–59 (*Itaque hunc . . . dignum existimarunt*), we learn that the people of Tarentum, Locri, Rhegium and Naples
    a. gave Archias money to visit them
    b. granted citizenship to Archias
    c. thought that Archias was dignified
    d. considered Archias to be a genius

28. From lines 59–61 (*Hac tanta celebritate . . . et Catulo*), we learn that Archias
    a. was a very well-known poet
    b. was known to those he hadn't met
    c. came to Rome with the consul
    d. took advice from Marius and Catulus

29. The antecedent of *quorum* (line 62) is
    a. *consules* (line 61)
    b. *alter . . . alter* (line 62)
    c. *res . . . maximas* (line 62)
    d. *res gestas* (lines 62–63)

30. The phrase *res gestas* in lines 62–63 is the object of
    a. *nactus est* (line 61)
    b. *scribendum* (line 62)
    c. *adhibere* (line 63)
    d. *posset* (line 63)

31. The tense and mood of *posset* (line 63) is
    a. present subjunctive
    b. imperfect subjunctive
    c. present indicative
    d. imperfect indicative

32. From lines 61–63 (*Nactus est . . . adhibere posset*), we learn that
    a. the consul had written about his deeds
    b. both consuls' deeds were worth writing about
    c. writing is the greatest possible thing
    d. enthusiasm is necessary for writing well

33. In line 64, *cum . . . tum etiam* is translated
    a. not only . . . but also
    b. since . . . also then
    c. although . . . even then
    d. when . . . then too

34. In lines 64–65 (*Statim . . . receperunt*), Cicero tells us that
    a. Archias immediately received his own home
    b. Archias was no longer wearing his boyhood toga
    c. The Luculli admitted Archias into their home
    d. Archias was sent home because he was very young

35. The adjective *prima* (line 67) modifies
    a. *naturae atque virtutis* (lines 66–67)
    b. *domus* (line 67)
    c. *adulescentiae* (line 67)
    d. *eadem* (line 67)

Translation *Suggested time: 15 minutes*

> Itaque hunc et Tarentini et Locrenses et Regini et Nea-
> politani civitate ceterisque praemiis donarunt, et omnes
> qui aliquid de ingeniis poterant iudicare cognitione atque
> hospitio dignum existimarunt. Hac tanta celebritate
> 5 famae cum esset iam absentibus notus, Romam venit
> Mario consule et Catulo.

_____

_____

_____

_____

_____

_____

_____

_____

Short Analysis Questions

> Nam ut primum ex pueris excessit Archias atque ab
> eis artibus quibus aetas puerilis ad humanitatem informari
> solet, se ad scribendi studium contulit. Primum Antiochiae
> —nam ibi natus est loco nobili—celebri quondam urbe et
> 5   copiosa atque eruditissimis hominibus liberalissimisque
> studiis adfluenti, celeriter antecellere omnibus ingeni gloria
> coepit. Post in ceteris Asiae partibus cunctaque Graecia sic
> eius adventus celebrabantur ut famam ingeni exspectatio
> hominis, exspectationem ipsius adventus admiratioque
> 10   superaret.

1. In lines 1–3, Cicero begins to narrate for the jury some details of Archias's life. At what point in Archias's life does Cicero begin his narrative?

   _____

2. To what studies did Archias apply himself from the outset (lines 2–3)?

   _____

3. In lines 4–6, how does Cicero describe Archias's birthplace? Cite the Latin that substantiates your answer and translate or accurately paraphrase.

   _____

   _____

   _____

4. Identify two reactions to Archias in cities that he visited (lines 7–10). Cite the Latin text which supports your answer.

   _____

   _____

   _____

Essay *Suggested time: 20 minutes*

> Erat Italia tum plena Graecarum artium ac dis-
> ciplinarum, studiaque haec et in Latio vehementius tum
> colebantur quam nunc isdem in oppidis, et hic Romae
> propter tranquillitatem rei publicae non neglegebantur.
> 5   Itaque hunc et Tarentini et Locrenses et Regini et Nea-
> politani civitate ceterisque praemiis donarunt, et omnes
> qui aliquid de ingeniis poterant iudicare cognitione atque
> hospitio dignum existimarunt.

In this passage Cicero includes a number of geographical references, beginning with *Italia* in line 1. In a short essay, discuss the different geographical locations he cites and his purpose in referring to them at this juncture in the oration.

Support your assertions with references to the Latin text throughout the passage above. All Latin words must be copied or their line numbers provided, AND they must be translated or paraphrased closely enough that it is clear you understand the Latin. It is your responsibility to convince the reader that you are basing your conclusions on the Latin text and not merely on a general recollection of the passage. Direct your answer to the question; do not merely summarize the passage. Please write your essay on a separate piece of paper.

CHAPTER 4: LINES 69–89

6 Erat temporibus illis iucundus Q. Metello, illi
70 Numidico, et eius Pio filio, audiebatur a M. Aemilio, vivebat cum Q. Catulo et patre et filio, a L. Crasso colebatur. Lucullos vero et Drusum et Octavios et Catonem et
totam Hortensiorum domum devinctam consuetudine
cum teneret, adficiebatur summo honore, quod eum non
75 solum colebant, qui aliquid percipere atque audire
studebant, verum etiam si qui forte simulabant. Interim
satis longo intervallo, cum esset cum M. Lucullo in Siciliam profectus et cum ex ea provincia cum eodem
Lucullo decederet, venit Heracleam. Quae cum esset
80 civitas aequissimo iure ac foedere, ascribi se in
eam civitatem voluit idque, cum ipse per se dignus
putaretur, tum auctoritate et gratia Luculli ab Hera-
cliensibus impetravit. 7 Data est civitas Silvani lege et Carbonis: SI QUI FOEDERATIS CIVITATIBUS ASCRIPTI FUISSENT, SI TUM
85 CUM LEX FEREBATUR IN ITALIA DOMICILIUM HABUISSENT ET
SI SEXAGINTA DIEBUS APUD PRAETOREM ESSENT PROFESSI.
Cum hic domicilium Romae multos iam annos haberet,
professus est apud praetorem Q. Metellum, familiarissimum suum.

Preparatory Questions

Line 69   Identify the subject of *erat.* _____

What is the the case and use of *temporibus illis?* _____

What is the case and use of *iucundus?* _____

What is the case and use of *Metello?* _____

What does *illi* modify? _____

Line 70   To whom does *eius* refer? _____

Identify the case and use of *Pio.* _____

What is the case and use of *Aemilio?* _____

Lines 70–72   Identify the subject of *audiebatur, vivebat* and *colebatur.* _____

Line 71   Find a correlative construction. _____

Line 72   What part of speech is *vero?* _____

Lines 72–73   What verb governs *Lucullos . . . totam Hortensiorum domum?* _____

                What rhetorical device is used in these lines? _____

Line 73   What part of speech is *devinctam?* Identify its case and use. _____

                Identify the case and use of *consuetudine.* _____

Line 74   Find a *cum* clause. _____

                What kind of *cum* clause is it? _____

                What is the tense and mood of *teneret?* _____

                Identify the subject of *teneret.* _____

                Find the main verb of the sentence and identify its subject. _____

                What is the case and use of *summo honore?* _____

                What kind of clause is introduced by *quod?* _____

                To whom does *eum* refer? _____

Lines 74–76   Find a correlative construction. _____

Line 75   Identify the subject of *colebant.* _____

                What is the case and use of *aliquid?* _____

Lines 75–76   Find a relative clause. _____

Line 76   Identify the case and use of *qui.* _____

                What is the antecedent of *qui?* _____

                What part of speech is *forte?* _____

Lines 76–79   Find the main verb of the sentence. _____

Line 77   What does *satis* modify? _____

                Identify the case and use of *longo intervallo.* _____

                Identify the subject of *esset.* _____

                What is the case and use of *M. Lucullo?* _____

Lines 77–78   What is the case and use of *Siciliam?* _____

Line 78   Identify the case and use of *provincia.* _____

                To what word does *provincia* refer? _____

                Identify the case and use of *eodem.* _____

Lines 77–78   Find a *cum* clause. _____

                What kind of *cum* clause is it? _____

Lines 78-79   Find another *cum* clause._____

Line 79   Identify the subject of *venit.* _____

       What is the case and use of *Heracleam.* _____

       Find a connecting relative. _____

       Find a *cum* clause. _____

       What kind of *cum* clause is it? _____

Line 80   What is the case and use of *civitas?* _____

       What does *aequissimo* modify? _____

       Identify the case and use of *iure* and *foedere.* _____

       To whom does *se* refer? _____

       Identify the form of *ascribi.* On what word does it depend? _____

Line 81   Identify the subject of *voluit.* _____

       To what does *id* (*idque*) refer? _____

       What words does *-que* connect? _____

       To whom does *ipse* refer? _____

       What is the case and use of *dignus?* _____

Line 82   What infinitive is understood with *putaretur?* _____

       What part of speech is *tum?* What does it modify? _____

       Identify the case and use of *auctoritate* and *gratia.* _____

Lines 81–82   Find a *cum* clause. _____

       What kind of *cum* clause is it? _____

Line 83   Identify the subject of *impetravit.* _____

       Identify the subject of *data est.* _____

       What is the case and use of *lege?* _____

Lines 84–86   Find three conditional clauses. _____

       Identify the conclusion (apodosis) of the conditions._____

Line 84   What is the case and use of *QUI?* _____

       Identify the tense, mood and voice of *ASCRIPTI FUISSENT.*_____

Lines 84–85   What does *TUM* modify? _____

Line 85   What kind of clause is *CUM . . . FEREBATUR?* _____

           With which word should *IN ITALIA* be taken? _____

Line 86   Identify the case and use of *SEXAGINTA DIEBUS.* _____

           Identify the case and use of *PRAETOREM.* _____

           What is the tense and mood of *ESSENT PROFESSI?* _____

Lines 87–89 Find the main verb of the sentence. _____

Line 87   Find a *cum* clause. _____

           What kind of *cum* clause is it? _____

           To whom does *hic* refer? _____

           Identify the case and use of *Romae.* _____

           Identify the case and use of *multos . . . annos.* _____

           What does *iam* modify? _____

Line 88   What is the case and use of *Q. Metellum?* _____

Lines 88–89 What part of speech is *familiarissimum?* _____

           What is its case and use? _____

Line 89   To whom does *suum* refer? _____

Multiple Choice Questions *Suggested time: 27 minutes*

1. The word *illi* in line 69 modifies
    a. *Metello* (line 69)   b. *Numidico* (line 70)
    c. *Pio* (line 70)   d. *Aemilio* (line 70)

2. From lines 69–72 (*Erat . . . colebatur*), we learn that
    a. Archias wrote poems about his friends
    b. A number of prominent people were Archias's pupils
    c. Many prominent men supported Archias
    d. Archias stayed with many famous men

3. Lines 69–72 (*Erat . . . colebatur*) contain an example of
    a. hyperbole   b. assonance
    c. asyndeton   d. polysyndeton

4. The adjective *totam* (line 73) modifies
    a. *Catonem* (line 72)   b. *domum* (line 73)
    c. *devinctam* (line 73)   d. *consuetudine* (line 73)

5. In line 73, *consuetudine* is translated
   a. habitually
   b. with society
   c. by friendship
   d. according to custom

6. In line 74, *cum* is translated
   a. with
   b. when
   c. since
   d. although

7. In line 75, *aliquid* is translated
   a. something
   b. anyone
   c. whatever
   d. whenever

8. In line 76, *interim* is a(n)
   a. adjective
   b. noun
   c. adverb
   d. verb

9. In line 77, the <u>second</u> *cum* is translated
   a. when
   b. since
   c. although
   d. with

10. The tense and mood of *decederet* (line 79) is
    a. present indicative
    b. present subjunctive
    c. imperfect indicative
    d. imperfect subjunctive

11. Lines 77–79 (*cum esset . . . decederet*) contain an example of
    a. litotes
    b. asyndeton
    c. chiasmus
    d. hyperbole

12. From lines 76–79 (*Interim . . . Heracleam*), we learn that
    a. Lucullus had a home in Sicily for many years
    b. Archias accompanied Lucullus to Sicily
    c. Lucullus died in Sicily
    d. Archias never visited Heraclea

13. The antecedent of *quae* (line 79) is
    a. *ea provincia* (line 78)
    b. *Heracleam* (line 79)
    c. *civitas* (line 80)
    d. *se* (line 80)

14. The subject of *ascribi* (line 80) is
    a. *Heracleam* (line 79)
    b. *se* (line 80)
    c. *civitatem* (line 81)
    d. *idque* (line 81)

15. The word *idque* (line 81) is the object of

    a. *ascribi* (line 80)

    b. *voluit* (line 81)

    c. *putaretur* (line 82)

    d. *impetravit* (line 83)

16. In line 82, *gratia* is translated

    a. thanks

    b. grace

    c. influence

    d. pleasing

17. From lines 79–83 (*Quae cum esset . . . impetravit*), we learn that

    a. Archias thought himself worthy of citizenship

    b. Heraclea did not have a treaty with Rome

    c. Lucullus held a magistracy in Heraclea

    d. Archias received citizenship from the Heracleans

18. The individuals *Silvani* and *Carbonis* (lines 83–84) are

    a. friends of Lucullus

    b. citizens of Heraclea

    c. authors of a law

    d. relatives of Archias

19. The subject of *HABUISSENT* (line 85) is

    a. *Silvani et Carbonis* (lines 83–84).

    b. *QUI* (line 84)

    c. *SEXAGINTA* (line 86)

    d. *PROFESSI* (line 86)

20. In line 86, *ESSENT PROFESSI* is translated

    a. they had registered

    b. they had been registered

    c. they would have registered

    d. they should have been registered

21. From lines 83–86 (*Data est . . . PROFESSI*), we learn that

    a. Rome had many different citizenship laws

    b. there were three requirements for citizenship

    c. a sixty day waiting period was necessary

    d. only people in allied towns could be citizens

22. The subject of *professus est* (line 88) is

    a. *hic* (line 87)

    b. *domicilium* (line 87)

    c. *praetorem* (line 88)

    d. *Q. Metellum* (line 88)

23. From lines 87–89 (*Cum hic . . . familiarissimum suum*), we learn that

    a. Metellus lived in Rome

    b. Archias lived in Rome

    c. the praetor was very friendly

    d. Rome had many houses

Translation *Suggested time: 15 minutes*

                            Interim
satis longo intervallo, cum esset cum M. Lucullo in Siciliam profectus et cum ex ea provincia cum eodem
Lucullo decederet, venit Heracleam. Quae cum esset
5   civitas aequissimo iure ac foedere, ascribi se in
eam civitatem voluit idque, cum ipse per se dignus
putaretur, tum auctoritate et gratia Luculli ab Hera-
cliensibus impetravit.

Short Analysis Questions

> Erat temporibus illis iucundus Q. Metello, illi
> Numidico, et eius Pio filio, audiebatur a M. Aemilio, vi-
> vebat cum Q. Catulo et patre et filio, a L. Crasso coleba-
> tur. Lucullos vero et Drusum et Octavios et Catonem et
> 5   totam Hortensiorum domum devinctam consuetudine
> cum teneret, adficiebatur summo honore, quod eum non
> solum colebant, qui aliquid percipere atque audire
> studebant, verum etiam si qui forte simulabant. Interim
> satis longo intervallo, cum esset cum M. Lucullo in Si-
> 10 ciliam profectus et cum ex ea provincia cum eodem
> Lucullo decederet, venit Heracleam.

1. In lines 4–5, what do the Luculli, Drusus, the Octavii, Cato and the entire household of the Hortensii have in common with respect to Archias? Cite the Latin that supports your answer and translate or accurately paraphrase it.

   _____

   _____

   _____

2. Identify the figure of speech found in lines 8–9. Quote the Latin that illustrates its use and comment on its effectiveness.

   _____

   _____

   _____

3. What point is Cicero trying to reinforce with the antithesis of *cum M. Lucullo . . . profectus* and *. . . cum eodem Lucullo decederet* (lines 9–11)?

   _____

   _____

   _____

Quae cum esset
civitas aequissimo iure ac foedere ascribi se in
eam civitatem voluit idque, cum ipse per se dignus
putaretur, tum auctoritate et gratia Luculli ab Hera-

5 cliensibus impetravit. 7 Data est civitas Silvani lege et Car-
bonis: SI QUI FOEDERATIS CIVITATIBUS ASCRIPTI FUISSENT, SI TUM
CUM LEX FEREBATUR IN ITALIA DOMICILIUM HABUISSENT ET
SI SEXAGINTA DIEBUS APUD PRAETOREM ESSENT PROFESSI.
Cum hic domicilium Romae multos iam annos haberet,

10 professus est apud praetorem Q. Metellum, familiarissimum suum.

4. What does the phrase *aequissimo iure ac foedere* (line 2), reveal about the status of Heraclea and its citizens?

_____

_____

_____

5. According to Cicero, what two factors brought the privilege of citizenship in Heraclea to Archias? Quote the Latin that supports your answer and translate or paraphrase accurately.

_____

_____

_____

_____

6. Lines 5–8 state the terms of a law authored by Silvanus and Carbo, tribunes of 89 B.C., granting full Roman citizenship to the citizens of states allied with Rome. What are the three conditions that must be met to attain citizenship? Which two conditions of this law did Archias fulfill? Cite the Latin which supports your answer and translate or paraphrase accurately.

_____

_____

_____

_____

Essay *Suggested time: 20 minutes*

      Erat temporibus illis iucundus Q. Metello, illi
Numidico, et eius Pio filio, audiebatur a M. Aemilio, vivebat cum Q. Catulo et patre et filio, a L. Crasso colebatur. Lucullos vero et Drusum et Octavios et Catonem et
5   totam Hortensiorum domum devinctam consuetudine
cum teneret, adficiebatur summo honore, quod eum non
solum colebant, qui aliquid percipere atque audire
studebant, verum etiam si qui forte simulabant. Interim
satis longo intervallo, cum esset cum M. Lucullo in Si-
10   ciliam profectus et cum ex ea provincia cum eodem
Lucullo decederet, venit Heracleam.

In this passage the name of Archias is closely linked with that of the Luculli. In a short essay, discuss the nature of this relationship and how Cicero underscores the closeness of the relationship between the two.

Support your assertions with references to the Latin text throughout the passage above. All Latin words must be copied or their line numbers provided, AND they must be translated or paraphrased closely enough that it is clear you understand the Latin. It is your responsibility to convince the reader that you are basing your conclusions on the Latin text and not merely on a general recollection of the passage. Direct your answer to the question; do not merely summarize the passage. Please write your essay on a separate piece of paper.

CHAPTER 5: LINES 90–106

90   8 Si nihil aliud nisi de civitate ac lege dicimus,
nihil dico amplius: causa dicta est. Quid enim horum
infirmari, Gratti, potest? Heracleaene esse tum ascriptum negabis? Adest vir summa auctoritate et religione
et fide, M. Lucullus, qui se non opinari sed scire, non
95   audisse sed vidisse, non interfuisse sed egisse dicit.
Adsunt Heraclienses legati, nobilissimi homines, huius
iudici causa cum mandatis et cum publico testimonio
venerunt, qui hunc ascriptum Heracleae esse dicunt. Hic tu
tabulas desideras Heracliensium publicas, quas Italico bello
100   incenso tabulario interisse scimus omnes? Est ridiculum
ad ea quae habemus nihil dicere, quaerere quae habere
non possumus, et de hominum memoria tacere, litterarum
memoriam flagitare et, cum habeas amplissimi viri re-
ligionem, integerrimi municipi ius iurandum fidemque,
105   ea quae depravari nullo modo possunt repudiare, tabulas
quas idem dicis solere corrumpi desiderare.

Preparatory Questions

Lines 90–91   Identify the type of conditional sentence. _____

Line 90   Identify the case and use of *aliud*. _____

Line 91   What part of speech is *amplius?* _____

    Identify the tense, voice and mood of *dicta est*. _____

    What part of speech is *quid?* _____

    Identify the case and use of *horum*. _____

Line 92   Identify the form and use of *infirmari*. _____

    Identify the case and use of *Gratti*. _____

    What does the enclitic *-ne* indicate? _____

    What is the case of *Heracleae?* _____

    Identify the form and function of *esse . . . ascriptum*. _____

Lines 92–93   What word must be understood with *esse . . . ascriptum negabis?* _____

Line 93   Identify the subject of *adest*. _____

From what verb does *adest* come? _____

What does *summa* modify? _____

Lines 93–94   Identify the case and use of *auctoritate* and *religione* and *fide*. _____

Line 94   Identify the case and use of *M. Lucullus*. _____

Lines 94–95   Find a relative clause. _____

List all the infinitives in these lines and give the tense of each. _____

What is the function of these infinitives? _____

On what word do they depend? _____

What three rhetorical devices are used in these lines? _____

Line 96   What is the case and use of *nobilissimi homines?* _____

Lines 96–97   What is the case and use of *huius iudici?* _____

Line 98   Find a relative clause. _____

Identify the subject of *venerunt*. _____

What is the antecedent of *qui?* Of what verb is *qui* the subject? _____

Identify the case and use of *hunc*. To whom does *hunc* refer? _____

What is the function of *ascriptum . . . esse?* _____

What part of speech is *hic?* _____

Line 99   Identify the case and use of *tabulas*. _____

What word modifies it? _____

What is the tense of *desideras?* _____

Identify the case and use of *Heracliensium*. _____

Lines 99–100   Find a relative clause. _____

Line 99   What is the antecedent of *quas?* Identify the case and use of *quas*. _____

Identify the case and use of *Italico bello*. _____

Line 100   Identify the form of *incenso*. _____

What construction is *incenso tabulario?* _____

Identify the form of *interisse*. _____

From what verb is it derived? _____

Identify the case and use of *omnes*. _____

What is the function of *ridiculum?* _____

Lines 101–2   Find two relative clauses. _____

Line 101   Identify the case and use of *ea*. _____

       What is the case and use of *nihil*? _____

       What is the function of *dicere*? _____

       Identify the case and use of the <u>second</u> *quae*. _____

       What rhetorical device is used in this line? _____

Line 102   What word does *non possumus* govern? _____

       Identify the case and use of *memoria*. _____

Line 103   Identify the case and use of *amplissimi viri*. _____

Line 104   Identify the case and use of *ius iurandum*. _____

       What words does *-que* connect? _____

Lines 103–4   Find a *cum* clause. _____

       What kind of *cum* clause is it? _____

Line 105   Find a relative clause. _____

       What is the case and use of *ea*? _____

       Identify the tense and voice of *depravari*. _____

       What word governs it? _____

       Identify the case and use of *nullo modo*. _____

       Identify the case and use of *tabulas*. _____

Line 106   Find a relative clause. _____

       What is the antecedent of *quas*? _____

       What is the case and use of *quas*? _____

       What is the case and use of *idem*? _____

       Identify the form of *corrumpi*. _____

       What word governs it? _____

Lines 100–6   What rhetorical devices are used in this sentence? _____

       _____

Multiple Choice Questions *Suggested time: 32 minutes*

1. In lines 90–91 (*Si nihil . . . dicta est*), we learn that Cicero
    a. has a lot more to say
    b. has presented his evidence in the case
    c. will say nothing about the law
    d. will speak more loudly

2. In line 91, *causa* is translated
    a. cause
    b. reason
    c. case
    d. pretext

3. The word *horum* in line 91 refers to
    a. *nihil aliud* (line 90)
    b. *civitate ac lege* (line 90)
    c. Archias and Cicero
    d. Archias and Lucullus

4. The subject of *esse ascriptum* (lines 92–93) is
    a. *Gratti* (line 92)
    b. *Heracleaene* (line 92)
    c. Archias (understood)
    d. *Lucullus* (line 94)

5. The subject of *negabis* (line 93) is
    a. *Gratti* (line 92)
    b. *vir* (line 93)
    c. *Lucullus* (line 94)
    d. Archias (understood)

6. The antecedent of *qui* (line 94) is
    a. *Gratti* (line 92)
    b. *vir* (line 93)
    c. *fide* (line 94)
    d. *Lucullus* (line 94)

7. The pronoun *se* in line 94 refers to
    a. *Gratti* (line 92)
    b. *Heracleaene* (line 92)
    c. *Lucullus* (line 94)
    d. Archias (understood)

8. The subject of *audisse* (line 95) is
    a. *vir* (line 93)
    b. *Lucullus* (line 94)
    c. *qui* (line 94)
    d. *se* (line 94)

9. The subject of *dicit* (line 95) is
    a. *vir* (line 93)
    b. *Lucullus* (line 94)
    c. *qui* (line 94)
    d. *se* (line 94)

10. In lines 93–95 (*Adest vir . . . egisse dicit*), we learn that Lucullus
    a. was a very religious man
    b. had no opinion about the case
    c. was present at the court
    d. couldn't see or hear very well

11. Lines 93–95 (*Adest vir . . . egisse dicit*) contain an example of

    a. asyndeton
           b. hyperbole

    c. tricolon
           d. alliteration

12. In line 97, *causa* is translated

    a. the case
           b. with reason

    c. the cause
           d. for the sake of

13. In line 97, the <u>first</u> *cum* is translated

    a. when
           b. since

    c. although
           d. with

14. The subject of *dicunt* (line 98) is

    a. *Heraclienses legati* (line 96)
           b. *nobilissimi homines* (line 96)

    c. *qui* (line 98)
           d. *Heracleae* (line 98)

15. From lines 96–98 (*Adsunt . . . esse dicunt*), we learn that the representatives from Heraclea

    a. were ordered to come to court
           b. gave public testimony in Rome

    c. said that Archias was enrolled
           d. expressed opposition to Archias

16. The pronoun *tu* (line 98) refers to

    a. the prosecutor
           b. the defendant

    c. the jury
           d. the delegation from Heraclea

17. The word *omnes* in line 100 refers to

    a. the jurymen
           b. the defense team

    c. everyone present in the court
           d. the delegation from Heraclea

18. In lines 98–100 (*Hic tu . . . scimus omnes*), we learn that

    a. the records of Heraclea were public knowledge
           b. the Heracleans took good care of their records

    c. the records office was burned during a war
           d. accurate records were never kept

19. The antecedent of the <u>first</u> *quae* in line 101 is

    a. *ea* (line 101)
           b. *nihil* (line 101)

    c. *memoria* (line 102)
           d. *litterarum* (line 102)

20. The object of *habere* (line 101) is

    a. *ea* (line 101)
           b. the first *quae* (line 101)

    c. *nihil* (line 101)
           d. the second *quae* (line 101)

21. The tense and mood of *habeas* (line 103) is
    a. present indicative
    b. present subjunctive
    c. imperfect indicative
    d. imperfect subjunctive

22. The phrase *amplissimi viri* (line 103) refers to
    a. Archias
    b. Cicero
    c. Lucullus
    d. Grattius

23. The object of *repudiare* (line 105) is
    a. *ius iurandum fidemque* (line 104)
    b. *ea* (line 105)
    c. *quae* (line 105)
    d. *tabulas* (line 105)

24. In line 106, *idem* is the subject of
    a. *dicis* (line 106)
    b. *solere* (line 106)
    c. *corrumpi* (line 106)
    d. *desiderare* (line 106)

25. In line 106, *idem* refers to
    a. Archias
    b. the jury
    c. the prosecutor
    d. Lucullus

26. The main verb of the sentence in lines 100–106 (*Est ridiculum . . . corrumpi desiderare*) is
    a. *est* (line 100)
    b. *habemus* (line 101)
    c. *possunt* (line 105)
    d. *dicis* (line 106)

27. From lines 100–106 (*Est ridiculum . . . corrumpi desiderare*), we learn that
    a. the Heracleans have sworn an oath
    b. many records have been forged
    c. human memory is unreliable
    d. bribery of the court is possible

Translation *Suggested time: 15 minutes*

Adsunt Heraclienses legati, nobilissimi homines, huius
iudici causa cum mandatis et cum publico testimonio
venerunt, qui hunc ascriptum Heracleae esse dicunt. Hic tu
tabulas desideras Heracliensium publicas, quas Italico bello
5   incenso tabulario interisse scimus omnes?

_____

_____

_____

_____

_____

_____

_____

_____

Short Analysis Questions

Si nihil aliud nisi de civitate ac lege dicimus,
nihil dico amplius: causa dicta est. Quid enim horum
infirmari, Gratti, potest? Heracleaene esse tum ascriptum negabis? Adest vir summa auctoritate et religione
5   et fide, M. Lucullus, qui se non opinari sed scire, non
audisse sed vidisse, non interfuisse sed egisse dicit.

1. Identify the case of *Gratti*, line 3. _____ What is the significance of Grattius
    to this trial?

    _____

2. How is Marcus Lucullus described in lines 4–5? Cite the Latin that supports your answer and
    translate or accurately paraphrase.

    _____

    _____

    _____

3. Identify the figure of speech in lines 5–6. Quote the Latin that illustrates this rhetorical figure.

    _____

> Adsunt Heraclienses legati, nobilissimi homines, huius
> iudici causa cum mandatis et cum publico testimonio
> venerunt, qui hunc ascriptum Heracleae esse dicunt. Hic tu
> tabulas desideras Heracliensium publicas, quas Italico bello
> 5   incenso tabulario interisse scimus omnes? Est ridiculum
> ad ea quae habemus nihil dicere, quaerere quae habere
> non possumus, et de hominum memoria tacere, litterarum
> memoriam flagitare et, cum habeas amplissimi viri re-
> ligionem, integerrimi municipi ius iurandum fidemque,
> 10 ea quae depravari nullo modo possunt repudiare, tabulas
> quas idem dicis solere corrumpi desiderare.

4. According to lines 3–5, what happened to the public records that would have proved the validity of Archias's enrollment as a citizen of Heraclea? Cite the Latin that answers the question and translate or accurately paraphrase.

_____

_____

_____

_____

5. What evidence has Cicero produced in the absence of the written records? Cite the Latin that supports your answer and translate or accurately paraphrase.

_____

_____

_____

Essay *Suggested time: 20 minutes*

Est ridiculum
ad ea quae habemus nihil dicere, quaerere quae habere
non possumus, et de hominum memoria tacere, litterarum
memoriam flagitare et, cum habeas amplissimi viri re-
5   ligionem, integerrimi municipi ius iurandum fidemque,
ea quae depravari nullo modo possunt repudiare, tabulas
quas idem dicis solere corrumpi desiderare.

In this passage Cicero uses a tricolon of antithetical pairs of infinitives to ridicule the prosecution's request for the records that had been destroyed. In a short essay, discuss specifically what Cicero finds ridiculous about the prosecution's demands and in each instance what he suggests as a more reasonable approach.

Support your assertions with references to the Latin text throughout the passage above. All Latin words must be copied or their line numbers provided, AND they must be translated or paraphrased closely enough that it is clear you understand the Latin. It is your responsibility to convince the reader that you are basing your conclusions on the Latin text and not merely on a general recollection of the passage. Direct your answer to the question; do not merely summarize the passage. Please write your essay on a separate piece of paper.

CHAPTER 6: LINES 107–131

9 An domicilium Romae non habuit is qui tot annis ante civitatem datam sedem omnium rerum ac fortunarum suarum Romae conlocavit? An non est professus? Immo
110 vero eis tabulis professus quae solae ex illa professione conlegioque praetorum obtinent publicarum tabularum auctoritatem. Nam, cum Appi tabulae neglegentius adservatae dicerentur, Gabini, quam diu incolumis fuit, levitas, post damnationem calamitas omnem tabularum
115 fidem resignasset, Metellus, homo sanctissimus modestissimusque omnium, tanta diligentia fuit ut ad L. Lentulum praetorem et ad iudices venerit et unius nominis litura se commotum esse dixerit. His igitur in tabulis nullam lituram in nomine A. Licini videtis. 10 Quae cum
120 ita sint, quid est quod de eius civitate dubitetis, praesertim cum aliis quoque in civitatibus fuerit ascriptus? Etenim cum mediocribus multis et aut nulla aut humili aliqua arte praeditis gratuito civitatem in Graecia homines impertiebant, Reginos credo aut Locrensis aut Neapolitanos
125 aut Tarentinos, quod scaenicis artificibus largiri solebant, id huic summa ingeni praedito gloria noluisse! Quid? Cum ceteri non modo post civitatem datam sed etiam post legem Papiam aliquo modo in eorum municipiorum tabulas inrepserunt, hic qui ne utitur quidem illis in quibus
130 est scriptus, quod semper se Heracliensem esse voluit, reicietur?

Preparatory Questions

Line 107   What part of speech is *an?* _____

What is the case of *Romae?* _____

Identify the subject of *habuit.* What is its object?_____

Lines 107–9   Find a relative clause. _____

Line 107   What is the antecedent of *qui?* _____

What word does *tot* modify? _____

Identify the case and use of *annis.* _____

Line 108   What part of speech is *datam?* What word does it modify?_____

            Identify the case and use of *sedem.* _____

Line 109   What words does *suarum* modify? _____

            To whom does it refer? _____

            What is the tense and mood of *est professus?*. _____

            Identify the subject of *est professus.* _____

            What part of speech is *immo?*_____

Line 110   Identify the case and use of *eis tabulis.* _____

            What word must be understood with *professus* to make a finite verb? _____

Lines 110–12 Find a relative clause. _____

Line 110   What is the antecedent of *quae?* _____

            What word does *solae* modify?_____

Line 111   What is the case and use of *conlegio(que)?* _____

            Identify the subject of *obtinent.* What is its object? _____

Lines 112–13 Find a *cum* clause. _____

            What kind of *cum* clause is it? _____

Line 112   Identify the case and use of *Appi.* _____

            What part of speech is *neglegentius?* What word does it modify? _____

Lines 112–13 What is the form and use of *adservatae?* _____

Line 113   Identify the subject of *dicerentur.* _____

            What is the case and use of *Gabini?*_____

            What does *incolumis* modify? _____

            Identify the subject of *fuit.* _____

Line 114   What is the case and use of *levitas?* _____

            What is the case and use of *calamitas?* _____

            What word does *omnem* modify?_____

            Identify the case and use of *tabularum.* _____

Line 115   What are the subjects of *resignasset?* What is its object?_____

            Identify the case and use of *Metellus.* _____

Lines 115–16   Identify the case and use of *homo sanctissimus modestissimusque.* _____

Line 116   Identify the case and use of *omnium.* _____

                Identify the case and use of *tanta diligentia.* _____

Lines 116–18   Find a result clause. _____

                What word signals the result clause? _____

Line 117   Identify the case and use of *praetorem.* _____

Lines 117–18   Identify the tense and mood of *venerit* and *dixerit.* _____

Line 118   Identify the case and use of *litura.* _____

                Find an indirect statement. _____

                Identify the subject of *dixerit.* _____

                What part of speech is *igitur?* _____

                What word does *his* modify? _____

Line 119   What is the case and use of *nullam lituram?* _____

                What is the case and use of *A. Licini?* _____

                Identify the subject of *videtis.* _____

Lines 119–120   Find a *cum* clause. _____

                What is the subject of the *cum* clause? _____

Line 120   What part of speech is *quid?* _____

                Identify the case and use of *quod.* _____

                To whom does *eius* refer? _____

                What is the tense and mood of *dubitetis?* _____

                What part of speech is *praesertim?* _____

Line 121   Find a *cum* clause. _____

                Identify the subject of the *cum* clause. _____

                What word does *aliis* modify? _____

Lines 122–24   Find a *cum* clause. _____

                What kind of *cum* clause is it? _____

Line 122   Identify the case and use of *multis.* _____

                What two words modify *multis?* _____

Line 123   Identify the case and use of *arte*. _____

What words modify *arte?* _____

What part of speech is *gratuito?* What word does it modify? _____

Identify the case and use of *civitatem.* _____

Identify the case and use of *homines.* _____

Lines 124–26   Find an indirect statement. _____

What word introduces it? _____

Lines 124–25   What words are the subjects of the indirect statement? _____

Line 125   What is the antecedent of *quod?* _____

What is the case and use of *scaenicis artificibus?* _____

Identify the form and use of *largiri.* _____

Identify the subject of *solebant.* _____

What is the case and use of *id?* _____

Line 126   To whom does *huic* refer? _____

What is the case and use of *huic?* _____

What word modifies *huic?* _____

Identify the case and use of *gloria.* What word modifies it? _____

Identify the case and use of *ingeni.* _____

What is the object of *noluisse?* _____

What part of speech is *quid?* _____

Lines 126–29   Find a *cum* clause. _____

What kind of *cum* clause is it? _____

Line 127   Identify the case and use of *ceteri.* _____

What word does *datam* modify? _____

Line 128   Identify the case and use of *aliquo modo.* _____

What does *eorum* modify? _____

What is the case and use of *tabulas?* _____

Line 129   Identify the subject of *inrepserunt.* _____

What is the case and use of *hic?* _____

To whom does *hic* refer? _____

What is the antecedent of *qui*? _____

What is the case and use of *qui*? _____

Identify the case and use of *illis*. _____

What is the antecedent of *quibus*? _____

Line 130   Identify the subject of *est scriptus*. _____

What kind of clause does *quod* introduce? _____

Identify the case and use of *se*. To whom does *se* refer? _____

Identify the case and use of *Heracliensem*. _____

Lines 130–31   Identify the subject of *voluit*. _____

Line 131   Identify the subject of *reicietur*. _____

Multiple Choice Questions *Suggested time: 34 minutes*

1. In line 107, *tot annis* is translated
    a. within so many years
    b. during so many years
    c. for so many years
    d. after so many years

2. The subject of *conlocavit* (line 109) is
    a. Archias (understood)
    b. *is* (line 107)
    c. *qui* (line 107)
    d. *Romae* (line 109)

3. From lines 107–109 (*An domicilium . . . Romae conlocavit?*), we learn that Archias
    a. never lived in Rome
    b. had a house at Rome
    c. was a citizen of Rome
    d. had a large fortune

4. The case of *praetorum* (line 111) is
    a. nominative
    b. genitive
    c. accusative
    d. locative

5. From lines 109–112 (*Immo . . . auctoritatem*), we learn that
    a. some records of the praetors have been lost
    b. Archias is registered in valid records
    c. only some records are kept by the praetors
    d. no valid records are available

6. The subject of *venerit* (line 117) is
    a. *Appius* (line 112)
    b. *Gabinius* (line 113)
    c. *Metellus* (line 115)
    d. *homo* (line 115)

7. The adjective *unius* (line 117) modifies
   a. *homo* (line 115)
   b. *diligentia* (line 116)
   c. *nominis* (line 117)
   d. *litura* (line 118)

8. In line 118, *se* refers to
   a. *Metellus* (line 115)
   b. *Lentulum* (lines 116–117)
   c. *iudices* (line 117)
   d. *litura* (line 118)

9. The subject of *commotum esse* (line 118) is
   a. *Metellus* (line 115)
   b. *Lentulum* (lines 116–117)
   c. *praetorem* (line 117)
   d. *se* (line 118)

10. From lines 112–115 (*Nam . . . resignasset*), we learn that
    a. Appius and Gabinius were praetors
    b. Gabinius resigned his post
    c. Appius spoke rather carelessly
    d. Appius and Gabinius kept poor records

11. From lines 115–118 (*Metellus, homo . . . dixerit*), we learn that Metellus
    a. guarded the records carefully
    b. was diligent toward the judges
    c. went to see the praetor Lentulus
    d. said that he had erased one name

12. In line 119, *cum* is translated
    a. when
    b. since
    c. although
    d. with

13. In line 120, *sint* is translated
    a. might be
    b. were
    c. are
    d. would be

14. The tense and mood of *fuerit ascriptus* (line 121) is
    a. future indicative
    b. future perfect indicative
    c. present subjunctive
    d. perfect subjunctive

15. The subject of *fuerit ascriptus* (line 121) is
    a. *quid* (line 120)
    b. *quod* (line 120)
    c. Archias (understood)
    d. Metellus (understood)

16. From lines 119–121 (*Quae cum . . . fuerit ascriptus?*), we learn that
    a. the jury should have doubts about Archias's citizenship
    b. no city would hesitate to enroll Archias as a citizen
    c. Archias was already enrolled as a citizen in other cities
    d. because of special circumstances, Archias could not enroll

17. The word *etenim* (lines 121–122) is

    a. an adverb   b. an adjective

    c. a preposition   d. a conjunction

18. In line 122, *aliqua* is translated

    a. any   b. another

    c. some   d. whatever

19. The case of *praeditis* (line 123) is

    a. genitive   b. dative

    c. accusative   d. ablative

20. The verb *credo* (line 124) governs

    a. *impertiebant* (lines 123–124)   b. *largiri* (line 125)

    c. *solebant* (line 125)   d. *noluisse* (line 126)

21. In line 125, *scaenicis artificibus* is translated

    a. fake scenery   b. stage actors

    c. set painters   d. clever storytellers

22. The word *praedito* (line 126) modifies

    a. *id* (line 125)   b. *huic* (line 126)

    c. *ingeni* (line 126)   d. *noluisse* (line 126)

23. From lines 121–126 (*Etenim cum . . . gloria noluisse*), we learn that

    a. certain cities only granted citizenship to talented people   b. mediocre actors never held citizenship in some cities

    c. certain cities were not unwilling to grant citizenship to Archias   d. Archias had never even visited some of these cities

24. The phrase *non modo* (line 127) should be taken with

    a. *post civitatem* (line 127)   b. *sed etiam* (line 127)

    c. *post legem* (lines 127–128)   d. *aliquo modo* (line 128)

25. In line 127, the phrase *post civitatem datam* is translated

    a. after granting citizenship   b. when citizenship had been granted

    c. although citizenship was granted   d. to grant citizenship later

26. *Papiam* (line 128) modifies

    a. *civitatem* (line 127)   b. *datam* (line 127)

    c. *etiam* (line 127)   d. *legem* (lines 127–128)

27. The word *eorum* in line 128 refers to

    a. *Regino . . . Locrensis . . . Neapolitanos . . . Tarentinos* (lines 124–125)

    b. *scaenicis artificibus* (line 125)

    c. *ceteri* (line 127)

    d. *tabulas* (lines 128–129)

28. In lines 126–131 (*Cum ceteri . . . reicietur*), we learn that

    a. Archias wanted to be a citizen of Heraclea

    b. other people wanted to be citizens of Heraclea

    c. other people were illegally on the citizen rolls

    d. Archias made use of several citizenship rolls

Translation *Suggested time: 15 minutes*

Quid? Cum
ceteri non modo post civitatem datam sed etiam post legem Papiam aliquo modo in eorum municipiorum tabulas inrepserunt, hic qui ne utitur quidem illis in quibus
5   est scriptus, quod semper se Heracliensem esse voluit, reicietur?

_____

_____

_____

_____

_____

_____

_____

Short Analysis Questions

> Nam, cum Appi tabulae neglegentius ad-
> servatae dicerentur, Gabini, quam diu incolumis fuit,
> levitas, post damnationem calamitas omnem tabularum
> fidem resignasset, Metellus, homo sanctissimus modes-
> 5   tissimusque omnium, tanta diligentia fuit ut ad L. Len-
> tulum praetorem et ad iudices venerit et unius nominis
> litura se commotum esse dixerit.

1.   Who are Appius and Gabinius and what criticisms have been leveled against them in lines 1–4? Cite the Latin that supports your answer and translate or accurately paraphrase.

    _____

    _____

    _____

    _____

2.   According to Cicero how did the diligence and care employed by Metellus in handling the job of praetor manifest itself? How did his dutiful performance support Archias's claim to citizenship? Cite the Latin that supports your answer and translate or accurately paraphrase.

    _____

    _____

    _____

    _____

    _____

Quae cum
ita sint, quid est quod de eius civitate dubitetis, praesertim cum aliis quoque in civitatibus fuerit ascriptus? Etenim cum mediocribus multis et aut nulla aut humili aliqua
5   arte praeditis gratuito civitatem in Graecia homines impertiebant, Reginos credo aut Locrensis aut Neapolitanos
aut Tarentinos, quod scaenicis artificibus largiri solebant, id
huic summa ingeni praedito gloria noluisse! Quid? Cum
ceteri non modo post civitatem datam sed etiam post le-
10   gem Papiam aliquo modo in eorum municipiorum tabulas inrepserunt, hic qui ne utitur quidem illis in quibus
est scriptus, quod semper se Heracliensem esse voluit, reicietur?

3.   How does the mention of *aliis civitatibus* in line 3 help to reinforce the point that Cicero is making about Archias?

_____

_____

_____

4.   To people of what occupation were the Regini, Locrenses, Neapolitani and Tarentini accustomed to offer citizenship? Cite the Latin that answers the question and translate or accurately paraphrase.

_____

_____

5.   According to line 12, why did Archias not take advantage of his enrollment in the ranks of other municipalities?

_____

_____

Essay *Suggested time: 20 minutes*

                         Quae cum ita sint, quid est quod de eius civitate dubitetis, praesertim cum aliis quoque in civitatibus fuerit ascriptus? Etenim cum mediocribus multis et aut nulla aut humili aliqua

5   **arte praeditis gratuito civitatem in Graecia homines impertiebant, Reginos credo aut Locrensis aut Neapolitanos aut Tarentinos, quod scaenicis artificibus largiri solebant, id huic summa ingeni praedito gloria noluisse! Quid? Cum ceteri non modo post civitatem datam sed etiam post le-**

10   **gem Papiam aliquo modo in eorum municipiorum tabulas inrepserunt, hic qui ne utitur quidem illis in quibus est scriptus, quod semper se Heracliensem esse voluit, reicietur?**

In this passage Cicero sets up a clear contrast between the many (*multis*) who have been granted the rights of citizenship and the one person (*huic*) whose citizenship was being debated, i.e., Archias. In a short essay, discuss the methods Cicero uses to develop this contrast.

Support your assertions with references to the Latin text throughout the passage above. All Latin words must be copied or their line numbers provided, AND they must be translated or paraphrased closely enough that it is clear you understand the Latin. It is your responsibility to convince the reader that you are basing your conclusions on the Latin text and not merely on a general recollection of the passage. Direct your answer to the question; do not merely summarize the passage. Please write your essay on a separate piece of paper.

CHAPTER 7: LINES 131–157

        11 Census nostros requiris. Scilicet! Est enim obscurum proximis censoribus hunc cum clarissimo imperatore L. Lucullo apud exercitum fuisse, superioribus cum eodem quaestore fuisse in Asia, primis
135 Iulio et Crasso nullam populi partem esse censam. Sed, quoniam census non ius civitatis confirmat ac tantum modo indicat eum, qui sit census, ita se iam tum gessisse pro cive, eis temporibus is quem tu criminaris ne ipsius quidem iudicio in civium Romanorum iure esse versatum et testa-
140 mentum saepe fecit nostris legibus, et adiit hereditates civium Romanorum, et in beneficiis ad aerarium delatus est a L. Lucullo pro consule. Quaere argumenta, si quae potes; numquam enim hic neque suo neque amicorum iudicio revincetur.
        12 Quaeres a nobis, Gratti, cur tanto opere hoc
145 homine delectemur. Quia suppeditat nobis ubi et animus ex hoc forensi strepitu reficiatur et aures convicio defessae conquiescant. An tu existimas aut suppetere nobis posse quod cotidie dicamus in tanta varietate rerum, nisi animos nostros doctrina excolamus, aut ferre animos tantam posse
150 contentionem, nisi eos doctrina eadem relaxemus? Ego vero fateor me his studiis esse deditum. Ceteros pudeat, si qui ita se litteris abdiderunt ut nihil possint ex eis neque ad communem adferre fructum neque in aspectum lucemque proferre; me autem quid pudeat qui tot annos ita
155 vivo, iudices, ut a nullius umquam me tempore aut commodo aut otium meum abstraxerit aut voluptas avocarit aut denique somnus retardarit?

Preparatory Questions

Line 131   Identify the subject of *requiris*. _____

              What part of speech is *scilicet?* _____

              Identify the subject of *est*. _____

Line 132   What is the case and use of *proximis censoribus?* _____

              What is the case and use of *hunc?* _____

              To whom does *hunc* refer? _____

Lines 132–33   What is the case and use of *clarissimo imperatore?* _____

Line 133   Identify the case and use of *L. Lucullo.* _____

What is the form of *fuisse?* _____

Identify the subject of *fuisse.* _____

What word should be supplied with *superioribus?* _____

Line 134   Identify the subject of *fuisse.* _____

What word should be supplied with *primis?* _____

Line 135   Identify the case and use of *Iulio et Crasso.* _____

Find an infinitive. Identify the subject of the infinitive. _____

_____

What does *nullam* modify? _____

Identify the case and use of *populi.* _____

Line 136   What part of speech is *quoniam?* _____

Identify the case and use of *census.* _____

Identify the case and use of *ius.* _____

What part of speech is *tantum?* _____

Lines 136–37   What do *tantum modo* modify? _____

Line 137   What part of speech is *modo?* _____

Identify the case and use of *eum.* _____

What is the antecedent of *qui?* _____

Identify and explain the mood of *sit census.* _____

What is the case and use of *se?* _____

Identify the subject of *gessisse.* _____

Line 138   What is the case and use of *eis temporibus?* _____

To whom does *is* refer? _____

What is the antecedent of *quem?* _____

To whom does *ipsius* refer? _____

Line 139   Find the word that *in* governs. _____

Identify the subject of *esse versatum.* _____

Line 140   Identify the subject of *fecit.* _____

                       What is the case and use of *nostris legibus?* _____

                       Identify the subject of *adiit.* _____

Line 141   Identify the subject of *delatus est.* _____

                       What is the case and use of *Lucullo?* _____

Line 142   What is the form of *quaere?* _____

                       What is the object of *quaere?* _____

                       To what does *quae* refer? _____

Line 143   To whom does *hic* refer? _____

                       What is the case and use of *suo?* _____

                       What is the case and use of *iudicio?* _____

                       Identify the subject of *revincetur.* _____

Line 144   Identify the tense and mood of *quaeres.* _____

                       Find a vocative. _____

Line 145   Identify and explain the tense and mood of *delectemur.* _____

                       _____

                       Identify the subject of *suppeditat.* _____

                       What is the case and use of *nobis?* _____

Line 146   Identify the subject of *reficiatur.* _____

                       What is the case and use of *convicio?* _____

                       What does *defessae* modify? _____

Line 147   What is the function of *suppetere?* _____

                       Identify the subject of *posse.* _____

Lines 146–47   Identify and explain the tense and mood of *reficiatur* and *conquiescant.* _____

                       _____

Line 148   Identify and explain the mood of *dicamus.* _____

Lines 147–48   Find an indirect statement. _____

Line 149   What is the case and use of *doctrina?* _____

                       Identify and explain the tense and mood of *excolamus.* _____

                       _____

What is the function of *ferre?* _____

What is the object of *ferre?* _____

Identify the subject of *posse?* _____

Line 150   To what/whom does *eos* refer? _____

What does *eadem* modify? _____

Line 151   Find an indirect statement. _____

Identify the case and use of *me.* _____

Identify the case and use of *his studiis.* _____

Identify the mood and use of *pudeat.* _____

Line 152   What is the antecedent of *qui?* _____

Identify the case and use of *se.* _____

Identify the case and use of *litteris.* _____

Find a result clause. _____

To what does *eis* refer? _____

Lines 153–54   Find two infinitives dependent on *possint.* _____

Line 153   What is the object of *adferre?* _____

Line 154   What is the object of *proferre?* _____

What part of speech is *quid?* _____

What is the antecedent of *qui?* _____

Identify the case and use of *annos.* _____

Lines 154–55   Find a result clause. _____

Line 155   Identify the case and use of *me.* _____

Identify the case and use of *tempore.* _____

Line 156   Identify the subject of *abstraxerit.* _____

Line 157   What is the unsyncopated form of *retardit?* _____

Multiple Choice Questions *Suggested time: 31 minutes*

1. In line 133, *apud* is translated
   a. at the home of
   c. with
   b. in the presence of
   d. near

2. *eodem* (line 134) refers to
   a. Archias (understood)
   c. *Iulio* (line 135)
   b. *Lucullo* (line 133)
   d. *Crasso* (line 135)

3. From lines 131–135 (*Est enim . . . esse censam*), we learn that
   a. the census records were obscure
   c. Archias served in the army
   b. the superior censors were in Asia
   d. Iulius and Crassus were censors

4. The subject of *confirmat* (line 136) is
   a. *census* (line 136)
   c. *modo* (line 137)
   b. *ius* (line 136)
   d. *qui* (line 137)

5. The subject of *indicat* (line 137) is
   a. *census* (line 136)
   c. *modo* (line 137)
   b. *ius* (line 136)
   d. *qui* (line 137)

6. The subject of *sit census* (line 137) is
   a. *census* (line 136)
   c. *tantum* (line 136)
   b. *ius* (line 136)
   d. *qui* (line 137)

7. The pronoun *se* in line 137 refers to
   a. *ius* (line 136)
   c. *qui* (line 137)
   b. *eum* (line 137)
   d. *cive* (line 138)

8. In line 137, *pro* is translated
   a. for
   c. as
   b. on behalf of
   d. in place of

9. In line 139, *iudicio* is translated
   a. court
   c. sentence
   b. trial
   d. opinion

10. The tense of *adiit* (line 140) is
    a. present
    c. perfect
    b. future
    d. future perfect

11. The words *testamentum saepe fecit nostris legibus* (lines 139–140) tell us that Archias

    a. was a witness in court

    b. gave testimony about the laws

    c. made a will legally

    d. made Lucullus his heir

12. From lines 136–142 (*Sed, quoniam . . . pro consule*), we learn that

    a. a person is automatically a citizen if he is counted in the census

    b. Archias often acted as if he were a Roman citizen

    c. the prosecution claimed that Archias had broken the laws

    d. the proconsul L. Lucullus was a friend of Archias

13. From lines 142–143 (*Quaere . . . revincetur*), we learn that

    a. the prosecution has a strong case

    b. the defense has a strong case

    c. Archias has many friends

    d. Archias will not be convicted

14. *tanto* (line 144) modifies

    a. *Gratti* (line 144)

    b. *opere* (line 144)

    c. *hoc* (line 144)

    d. *homine* (line 145)

15. In line 145, *quia* is translated

    a. therefore

    b. because

    c. which

    d. that

16. *hoc* in line 146 modifies

    a. *forensi* (line 146)

    b. *strepitu* (line 146)

    c. *aures* (line 146)

    d. *convicio* (line 146)

17. The case of *forensi* (line 146) is

    a. nominative

    b. genitive

    c. dative

    d. ablative

18. In line 149, *ferre* is translated

    a. to endure

    b. to carry

    c. to convey

    d. to mention

19. From lines 147–150 (*An tu existimas . . . eadem relaxemus*), we learn that

    a. everyone needs an education

    b. educated people tend to talk too much

    c. education is relaxing and nourishing

    d. our minds cannot bear too much education

20. The subject of *esse deditum* (line 151) is

    a. *ego* (line 150)

    b. *vero* (line 151)

    c. *me* (line 151)

    d. *his* (line 151)

21. In line 152, *qui* is translated
    a. who
    b. those
    c. any
    d. which

22. The adjective *communem* (line 153) modifies
    a. *se* (line 152)
    b. *nihil* (line 152)
    c. *fructum* (line 153)
    d. *aspectum* (line 153)

23. In lines 151–154 (*Ceteros . . . lucemque proferre*), we find an example of
    a. hyperbole
    b. asyndeton
    c. hendiadys
    d. alliteration

24. In lines 151–154 (*Ceteros . . . lucemque proferre*), we learn that educated people
    a. are sometimes hermits
    b. should make a contribution
    c. are able to offer nothing
    d. rarely come outside in the daylight

25. In lines 154–157 (*me autem . . . retardarit*), we find an example of
    a. anaphora
    b. alliteration
    c. asyndeton
    d. assonance

26. In lines 154–157 (*me autem . . . retardarit*), we learn that Cicero
    a. never sleeps
    b. always helps his friends
    c. spends his leisure time studying
    d. does not have many pleasures

Translation *Suggested time: 15 minutes*

Sed, quoniam census non ius civitatis confirmat ac tantum modo indicat eum, qui sit census, ita se iam tum gessisse pro cive, eis temporibus is quem tu criminaris ne ipsius quidem iudicio in civium Romanorum iure esse versatum et testa-
5 mentum saepe fecit nostris legibus, et adiit hereditates civium Romanorum, et in beneficiis ad aerarium delatus est a L. Lucullo pro consule.

_____

_____

_____

_____

_____

_____

_____

Short Analysis Questions

Census nostros requiris. Scilicet! Est enim obscurum proximis censoribus hunc cum claris-simo imperatore L. Lucullo apud exercitum fuisse, su-perioribus cum eodem quaestore fuisse in Asia, primis
5 Iulio et Crasso nullam populi partem esse censam. Sed, quoniam census non ius civitatis confirmat ac tantum modo indicat eum, qui sit census, ita se iam tum gessisse pro cive, eis temporibus is quem tu criminaris ne ipsius quidem iudicio in civium Romanorum iure esse versatum et testa-
10 mentum saepe fecit nostris legibus, et adiit hereditates civium Romanorum, et in beneficiis ad aerarium delatus est a L. Lucul-lo pro consule. Quaere argumenta, si quae potes; numquam enim hic neque suo neque amicorum iudicio revincetur.

1. Where was Archias during the most recent census noted by Cicero, i.e., in 70 BCE?

_____

_____

2. Where was Archias during the previous census, i.e., the one held in 86 BCE?

_____

_____

3. Why was his name not included in the census sponsored by Julius Caesar and Crassus in 70 BCE?

_____

_____

4. In what activities did Archias engage which are particular to those who are Roman citizens (lines 9–12)? Quote the Latin that supports your answer and translate or accurately paraphrase.

_____

_____

_____

_____

> Quaeres a nobis, Gratti, cur tanto opere hoc
> homine delectemur. Quia suppeditat nobis ubi et animus
> ex hoc forensi strepitu reficiatur et aures convicio defessae
> conquiescant. An tu existimas aut suppetere nobis posse
> 5   quod cotidie dicamus in tanta varietate rerum, nisi animos
> nostros doctrina excolamus, aut ferre animos tantam posse
> contentionem, nisi eos doctrina eadem relaxemus?

5. In lines 1–2, what question does Cicero anticipate from the prosecution?

_____

_____

6. What is his explanatory reply to this hypothetical question (lines 2–4)? Quote the Latin that supports your answer and translate or accurately paraphrase.

_____

_____

_____

7. In a carefully balanced sentence, lines 4–7, Cicero conveys the value of formal learning for a person daily involved in public life. How does Cicero define these benefits and how does he convey their value? Quote the Latin that supports your answer and translate or accurately paraphrase.

_____

_____

_____

_____

_____

Essay _Suggested time: 20 minutes_

Ceteros pudeat,

si qui ita se litteris abdiderunt ut nihil possint ex eis neque
ad communem adferre fructum neque in aspectum lucemque proferre; me autem quid pudeat qui tot annos ita
5   vivo, iudices, ut a nullius umquam me tempore aut commodo aut otium meum abstraxerit aut voluptas avocarit
aut denique somnus retardarit?

In this passage Cicero sets up a contrast between others (_ceteros_, line 1) and himself (_me_, line 4). In a short essay, discuss the distinctions he makes between himself and the rest of humanity and how stylistically he underscores these differences.

Support your assertions with references to the Latin text throughout the passage above. All Latin words must be copied or their line numbers provided, AND they must be translated or paraphrased closely enough that it is clear you understand the Latin. It is your responsibility to convince the reader that you are basing your conclusions on the Latin text and not merely on a general recollection of the passage. Direct your answer to the question; do not merely summarize the passage. Please write your essay on a separate piece of paper.

CHAPTER 8: LINES 157–183

13 Quare quis tandem me reprehendat, aut quis mihi iure suscenseat, si, quantum ceteris ad suas res obeundas, quantum ad festos dies ludorum
160 celebrandos, quantum ad alias voluptates et ad ipsam requiem animi et corporis conceditur temporum, quantum alii tribuunt tempestivis conviviis, quantum denique alveolo, quantum pilae, tantum mihi egomet ad haec studia recolenda sumpsero? Atque id eo mihi concedendum est magis quod
165 ex his studiis haec quoque crescit oratio et facultas quae, quantacumque est in me, numquam amicorum periculis defuit. Quae si cui levior videtur, illa quidem certe quae summa sunt ex quo fonte hauriam sentio. 14 Nam nisi multorum praeceptis multisque litteris mihi ab adulescentia
170 suasissem nihil esse in vita magno opere expetendum nisi laudem atque honestatem, in ea autem persequenda omnis cruciatus corporis, omnia pericula mortis atque exsili parvi esse ducenda, numquam me pro salute vestra in tot ac tantas dimicationes atque in hos profligatorum hominum
175 cotidianos impetus obiecissem. Sed pleni omnes sunt libri, plenae sapientium voces, plena exemplorum vetustas; quae iacerent in tenebris omnia, nisi litterarum lumen accederet. Quam multas nobis imagines non solum ad intuendum verum etiam ad imitandum fortissimorum virorum
180 expressas scriptores et Graeci et Latini reliquerunt! Quas ego mihi semper in administranda re publica proponens animum et mentem meam ipsa cogitatione hominum excellentium conformabam.

Preparatory Questions

Line 157   What part of speech is *quis?* _____

Line 158   Identify the case and use of *mihi.* _____

              What part of speech is *iure?* _____

              Identify and explain the mood of *suscenseat.* _____

              Find the verb that *si* governs. _____

              Identify the case and use of *quantum.* _____

              Identify the case and use of *ceteris.* _____

Lines 158–59   Find two examples of a gerundive of purpose. _____

Line 161   Identify the case and use of *temporum*. _____

Line 162   Identify the case and use of *conviviis*. _____

Line 163   Identify the case and use of *pilae*. _____

Identify the case and use of *tantum*. _____

Identify the case and use of *mihi*. _____

What part of speech is *egomet*? _____

Line 164   What is the case and use of *eo*? _____

What is the case and use of *mihi*? _____

Find a gerundive of obligation. _____

Identify the subject of *concedendum est*. _____

What part of speech is *magis*? _____

Line 165   What does *haec* modify? _____

What is the antecedent of *quae*? _____

Line 166   Identify the subject of *est*. _____

What is the case and use of *periculis*? _____

Line 167   Identify the subject of *defuit*. _____

Lines 167–68   Find the two verbs in the conditional sentence. _____

Line 167   What is the antecedent of *quae*? _____

Identify the case and use of *cui*. _____

Identify the case and use of *illa*. _____

What is the antecedent of the <u>second</u> *quae*? _____

Line 168   Identify and explain the mood of *hauriam*. _____

Lines 168–75   Identify the condition in this sentence. _____

Line 169   What is the case and use of *praeceptis*? _____

What is the case and use of *mihi*? _____

Line 170   Identify and explain the tense and mood of *suasissem*. _____

_____

What is the case and use of *nihil*? _____

What is the case and use of *magno opere*? _____

Line 171   What is the case and use of *laudem?* _____

Line 172   What is the case and use of *parvi?* _____

Line 173   Identify the subject of *esse ducenda.* _____

            What is the case and use of *me?* _____

Line 174   What is the object of *in?* _____

            What does *hos* modify? _____

Line 175   Identify and explain the mood and tense of *obiecissem.* _____

            _____

            What does *omnes* modify? _____

Line 176   Identify the case and use of *sapientium.* _____

            Identify the case and use of *exemplorum.* _____

Line 177   What is the antecedent of *quae?* _____

            Identify and explain the tense and mood of *iacerent.* _____

            _____

            What is the case and use of *lumen?* _____

Line 178   What part of speech is *quam?* _____

            Identify the case and use of *nobis.* _____

Lines 178–79   Find two gerunds expressing purpose. _____

Line 179   Identify the case and use of *virorum.* _____

Line 180   What does *expressas* modify? _____

            Identify the subject of *reliquerunt.* _____

            What is the antecedent of *quas?* _____

Line 181   Identify the case and use of *mihi.* _____

            What is the object of *proponens?* _____

            What does *proponens* modify? _____

Line 182   Identify the case and use of *ipsa cogitatione.* _____

Line 183   What is the object of *conformabam?* _____

Multiple Choice Questions *Suggested time: 34 minutes*

1. In line 157, *quis* is translated
   - a. what
   - c. anyone
   - b. who
   - d. some

2. In line 158, the tense and mood of *reprehendat* is
   - a. present indicative
   - c. perfect subjunctive
   - b. present subjunctive
   - d. future indicative

3. The word *suas* (line 159) refers to
   - a. *me* (line 157)
   - c. *ceteris* (line 158)
   - b. *quis* (line 158)
   - d. *obeundas* (line 159)

4. The two words *ad . . . celebrandos* (lines 159–160) are translated
   - a. to celebrate
   - c. to crowd around
   - b. to attend
   - d. to hide

5. In line 160, *ipsam* is translated
   - a. same
   - c. other
   - b. very
   - d. own

6. The tense of *sumpsero* in line 164 is
   - a. present
   - c. future perfect
   - b. future
   - d. perfect

7. In line 164, *quod* is translated
   - a. which
   - c. because
   - b. that
   - d. what

8. In lines 157–164 (*Quare quis . . . sumpsero*), we find an example of
   - a. hyperbole
   - c. assonance
   - b. polysyndeton
   - d. anaphora

9. From lines 157–164 (*Quare quis . . . sumpsero*), we learn that Cicero
   - a. often attends the games
   - c. goes to dinner parties
   - b. has little time for pleasures
   - d. pursues his studies

10. In line 166, *quantacumque* is translated
    - a. however great
    - c. of such a size
    - b. how much
    - d. as big as

11. In lines 164–167 (*atque id . . . defuit*), we find an example of

    a. asyndeton

    b. assonance

    c. hendiadys

    d. hyperbole

12. From lines 164–167 (*atque id . . . defuit*), we learn that

    a. Cicero's oratory help his studies

    b. more time is needed for these studies

    c. Cicero supports his friends in trouble

    d. oratory is more important than study

13. The subject of *sunt* (line 168) is

    a. *Quae* (the <u>first</u> one, line 167)

    b. *illa* (line 167)

    c. *quae* (the <u>second</u> one, line 167)

    d. *summa* (line 168)

14. In line 168, *fonte* is translated

    a. spring

    b. origin

    c. fountain

    d. source

15. In line 169, *ab adulescentia* is translated

    a. by a young woman

    b. from a youth

    c. after adolescence

    d. from boyhood

16. The word *ea* (line 171) refers to

    a. *praeceptis* (line 169)

    b. *adulescentia* (line 169)

    c. *vita* (line 170)

    d. *laudem atquet honestatem* (line 171)

17. The word *ea* (line 171) is the object of

    a. *suasissem* (line 170)

    b. *esse . . . expetendum* (line 170)

    c. *in* (line 171)

    d. *persequenda* (line 171)

18. The adjective *omnis* (line 171) modifies

    a. *ea* (line 171)

    b. *cruciatus* (line 172)

    c. *corporis* (line 172)

    d. *mortis* (line 172)

19. In line 173, *esse ducenda* is translated

    a. ought to be led

    b. ought to be said

    c. ought to be considered

    d. ought to be guided

20. The word *numquam* (line 173) modifies

    a. *suasissem* (line 170)

    b. *esse . . . expetendum* (line 170)

    c. *esse ducenda* (line 173)

    d. *obiecissem* (line 175)

21. From lines 168–175 (*Nam nisi . . . impetus obiecissem*), we learn that

    a. gaining praise and honor is not worth much effort

    b. some people ought to be led into death and exile

    c. Cicero has undergone some dangers on behalf of others

    d. no one is able to accomplish much without an education

22. In lines 175–176 (*Sed pleni . . . vetustas*), there is an example of

    a. assonance

    b. asyndeton

    c. alliteration

    d. antithesis

23. The adjective *omnia* (line 177) modifies

    a. *voces* (line 176)

    b. *vetustas* (line 176)

    c. *quae* (line 177)

    d. *tenebris* (line 177)

24. The type of condition found in the clause *quae . . . accederet*, lines 177–178, is

    a. present general

    b. future less vivid

    c. present contrary to fact

    d. past contrary to fact

25. The adjective *multas* (line 178) modifies

    a. *nobis* (line 178)

    b. *imagines* (line 178)

    c. *expressas* (line 180)

    d. *scriptores* (line 180)

26. *quas* (line 180) is the object of

    a. *administranda* (line 181)

    b. *proponens* (line 181)

    c. *cogitatione* (line 182)

    d. *conformabam* (line 183)

27. The word *proponens* (line 181) modifies

    a. *ego* (line 181)

    b. *mihi* (line 181)

    c. *re publica* (line 181)

    d. *cogitatione* (line 182)

28. From lines 180–183 (*Quas ego . . . conformabam*), we learn that Cicero

    a. is inspired by thinking about excellent men

    b. manages the government with excellent men

    c. puts himself forward for administrative duties

    d. thinks of himself as a thoughtful person

Translation *Suggested time: 15 minutes*

                       Sed pleni omnes sunt libri,
plenae sapientium voces, plena exemplorum vetustas;
quae iacerent in tenebris omnia, nisi litterarum lumen accederet. Quam multas nobis imagines non solum ad intu-
5   endum verum etiam ad imitandum fortissimorum virorum
expressas scriptores et Graeci et Latini reliquerunt!

_____

_____

_____

_____

_____

_____

_____

_____

Short Analysis Questions

Quare quis tandem me
reprehendat, aut quis mihi iure suscenseat, si, quantum ceteris ad suas res obeundas, quantum ad festos dies ludorum
celebrandos, quantum ad alias voluptates et ad ipsam re-
5   quiem animi et corporis conceditur temporum, quantum alii
tribuunt tempestivis conviviis, quantum denique alveolo,
quantum pilae, tantum mihi egomet ad haec studia recolenda
sumpsero? Atque id eo mihi concedendum est magis quod
ex his studiis haec quoque crescit oratio et facultas quae,
10   quantacumque est in me, numquam amicorum periculis
defuit. Quae si cui levior videtur, illa quidem certe quae
summa sunt ex quo fonte hauriam sentio.

1. To what kind of pursuits do others devote themselves as represented by Cicero in lines 2–8? Cite four examples in Latin to support your answer and translate or accurately paraphrase each.

_____

_____

_____

_____

2. In contrast, to what pursuits does Cicero dedicate himself?

_____

_____

3. Identify the figure of speech found in line 9. Write out the Latin and name the device.

_____

_____

4. According to lines 9–11, what particular skill has Cicero developed in pursuing the studies of which he speaks and how has he employed that skill? Write out the Latin to support your answer and translate or accurately paraphrase.

_____

_____

_____

Essay *Suggested time: 20 minutes*

Nam nisi mul-
torum praeceptis multisque litteris mihi ab adulescentia
suasissem nihil esse in vita magno opere expetendum nisi
laudem atque honestatem, in ea autem persequenda omnis
5 cruciatus corporis, omnia pericula mortis atque exsili parvi
esse ducenda, numquam me pro salute vestra in tot ac
tantas dimicationes atque in hos profligatorum hominum
cotidianos impetus obiecissem. Sed pleni omnes sunt libri,
plenae sapientium voces, plena exemplorum vetustas;
10 quae iacerent in tenebris omnia, nisi litterarum lumen accederet. Quam multas nobis imagines non solum ad intuendum verum etiam ad imitandum fortissimorum virorum
expressas scriptores et Graeci et Latini reliquerunt! Quas
ego mihi semper in administranda re publica proponens
15 animum et mentem meam ipsa cogitatione hominum excellentium conformabam.

In this passage Cicero uses some very strong language to convey the importance of literature in shaping his own value system. In a short essay, discuss how Cicero uses language and syntax in this passage to show the impact of literature on his own life.

Support your assertions with references to the Latin text throughout the passage above. All Latin words must be copied or their line numbers provided, AND they must be translated or paraphrased closely enough that it is clear you understand the Latin. It is your responsibility to convince the reader that you are basing your conclusions on the Latin text and not merely on a general recollection of the passage. Direct your answer to the question; do not merely summarize the passage. Please write your essay on a separate piece of paper.

CHAPTER 9: LINES 184–211

15 Quaeret quispiam: "Quid? Illi ipsi summi viri,
185 quorum virtutes litteris proditae sunt, istane doctrina
quam tu effers laudibus eruditi fuerunt?" Difficile est hoc
de omnibus confirmare, sed tamen est certum quid respondeam. Ego multos homines excellenti animo ac virtute fuisse et sine doctrina, naturae ipsius habitu prope
190 divino per se ipsos et moderatos et gravis exstitisse fateor;
etiam illud adiungo: saepius ad laudem atque virtutem
naturam sine doctrina quam sine natura valuisse doctrinam.
Atque idem ego hoc contendo: cum ad naturam eximiam
et inlustrem accesserit ratio quaedam conformatioque
195 doctrinae, tum illud nescioquid praeclarum ac sing-
ulare solere exsistere. 16 Ex hoc esse hunc numero quem
patres nostri viderunt, divinum hominem, Africanum,
ex hoc C. Laelium, L. Furium, moderatissimos homines et continentissimos, ex hoc fortissimum virum et illis
200 temporibus doctissimum, M. Catonem illum senem. Qui
profecto si nihil ad percipiendam colendamque virtutem
litteris adiuvarentur, numquam se ad earum studium
contulissent. Quod si non hic tantus fructus ostenderetur,
et si ex his studiis delectatio sola peteretur, tamen,
205 ut opinor, hanc animi remissionem humanissimam ac liberalissimam iudicaretis. Nam ceterae neque temporum sunt
neque aetatum omnium neque locorum; at haec studia ad-
ulescentiam acuunt, senectutem oblectant, secundas res
ornant, adversis perfugium ac solacium praebent, delectant
210 domi, non impediunt foris, pernoctant nobiscum, peregri-
nantur, rusticantur.

Preparatory Questions

Line 184 Identify the subject of *quaeret*. _____

What is the tense of *quaeret?* _____

What part of speech is *quid?* _____

Lines 184–86 Find the main verb of the sentence. _____

Find the subject of the sentence. _____

Line 185 What is the antecedent of *quorum?* _____

Identify the case and use of *virtutes*. _____

Identify the case and use of *litteris*. _____

Identify the function of the *–ne* of *istane*. _____

Identify the case and use of *doctrina*. _____

Line 186   What is the antecedent of *quam?* _____

Identify the case and use of *quam*. _____

What is the tense and mood of *effers?* _____

What is the case and use of *laudibus?* _____

Lines 186–87   Identify the subject of *est*. _____

Line 186   What is the case and use of *hoc?* _____

Lines 186–88   Find an indirect question. _____

Lines 188–190 Find the main verb. _____

Line 188   Identify the case and use of *homines*. _____

What word does *excellenti* modify? _____

Lines 188–89   Identify the case and use of *animo ac virtute*. _____

Line 189   Explain the function of *fuisse*. _____

What word does *ipsius* modify? _____

Identify the case and use of *habitu*. _____

What part of speech is *prope?* _____

What word does it modify? _____

Line 190   Identify the case and use of *ipsos*. _____

Lines 191–92   Find an indirect statement. _____

Line 191   What part of speech is *saepius?* _____

What word does it modify? _____

Line 192   Identify the case and use of *naturam*. _____

Identify the case and use of *doctrinam*. _____

Lines 193–96   Find an indirect statement. _____

Line 193   What part of speech is *idem?* _____

What word does it modify? _____

Lines 193–94   Find a *cum* clause. _____

Line 194   Identify the subject of *accesserit.*_____

              What word does *quaedam* modify? _____

Line 195   Find three words that modify *nescioquid.*_____

Line 196   Identify the subject of *solere.*_____

              Explain the form and function of *exsistere.*_____

              Explain the function of *esse.* _____

              What is the case and use of *hunc?* _____

              Find the antecedent of *quem.* _____

              What is the case and use of *quem?*_____

Line 197   With what word are the words *divinum hominem, Africanum* in apposition? _____

              _____

Line 198   What word must be understood with *hoc?* _____

Lines 198–200 Why are *Laelium, Furium, Catonem* (and all their modifiers) in the accusative? _____

              _____

Lines 199–200 Identify the case and use of *illis temporibus.*_____

Line 200   What is the antecedent of *qui?* _____

Line 201   What part of speech is *profecto?* _____

Lines 201–3   Find a conditional sentence._____

              What type of condition is it? _____

Line 201   Identify the form, the case and the use of *percipiendam.*_____

              _____

              What is the case and use of *virtutem?* _____

Line 202   What is the case and use of *litteris?* _____

              Identify the subject of *adiuvarentur.*_____

              What is the case and use of *se?*_____

              To what does *earum* refer? _____

              What is the case and use of *studium?* _____

Line 203   Identify the subject of *contulissent.* _____

              What is the case and use of *fructus?* _____

Line 204   What word does *sola* modify? _____

Line 205   Explain the function of *ut opinor.* _____

Lines 205–6   Find the apodosis of the condition. _____

Line 205   What word modifies *remissionem?* _____

Lines 205–6   Identify the case and use of *humanissimam ac liberalissimam.* _____

_____

Line 206   Identify the subject of *iudicaretis.* _____

Lines 206–7   Find the main verb of the clause (*Nam . . . locorum*). _____

Line 206   To what does *ceterae* refer? _____

Line 207   What words does *omnium* modify? _____

Lines 207–211   Find all the verbs of which *haec studia* is the subject. _____

_____

Line 209   Identify the case and use of *adversis.* _____

Line 210   What is the case of *domi?* _____

                What part of speech is *foris?* _____

Multiple Choice Questions *Suggested time: 40 minutes*

1. In line 184, *quispiam* is translated
    a. someone   b. something
    c. whoever   d. whatever

2. The word *istane* (line 185) modifies
    a. *virtutes* (line 185)   b. *litteris* (line 185)
    c. *doctrina* (line 185)   d. *laudibus* (line 186)

3. The word *eruditi* (line 186) agrees with
    a. *viri* (line 184)   b. *virtutes* (line 185)
    c. *tu* (line 186)   d. *laudibus* (line 186)

4. In line 187, *quid* is translated
    a. why   b. what
    c. that   d. which

5. The tense and mood of *respondeam* (lines 187–188) is

    a. present indicative

    b. future indicative

    c. present subjunctive

    d. perfect subjunctive

6. The word *se* (line 190) refers to

    a. *homines* (line 188)

    b. *doctrina* (line 189)

    c. *naturae* (line 189)

    d. *habitu* (line 189)

7. The adjectives *moderatos* and *gravis* (line 190) modify

    a. *homines* (line 188)

    b. *animo ac virtute* (lines 188–189)

    c. *se* (line 190)

    d. *ipsos* (line 190)

8. In lines 188–190 (*Ego . . . fateor*), we find an example of

    a. hyperbaton

    b. alliteration

    c. hyperbole

    d. anaphora

9. From lines 188–190 (*Ego . . . fateor*), we learn that

    a. training is necessary for men to be outstanding

    b. an excellent mind is the result of education

    c. nature alone makes some men excellent

    d. without divine influence, men are too serious

10. In line 191, *saepius* is translated

    a. often

    b. too often

    c. more often

    d. rather often

11. In line 192, *quam* is translated

    a. that

    b. than

    c. which

    d. how

12. From lines 191–192 (*etiam illud . . . valuisse doctrinam*), we learn that

    a. either nature or education alone is powerful

    b. nature is only powerful with education

    c. education is more powerful than nature

    d. nature is more powerful than education

13. In line 193, *contendo* is translated

    a. I strive

    b. I hasten

    c. I assert

    d. I compare

14. The tense and mood of *accesserit* (line 194) is

    a. present indicative

    b. perfect indicative

    c. present subjunctive

    d. perfect subjunctive

15. The enclitic *–que* (line 194) connects
    a. *ego* (line 193) and *ratio* (line 194)
    b. *contendo* (line 193) and *accesserit* (line 194)
    c. *ratio* (line 194) and *conformatio* (line 194)
    d. *quaedam* (line 194) and *doctrinae* (line 195)

16. The word *nescioquid* (line 195) is the
    a. object of *solere* (line 196)
    b. object of *exsistere* (line 196)
    c. subject of *solere* (line 196)
    d. subject of *exsistere* (line 196)

17. From lines 193–196 (*Atque idem . . . exsistere*), we learn that
    a. one's nature is only outstanding if it is educated
    b. the value of education is not fully understood
    c. education enhances an already outstanding nature
    d. education must conform to a certain plan

18. In lines 198–199, the words *moderatissimos homines et continentissimos* apply to
    a. *patres* (line 197)
    b. *Africanum* (line 197) and *C. Laelium, L. Furium* (line 198)
    c. *C. Laelium, L. Furium* (line 198)
    d. *C. Laelium, L. Furium* (line 198) and *M. Catonem* (line 200)

19. Of the men mentioned in lines 196–200 (*Ex hoc . . . illum senem*), which one is described as "most learned"?
    a. Africanus
    b. Laelius
    c. Furius
    d. Cato

20. In lines 196–200 (*Ex hoc . . . illum senem*), we find an example of
    a. alliteration
    b. hyperbole
    c. hyperbaton
    d. anaphora

21. In line 201, *nihil* is translated
    a. none
    b. nothing
    c. not at all
    d. neither

22. The tense and mood of *adiuvarentur* (line 202) is
    a. present indicative
    b. present subjunctive
    c. imperfect subjunctive
    d. future indicative

23. From lines 200–203 (*Qui profecto . . . contulissent*), we learn that
    a. people study literature to develop virtue
    b. learning is not helped by virtue
    c. nothing is contentious if virtue is present
    d. with virtue, one can learn everything easily

24. In line 203, *quod* is translated
    a. that
    c. what
    b. because
    d. but

25. The subject of *ostenderetur* (line 203) is
    a. *quod* (line 203)
    c. *tantus* (line 203)
    b. *hic* (line 203)
    d. *fructus* (line 203)

26. The tense and mood of *iudicaretis* (line 206) is
    a. present indicative
    c. imperfect subjunctive
    b. future indicative
    d. perfect subjunctive

27. The type of condition found in lines 203–206 (*Quod si . . . iudicaretis*) is
    a. present contrary to fact
    c. present general
    b. past contrary to fact
    d. future less vivid

28. Lines 203–206 (*Quod si . . . iudicaretis*) tell us that literature
    a. offers many delightful fruits
    c. is very relaxing for the mind
    b. is the only thing worth studying
    d. is especially suited to liberal thinkers

29. In lines 206–207, the words *temporum, aetatum* and *locorum* are genitives of
    a. quality
    c. the whole
    b. possession
    d. description

30. In lines 206–207 (*Nam ceterae . . . locorum*), we find an example of
    a. hyperbole
    c. litotes
    b. asyndeton
    d. polysyndeton

31. The subject of *rusticantur* (line 211) is
    a. *ceterae* (line 206)
    c. *res* (line 208)
    b. *studia* (line 207)
    d. *domi* (line 210)

32. Lines 206–211 (*Nam ceterae . . . rusticantur*) tell us that literature
    a. must be studied at all times
    c. should be studied mainly at home
    b. is a constant companion
    d. offers fleeting pleasures to people

33. In lines 207–211 (*at haec studia . . . rusticantur*), we find an example of
    a. litotes
    c. hendiadys
    b. hyperbole
    d. tricolon

Translation *Suggested time: 15 minutes*

etiam illud adiungo: saepius ad laudem atque virtutem
naturam sine doctrina quam sine natura valuisse doctrinam.
Atque idem ego hoc contendo: cum ad naturam eximiam
et inlustrem accesserit ratio quaedam conformatioque
5   doctrinae, tum illud nescioquid praeclarum ac sing-
ulare solere exsistere.

_____

_____

_____

_____

_____

_____

_____

Short Analysis Questions

Ego multos homines excellenti animo ac virtute fuisse et sine doctrina, naturae ipsius habitu prope
divino per se ipsos et moderatos et gravis exstitisse fateor;
etiam illud adiungo: saepius ad laudem atque virtutem
5   naturam sine doctrina quam sine natura valuisse doctrinam.
Atque idem ego hoc contendo: cum ad naturam eximiam
et inlustrem accesserit ratio quaedam conformatioque
doctrinae, tum illud nescioquid praeclarum ac sing-
ulare solere exsistere.

1.   Identify the figure of speech used in the clause that begins with *ego* (line 1) and ends with *fateor* (line 3). Quote the Latin that illustrates this figure.

_____

_____

2. Since it is possible, according to lines 1–3, to find men of outstanding character who have had no training in the liberal arts, what accounts for their exceptional qualities? Cite the Latin that supports your answer and translate or accurately paraphrase.

_____

_____

_____

3. In lines 4–5, what two ideas does Cicero compare in using the comparative adverb, *saepius*?

_____

_____

_____

4. In line 8, to what does the phrase *nescioquid illud* refer?

_____

                                        Ex hoc esse hunc numero quem
patres nostri viderunt, divinum hominem, Africanum,
ex hoc C. Laelium, L. Furium, moderatissimos homines et continentissimos, ex hoc fortissimum virum et illis
5   temporibus doctissimum, M. Catonem illum senem. Qui
profecto si nihil ad percipiendam colendamque virtutem
litteris adiuvarentur, numquam se ad earum studium
contulissent.

5. To what group of people does the phrase *ex hoc numero* (line 1) refer?

_____

6. Identify one of the figures of speech found in lines 1–5. Quote the Latin that illustrates it. Comment on the effect of its use in this passage.

_____

_____

_____

7. In lines 1–5, Cicero gives a list of historical *exempla*. What do these *exempla* have in common? Cite the Latin that supports your answer and translate or accurately paraphrase.

_____

_____

_____

_____

Essay *Suggested time: 20 minutes*

> Quod si non hic tantus fructus ostenderetur, et si ex his studiis delectatio sola peteretur, tamen, ut opinor, hanc animi remissionem humanissimam ac liberalissimam iudicaretis. Nam ceterae neque temporum sunt
>
> 5 neque aetatum omnium neque locorum; at haec studia adulescentiam acuunt, senectutem oblectant, secundas res ornant, adversis perfugium ac solacium praebent, delectant domi, non impediunt foris, pernoctant nobiscum, peregrinantur, rusticantur.

In the presentation of his case, Cicero distinguishes between the pleasure derived from liberal studies and other sources of pleasure. In a short essay, discuss how these pleasures differ and how Cicero underscores their differences.

Support your assertions with references to the Latin text throughout the passage above. All Latin words must be copied or their line numbers provided, AND they must be translated or paraphrased closely enough that it is clear you understand the Latin. It is your responsibility to convince the reader that you are basing your conclusions on the Latin text and not merely on a general recollection of the passage. Direct your answer to the question; do not merely summarize the passage. Please write your essay on a separate piece of paper.

CHAPTER 10: LINES 212–236

215

220

225

230

235

17 Quod si ipsi haec neque attingere neque sensu nostro gustare possemus, tamen ea mirari deberemus, etiam cum in aliis videremus. Quis nostrum tam animo agresti ac duro fuit ut Rosci morte nuper non commoveretur? qui cum esset senex mortuus, tamen propter excellentem artem ac venustatem videbatur omnino mori non debuisse. Ergo ille corporis motu tantum amorem sibi conciliarat a nobis omnibus; nos animorum incredibilis motus celeritatemque ingeniorum neglegemus? 18 Quotiens ego hunc Archiam vidi, iudices—utar enim vestra benignitate, quoniam me in hoc novo genere dicendi tam diligenter attenditis—quotiens ego hunc vidi, cum litteram scripsisset nullam, magnum numerum optimorum versuum de eis ipsis rebus quae tum agerentur dicere ex tempore, quotiens revocatum eandem rem dicere commutatis verbis atque sententiis! Quae vero accurate cogitateque scripsisset, ea sic vidi probari ut ad veterum scriptorum laudem perveniret. Hunc ego non diligam, non admirer, non omni ratione defendendum putem? Atque sic a summis hominibus eruditissimisque accepimus, ceterarum rerum studia ex doctrina et praeceptis et arte constare, poetam natura ipsa valere et mentis viribus excitari et quasi divino quodam spiritu inflari. Quare suo iure noster ille Ennius "sanctos" appellat poetas, quod quasi deorum aliquo dono atque munere commendati nobis esse videantur.

Preparatory Questions

Lines 212–13   Find the protasis of a conditional sentence. _____

Line 212   Identify the case and use of *ipsi*. _____

To what/whom does *ipsi* refer? _____

Identify the case and use of *haec*. _____

Lines 212–13   Identify the case and use of *sensu nostro*. _____

Line 213   On what word does *gustare* depend? _____

Identify the tense and mood of *possemus*. _____

To what does *ea* refer? _____

What is the case and use of *ea?* _____

Identify the form and use of *mirari.* _____

Explain the tense and mood of *deberemus.* _____

Line 214   Find a *cum* clause. _____

Lines 214–15   Find a result clause. _____

Line 214   What is the case and use of *nostrum?* _____

Lines 214–15   What is the case and use of *animo agresti ac duro?* _____

Line 215   Identify the subject of *fuit.* _____

Identify the case and use of *morte.* _____

What is the antecedent of *qui?* _____

Lines 216–17   Find a *cum* concessive clause. _____

Line 216   Identify the tense and mood of *esset . . . mortuus.* _____

To whom/what does *senex* refer? _____

Line 217   Identify the subject of *videbatur?* _____

What part of speech is *omnino?* _____

Identify the form and use of *mori.* _____

Line 218   To whom does *ille* refer? _____

Identify the case and use of *motu.* _____

To whom does *sibi* refer? _____

What is the unsyncopated form of *conciliarat?* _____

What is the direct object of *conciliarat?* _____

Line 219   Identify the case and use of *nos.* _____

What does *incredibilis* modify? _____

Line 220   What are the direct objects of *neglegemus?* _____

Identify the case and use of *ego.* _____

Identify the case and use of *hunc Archiam.* _____

Line 221   Identify the the tense and mood of *utar.* _____

What is the case and use of *vestra benignitate?* _____

What is the case and use of *me?* _____

Line 222   Identify the form of *dicendi*. _____

               What does *tam* modify?_____

               Identify the subject of *attenditis*. _____

Line 223   To whom does *hunc* refer? _____

               Find a *cum* clause. _____

               Identify the subject of *scripsisset*. _____

               What does *nullam* modify? _____

Lines 223–24   Identify the case and use of *magnum numerum*._____

Line 224   What does *optimorum* modify?_____

Line 225   What is the antecedent of *quae?* _____

               Explain the tense and mood of *agerentur*._____

               Identify the form and use of *dicere*. _____

               What does *revocatum* modify? _____

Line 226   Identify the case and use of *eandem rem*._____

               What/who is the subject of *dicere?* _____

               Identify the case and use of *commutatis verbis*. _____

Line 227   What is the antecedent of *quae?* _____

               Identify the subject of *scripsisset*. _____

               What is the case and use of *ea?* _____

               Identify the subject of *vidi*. _____

Line 228   Identify the form and use of *probari*._____

               Find a result clause._____

               What is the case and use of *laudem?* _____

               Identify the subject of *perveniret*. _____

               To whom does *hunc* refer? _____

               Identify the case and use of *hunc*. _____

Lines 229–230 Find three deliberative subjunctives. _____

Line 229   Identify the case and use of *omni ratione*. _____

Line 230   What word must be supplied with *defendendum?*_____

               Identify the case and use of *hominibus*. _____

Line 231   Identify the case and use of *studia*. _____

Line 232   Identify the case and use of *arte*. _____

                Identify the case and use of *poetam*. _____

                Identify the case and use of *natura ipsa*. _____

Line 233   What is the case and use of *mentis?*_____

                What is the case and use of *viribus?* _____

                Identify the subject of *excitari*. _____

                What does *quodam* modify? _____

Line 234   Explain the form and use of *inflari*. _____

                Identify the case and use of *suo iure*. _____

                What does *noster* modify?_____

                Identify the case and use of *"sanctos."* _____

Line 235   Identify the subject of *appellat*. _____

                What is the case and use of *poetas?* _____

                What does *aliquo* modify? _____

Line 236   Identify the case and use of *munere*. _____

                With what word does *commendati* agree?_____

                What is the case and use of *nobis?* _____

                Identify the subject of *videantur*. _____

Multiple Choice Questions *Suggested time: 40 minutes*

1. In line 212, *quod* is translated
    a. but   b. because
    c. that   d. which

2. In line 212, *attingere* depends on
    a. *gustare* (line 213)   b. *possemus* (line 213)
    c. *deberemus* (line 213)   d. *videremus* (line 214)

3. In line 214, *cum* is translated
    a. when   b. since
    c. with   d. although

4. In line 214, *quis* is

   a. a pronoun

   b. an adjective

   c. a conjunction

   d. a noun

5. The type of condition found in lines 212–214 (*Quod si . . . deberemus*) is

   a. future more vivid

   b. future less vivid

   c. present contrary to fact

   d. past contrary to fact

6. In line 215, *ut . . . commoveretur* is a

   a. purpose clause

   b. result clause

   c. characteristic clause

   d. jussive clause

7. In line 215, *nuper* modifies

   a. *quis* (line 214)

   b. *Rosci* (line 215)

   c. *morte* (line 215)

   d. *commoveretur* (line 215)

8. In line 217, *omnino* is translated

   a. together

   b. wholly

   c. at all

   d. at once

9. The tense and voice of *debuisse* (line 217) is

   a. present passive

   b. future active

   c. perfect active

   d. perfect passive

10. From lines 214–217 (*Quis nostrum . . . debuisse*), we learn that Roscius

    a. died as quite a young man

    b. lived a long and happy life

    c. had great skill and charm

    d. was a close friend of Cicero

11. In line 218, the tense of *conciliarat* is

    a. present

    b. perfect

    c. pluperfect

    d. future perfect

12. In lines 218–220 (*Ergo . . . neglegemus*), we find an example of

    a. hyperbole

    b. litotes

    c. anaphora

    d. antithesis

13. Lines 218–220 (*Ergo . . . neglegemus*) tell us that

    a. geniuses do not move quickly

    b. Roscius was much loved

    c. Archias was not a dancer

    d. a quick mind is a good asset

14. In lines 218–220 (*Ergo . . . neglegemus*), we find an example of
    a. chiasmus
    b. anacoluthon
    c. polysyndeton
    d. hyperbaton

15. The object of *utar* (line 221) is
    a. *hunc Archiam* (line 220)
    b. *iudices* (line 221)
    c. *benignitate* (line 221)
    d. *me* (line 221)

16. In line 223, *cum* is translated
    a. since
    b. with
    c. although
    d. when

17. From lines 220–226 (*Quotiens . . . sententiis*), we learn that Archias
    a. is using a new kind of speaking
    b. has a terrible memory
    c. creates verses on the spot
    d. writes his poems in advance

18. The tense and mood of *scripsisset* (line 227) is
    a. perfect indicative
    b. perfect subjunctive
    c. pluperfect indicative
    d. pluperfect subjunctive

19. The case of *veterum* (line 228) is
    a. nominative
    b. genitive
    c. accusative
    d. vocative

20. From lines 227–228 (*Quae vero . . . laudem perveniret*), we learn that Archias
    a. approved of old writers
    b. always wrote the truth
    c. wrote carefully and thoughtfully
    d. never was as famous as old writers

21. In line 229, *admirer* is
    a. deliberative
    b. jussive
    c. hortatory
    d. optative

22. In line 231, *accepimus* is translated
    a. we accept
    b. we are accepted
    c. we have taken
    d. we have learned

23. The subject of *constare* (line 232) is
    a. *hominibus* (line 230)
    b. the understood subject of *accepimus* (line 231)
    c. *studia* (line 231)
    d. *doctrina* (line 232)

24. In line 233, the words *mentis viribus* are translated
    a. with thoughtful men
    b. with force of mind
    c. by strong minds
    d. by capability of the mind

25. In line 233, *quodam* is translated
    a. formerly
    b. someone
    c. a certain
    d. wherever

26. The subject of *inflari* (line 234) is
    a. *studia* (line 231)
    b. *doctrina* (line 232)
    c. *poetam* (line 232)
    d. *spiritu* (line 234)

27. From lines 230–234 (*Atque sic . . . spiritu inflari*), we learn that
    a. the greatest men are very well educated
    b. poetry is written with skill and training
    c. a poet may be inspired by divine spirit
    d. nature and talent are necessary for education

28. Lines 230–234 (*Atque sic . . . spiritu inflari*), contain an example of
    a. chiasmus
    b. asyndeton
    c. hyperbole
    d. litotes

29. The word *suo* (line 234) refers to
    a. *noster* (line 234)
    b. *ille* (line 234)
    c. *Ennius* (line 234)
    d. Archias (understood)

30. In line 234, *suo iure* is translated
    a. according to his law
    b. with his own good reason
    c. by his own right
    d. because of his citizenship

31. In line 235, *aliquo* is translated
    a. some
    b. any
    c. a certain
    d. whichever

32. The understood subject of *commendati . . . esse* (line 236) is
    a. poets
    b. learned men
    c. the jurors
    d. Ennius' friends

33. From lines 234–236 (*Quare suo iure . . . esse videantur*), we learn that
    a. poets are to be recommended for gifts
    b. Ennius thinks that poets are holy
    c. holy men make the best poets
    d. the poet Ennius is favored by the gods

Translation *Suggested time: 10 minutes*

> Quis nostrum tam animo agresti ac
> duro fuit ut Rosci morte nuper non commoveretur? qui
> cum esset senex mortuus, tamen propter excellentem ar-
> tem ac venustatem videbatur omnino mori non debuisse.

_____

_____

_____

_____

_____

_____

_____

Short Analysis Questions

> Quotiens ego hunc Archiam
> vidi, iudices—utar enim vestra benignitate, quoniam me
> in hoc novo genere dicendi tam diligenter attenditis—quo-
> tiens ego hunc vidi, cum litteram scripsisset nullam, mag-
> 5 num numerum optimorum versuum de eis ipsis rebus
> quae tum agerentur dicere ex tempore, quotiens revoca-
> tum eandem rem dicere commutatis verbis atque senten-
> tiis! Quae vero accurate cogitateque scripsisset, ea sic vidi
> probari ut ad veterum scriptorum laudem perveniret. Hunc
> 10 ego non diligam, non admirer, non omni ratione
> defendendum putem? Atque sic a summis hominibus
> eruditissimisque accepimus, ceterarum rerum studia ex
> doctrina et praeceptis et arte constare, poetam natura ipsa
> valere et mentis viribus excitari et quasi divino quodam
> 15 spiritu inflari. Quare suo iure noster ille Ennius "sanctos"
> appellat poetas, quod quasi deorum aliquo dono atque
> munere commendati nobis esse videantur.

1. In line 2 Cicero addresses the *iudices* directly. What compliment does Cicero extend to them at this point in his oration? Quote and translate the Latin that supports your answer.

_____

_____

_____

2. In lines 3–7 (*quotiens . . . sententiis!*) how does Cicero assess Archias's effectiveness as a public speaker? Quote the Latin that supports your answer and either translate or accurately paraphrase.

_____

_____

_____

_____

_____

_____

3. How did Cicero assess Archias's effectiveness as a writer (line 8)? Quote and translate the Latin that supports your answer.

_____

_____

_____

4. According to learned men, from what source does a poet derive his power (lines 13–15)?

_____

_____

5. Who is Ennius and what is his opinion of poets in general (lines 15–17)? Quote the Latin that supports your answer to the second part of the question and translate or accurately paraphrase.

_____

_____

_____

_____

Essay *Suggested time: 20 minutes*

> Quis nostrum tam animo agresti ac
> duro fuit ut Rosci morte nuper non commoveretur? qui
> cum esset senex mortuus, tamen propter excellentem ar-
> tem ac venustatem videbatur omnino mori non debuisse.
> 5 Ergo ille corporis motu tantum amorem sibi conciliarat a nobis
> omnibus; nos animorum incredibilis motus celeritatemque
> ingeniorum neglegemus?

In line 2 Cicero recalls the death of the actor, Roscius. In a short essay, show how Cicero uses this recollection to make his case on behalf of Archias.

Support your assertions with references to the Latin text throughout the passage above. All Latin words must be copied or their line numbers provided, AND they must be translated or paraphrased closely enough that it is clear you understand the Latin. It is your responsibility to convince the reader that you are basing your conclusions on the Latin text and not merely on a general recollection of the passage. Direct your answer to the question; do not merely summarize the passage. Please write your essay on a separate piece of paper.

CHAPTER 11: LINES 237–260

19 Sit igitur, iudices, sanctum apud vos, humanissimos homines, hoc poetae nomen quod nulla umquam barbaria violavit. Saxa atque solitudines voci
240 respondent, bestiae saepe immanes cantu flectuntur atque consistunt; nos instituti rebus optimis non poetarum voce moveamur? Homerum Colophonii civem esse dicunt suum, Chii suum vindicant, Salaminii repetunt, Smyrnaei vero suum esse confirmant itaque etiam delubrum eius in
245 oppido dedicaverunt, permulti alii praeterea pugnant inter se atque contendunt. Ergo illi alienum, quia poeta fuit, post mortem etiam expetunt; nos hunc vivum qui et voluntate et legibus noster est repudiamus, praesertim cum omne olim studium atque omne ingenium contulerit Archias ad populi
250 Romani gloriam laudemque celebrandam? Nam et Cimbricas res adulescens attigit et ipsi illi C. Mario qui durior ad haec studia videbatur iucundus fuit. 20 Neque enim quisquam est tam aversus a Musis qui non mandari versibus aeternum suorum laborum praeconium facile
255 patiatur. Themistoclem illum, summum Athenis virum, dixisse aiunt, cum ex eo quaereretur quod acroama aut cuius vocem libentissime audiret: eius a quo sua virtus optime praedicaretur. Itaque ille Marius item eximie L. Plotium dilexit, cuius ingenio putabat ea quae gesserat
260 posse celebrari.

Preparatory Questions

Line 237   Identify the subject of *sit*. _____

What is the case and use of *sanctum?* _____

Lines 237–38 What is the case and use of *humanissimos homines?* _____

Line 238   What does *hoc* modify? _____

Line 239   What is the object of *violavit?* _____

Identify the case and use of *voci*. _____

Line 240   Identify the case and use of *immanes.* _____

Identify the case and use of *cantu.* _____

Line 241   What is the form of *instituti?* _____

Line 242   Explain the mood of *moveamur.* _____

                Explain the syntax of *esse.* _____

Line 243   What words must be understood with *Chii suum vindicant?* _____

                _____

                Identify the case and use of *suum.* _____

                To whom does *suum* refer? _____

Line 244   To whom does *eius* refer? _____

Line 246   Identify the case and use of *se.* _____

                Tto whom does *se* refer? _____

                Identify the case and use of *illi.* _____

                Identify the case and use of *alienum.* _____

Lines 246–48   Find at least two examples of antithesis. _____

                _____

Line 247   Identify the case and use of *vivum.* _____

                What is the antecedent of *qui?* _____

Lines 247–48   Identify the case and use of *voluntate et legibus.* _____

Line 248   What is the case and use of *noster?* _____

                Identify the subject of *est.* _____

Line 249   Identify the tense and mood of *contulerit.* _____

                What is its subject? _____

Line 250   Identify the case and use of *gloriam laudemque.* _____

                Identify the form and use of *celebrandam.* _____

Line 251   To whom does the word *adulescens* refer? _____

                Identify the case and use of *ipsi illi.* _____

                Whom/what do these words modify? _____

                What is the antecedent of *qui?* _____

Line 252   Identify the subject of *videbatur.* _____

                What does *iucundus* modify? _____

                Identify the subject of *fuit.* _____

Lines 253–55   What type of clause does *qui . . . patiatur* illustrate? _____

Line 253   What does *aversus* modify?_____

Identify the case and use of *a Musis*. _____

What is the antecedent of *qui*? _____

Explain the form and syntax of *mandari*. _____

Line 254   What is the case and use of *versibus?* _____

What word does *aeternum* modify? _____

To whom does *suorum* refer? _____

What does *facile* modify?_____

Line 255   Identify the subject of *patiatur*. _____

Identify the case and use of *summum . . . virum*. _____

What is the case and use of *Athenis?* _____

Line 256   Identify the form and use of *dixisse*. _____

To whom does *eo* refer?_____

Line 256   Identify the case and use of *quod*. _____

Line 257   What part of speech is *cuius?* _____

What is the case and use of *vocem?* _____

Identify the form and use of *libentissime*. _____

Explain the mood of *audiret*._____

Identify the subject of *audiret*. _____

What noun needs to be understood with *eius?* _____

Identify the case and use of *quo*. _____

Line 258   Explain the mood of *praedicaretur*._____

What part of speech is *eximie?* What does it modify?_____

Line 259   What is the antecedent of *cuius?* _____

Identify the case and use of *ingenio*. _____

Identify the subject of *putabat*. _____

What is the case and use of *ea?* _____

What is the antecedent of *quae?* _____

Identify the subject of *gesserat*. _____

Line 260   Explain the form and use of *posse*._____

Explain the form and use of *celebrari*. _____

Multiple Choice Questions *Suggested time: 38 minutes*

1. In line 237, the case of *iudices* is
   - a. nominative
   - b. genitive
   - c. accusative
   - d. vocative

2. In lines 237–239 (*Sit igitur . . . barbaria violavit*), we find an example of
   - a. hyperbole
   - b. anaphora
   - c. litotes
   - d. antithesis

3. In line 241, *instituti* is translated
   - a. established
   - b. institutionalized
   - c. educated
   - d. ordered

4. In line 241, *rebus optimis* is ablative of
   - a. means
   - b. manner
   - c. separation
   - d. time

5. From lines 239–242 (*Saxa . . . moveamur*), we learn that
   - a. poets are fond of animals
   - b. people are not affected by poetry
   - c. animals are influenced by music
   - d. voices are heard in the desert

6. Lines 239–242 (*Saxa . . . moveamur*) contain an example of
   - a. antithesis
   - b. rhetorical question
   - c. chiasmus
   - d. hendiadys

7. The subject of *esse* (line 242) is
   - a. *Homerum* (line 242)
   - b. *Colophonii* (line 242)
   - c. *civem* (line 242)
   - d. *Chii* (line 243)

8. In line 243, the first *suum* refers to
   - a. *poetarum* (line 241)
   - b. *Homerum* (line 242)
   - c. *Colophonii* (line 242)
   - d. *civem* (line 242)

9. In line 243, *vindicant* is translated
   - a. claim
   - b. vindicate
   - c. conquer
   - d. avenge

10. In line 243, *repetunt* is translated

    a. search for

    c. demand

    b. trace

    d. seek in return

11. In lines 242–246 (*Homerum . . . contendunt*), we find an example of

    a. litotes

    c. antithesis

    b. asyndeton

    d. chiasmus

12. From lines 242–246 (*Homerum . . . contendunt*), we learn that Homer

    a. lived in many different cities

    c. was claimed by many cities

    b. had citizenship in Colophon

    d. built his shrine in Smyrna

13. In line 246, *illi* refers to

    a. Greeks

    c. Romans

    b. poets

    d. citizens

14. In line 246, *alienum* refers to

    a. *Homerum* (line 242)

    c. *nos* (line 247)

    b. *alii* (line 245)

    d. *Archias* (line 249)

15. The object of *repudiamus* (line 248) is

    a. *nos* (line 247)

    c. *vivum* (line 247)

    b. *hunc* (line 247)

    d. *studium* (line 249)

16. In line 248, *cum* is translated

    a. with

    c. although

    b. when

    d. since

17. In line 249, *populi* is

    a. genitive of the source

    c. possessive genitive

    b. partitive genitive

    d. genitive of quality

18. From lines 246–250 (*Ergo illi . . . celebrandam*), we learn that Archias

    a. will be honored after his death

    c. has celebrated the glory of the Romans

    b. is in trouble with the law

    d. is a greater poet than Homer

19. In lines 246–250 (*Ergo illi . . . celebrandam*), we see an example of

    a. antithesis

    c. synecdoche

    b. litotes

    d. hyperbaton

20. From lines 250–252 (*Nam et . . . iucundus fuit*), we learn that
    a. Marius was hard on the Cimbrians
    b. Archias wrote poems when he was younger
    c. Archias found it hard to write poetry
    d. Marius was a very pleasant person

21. In line 252, *durior* is translated
    a. rather insensitive
    b. somewhat dull
    c. too harsh
    d. more obtuse

22. In line 253, *quisquam* is translated
    a. anyone
    b. anything
    c. whoever
    d. a certain one

23. The subject of *mandari* (line 253) is
    a. *quisquam* (line 253)
    b. *qui* (line 253)
    c. *laborum* (line 254)
    d. *praeconium* (line 254)

24. The word *suorum* (line 254) refers to
    a. *Mario* (line 251)
    b. *Musis* (line 253)
    c. *qui* (line 253)
    d. *versibus* (line 254)

25. From lines 252–255 (*Neque enim . . . patiatur*), we learn that
    a. some people dislike the Muses
    b. verses are only written with labor
    c. people like their deeds to be celebrated
    d. poetry is easily allowed to be recited

26. The subject of *dixisse* (line 256) is
    a. *Themistoclem* (line 255)
    b. *Athenis* (line 255)
    c. *virum* (line 255)
    d. *acroama* (line 256)

27. In line 256, *cum* is translated
    a. with
    b. when
    c. although
    d. since

28. The antecedent of *quo* (line 257) is
    a. *eo* (line 256)
    b. *acroama* (line 256)
    c. *vocem* (line 257)
    d. *eius* (line 257)

29. The word *sua* in line 257 refers to
    a. *Themistoclem* (line 255)
    b. *Athenis* (line 255)
    c. *acroama* (line 256)
    d. *quo* (line 257)

30. From lines 255–258 (*Themistoclem illum . . . praedicaretur*), we learn that Themistocles

    a. liked to hear his own voice

    b. lived in Athens

    c. was very well-known in Rome

    d. was famous for his virtue

31. In line 258, *item* is translated

    a. single

    b. likewise

    c. the same

    d. among

32. From lines 258–260 (*Itaque ille . . . celebrari*), we learn that Marius

    a. thought Plotius was talented

    b. esteemed Plotius highly

    c. had celebrated his own deeds

    d. was a good friend of Plotius

Translation *Suggested time: 15 minutes*

> Ergo illi alienum, quia poeta fuit, post
> mortem etiam expetunt; nos hunc vivum qui et voluntate et
> legibus noster est repudiamus, praesertim cum omne olim
> studium atque omne ingenium contulerit Archias ad populi
> 5   Romani gloriam laudemque celebrandam?

_____

_____

_____

_____

_____

_____

_____

_____

Short Analysis Questions

Sit igitur, iudices, sanctum apud vos, humanissimos homines, hoc poetae nomen quod nulla
umquam barbaria violavit. Saxa atque solitudines voci
respondent, bestiae saepe immanes cantu flectuntur atque
5 consistunt; nos instituti rebus optimis non poetarum
voce moveamur? Homerum Colophonii civem esse dicunt
suum, Chii suum vindicant, Salaminii repetunt, Smyrnaei
vero suum esse confirmant itaque etiam delubrum eius in
oppido dedicaverunt, permulti alii praeterea pugnant inter
10 se atque contendunt. Ergo illi alienum, quia poeta fuit, post
mortem etiam expetunt; nos hunc vivum qui et voluntate et
legibus noster est repudiamus, praesertim cum omne olim
studium atque omne ingenium contulerit Archias ad populi
Romani gloriam laudemque celebrandam? Nam et Cim-
15 bricas res adulescens attigit et ipsi illi C. Mario qui durior ad haec studia videbatur iucundus fuit.

1. What do *saxa, solitudines* and *bestiae* (lines 3–4) have in common?

    _____

    _____

2. What do the *Colophonii*, the *Chii*, the *Salaminii*, the *Smyrnaei* (lines 6–7) have in common?

    _____

    _____

3. According to lines 8–10, why should the Roman people in particular not reject but rather
    embrace the poet, Archias? Quote the Latin that supports your answer and translate or
    accurately paraphrase.

    _____

    _____

    _____

    _____

4. For what purpose does Cicero mention Gaius Marius in lines 15–16? Quote the Latin that supports your answer and translate or accurately paraphrase.

_____

_____

_____

_____

_____

                Neque
enim quisquam est tam aversus a Musis qui non mandari
versibus aeternum suorum laborum praeconium facile
patiatur. Themistoclem illum, summum Athenis virum,
5   **dixisse aiunt, cum ex eo quaereretur quod acroama aut**
cuius vocem libentissime audiret: eius a quo sua virtus
optime praedicaretur. Itaque ille Marius item eximie L.
Plotium dilexit, cuius ingenio putabat ea quae gesserat
posse celebrari.

5. When asked whose voice he would hear most willingly, what did the famous Athenian, Themistocles, say?

_____

_____

_____

6. What was the relationship between Gaius Marius and Lucius Plotius? Quote the Latin that supports your answer and translate or accurately paraphrase.

_____

_____

_____

_____

_____

Essay *Suggested time: 20 minutes*

Homerum Colophonii civem esse dicunt
suum, Chii suum vindicant, Salaminii repetunt, Smyrnaei
vero suum esse confirmant itaque etiam delubrum eius in
oppido dedicaverunt, permulti alii praeterea pugnant inter
5   se atque contendunt. Ergo illi alienum, quia poeta fuit, post
mortem etiam expetunt; nos hunc vivum qui et voluntate et
legibus noster est repudiamus, praesertim cum omne olim
studium atque omne ingenium contulerit Archias ad populi
Romani gloriam laudemque celebrandam?

Cicero conjures up the name of Homer to support his efforts on behalf of the poet, Archias. In a short essay, discuss how Cicero uses this reference to Homer to achieve his desired end.

Support your assertions with references to the Latin text throughout the passage above. All Latin words must be copied or their line numbers provided, AND they must be translated or paraphrased closely enough that it is clear you understand the Latin. It is your responsibility to convince the reader that you are basing your conclusions on the Latin text and not merely on a general recollection of the passage. Direct your answer to the question; do not merely summarize the passage. Please write your essay on a separate piece of paper.

CHAPTER 12: LINES 260–287

260   21 Mithridaticum vero bellum magnum atque difficile et in multa varietate terra marique versatum totum ab hoc expressum est; qui libri non modo L. Lucul-lum, fortissimum et clarissimum virum, verum etiam populi Romani nomen inlustrant. Populus enim Romanus

265 aperuit Lucullo imperante Pontum et regiis quondam opibus et ipsa natura et regione vallatum, populi Romani exercitus eodem duce non maxima manu innumerabilis Armeniorum copias fudit, populi Romani laus est urbem amicissimam Cyzicenorum eiusdem consilio ex omni impetu regio atque

270 totius belli ore ac faucibus ereptam esse atque servatam. Nostra semper feretur et praedicabitur L. Lucullo dimi-cante, cum interfectis ducibus depressa hostium classis est, incredibilis apud Tenedum pugna illa navalis, nostra sunt tropaea, nostra monumenta, nostri triumphi. Quae

275 quorum ingeniis efferuntur, ab eis populi Romani fama celebratur.

          22 Carus fuit Africano superiori noster Ennius, itaque etiam in sepulcro Scipionum putatur is esse con-stitutus ex marmore. At eis laudibus certe non solum

280 ipse qui laudatur sed etiam populi Romani nomen ornatur. In caelum huius proavus Cato tollitur; magnus honos populi Romani rebus adiungitur. Omnes denique illi Maximi, Marcelli, Fulvii non sine communi omnium nostrum laude decorantur. Ergo illum qui haec fecerat,

285 Rudinum hominem, maiores nostri in civitatem receperunt; nos hunc Heracliensem, multis civitatibus expetitum, in hac autem legibus constitutum, de nostra civitate eiciamus?

Preparatory Questions

Lines 260–61   Identify at least three adjectives or adjective phrases that modify *bellum*. _____

_____

Line 261   Identify the case and use of *terra marique*. _____

                     What is the form of *versatum?* _____

Line 262   To whom does *hoc* refer?_____

Line 263   What is the case and use of *virum?* _____

Line 265   What is the form of *imperante?* _____

Identify the use of the phrase *Lucullo imperante.* _____

Lines 265–66   Identify the figure of speech in these lines. _____

Line 266   What is the case and use of *natura?* _____

Line 267   Identify the construction of the phrase *eodem duce.* _____

To whom does the phrase *eodem duce* refer? _____

With which phrase is *non maxima manu* contrasted? _____

What does *innumerabilis* modify? _____

Line 268   What is the most appropriate meaning of *fudit* in this context? _____

Of which verbs is *urbem* the subject? _____

Line 269   On which noun does *Cyzicenorum* depend? _____

What is the case of *eiusdem?* _____

To whom does *eiusdem* refer? _____

What does *regio* modify? _____

Line 270   Which preposition should be supplied with *ore* and *faucibus?* _____

Line 271   What does *nostra* modify? _____

Identify the subject of *feretur.* _____

What is the tense and voice of *feretur?* _____

What is the best meaning for *feretur* in this context? _____

Line 272   What is the use of *interfectis ducibus?* _____

Lines 272–73   Identify the subject of the *cum* clause. _____

Line 273   What does *incredibilis* modify? _____

Line 273–74   What three literary devices are employed simultaneously in this line? _____

_____

What word should be supplied with *nostra monumenta* and *nostri triumphi?* _____

_____

Line 275   Find the word to which *quorum* refers. _____

Line 277   What is the case and use of *carus?* _____

Line 278   Identify the grammatical subject of *putatur.* _____

To whom does *is* refer? _____

Lines 278–79 Identify the form of *esse constitutus*. _____

Line 279 On what word does the ablative phrase *eis laudibus* depend? _____

Line 280 Of which verb is *ipse* the subject? _____

Line 281 What ablative of means should be supplied with *tollitur*? _____

Line 282 What is the best way to translate *rebus* in this context? _____

Line 283 Identify the rhetorical device used in the phrase *non sine communi*. _____

_____

What does *communi* modify? _____

Line 284 Identify the subject of *decorantur*. _____

Identify the case and use of *illum*. _____

To whom does *illum* refer? _____

Identify the case and use of *haec*. _____

To what does *haec* refer? _____

Line 285 Identify the case and use of *Rudinum hominem*. _____

What is the reference contained in the word *Rudinum?* _____

Line 286 To whom does *hunc* refer? _____

What is the reference contained in the word *Heracliensem?* _____

Identify the case and use of *multis civitatibus*. _____

What word needs to be supplied with *hac?* _____

Line 287 Identify the form of *constitutum* and find the word it modifies. _____

_____

Identify the form and use of *eiciamus*. _____

Multiple Choice Questions *Suggested time: 46 minutes*

1. In line 262, *totum* is translated
   a. whole
   b. entire
   c. entirely
   d. totally

2. The subject of *expressum est* (line 262) is
   a. *bellum* (line 260)
   b. *terra marique* (line 261)
   c. *versatum* (line 261)
   d. *hoc* (line 262)

3. In line 262, *qui* is translated

    a. who
                                        b. that

    c. these
                                          d. where

4. In line 263, *verum etiam* is translated

    a. and truly
                                      b. although true

    c. but also
                                        d. and even

5. The case of *nomen* (line 264) is

    a. nominative
                                      b. vocative

    c. accusative
                                        d. locative

6. In lines 260–264 (*Mithridaticum . . . inlustrant*), we learn that

    a. Lucullus wrote a book about war
                b. the Roman people defeated Mithridates

    c. the war was fought on land and sea
         d. it is difficult to write about war

7. *Pontum* (line 265) is the object of

    a. *aperuit* (line 265)
                                  b. *imperante* (line 265)

    c. *vallatum* (line 266)
                                 d. *fudit* (line 268)

8. In line 266, the phrase *ipsa natura et regione* is an example of

    a. hyperbole
                                      b. hendiadys

    c. hyperbaton
                                    d. hysteron proteron

9. The word *vallatum* (line 266) modifies

    a. *Romanus* (line 264)
                                 b. *Lucullo* (line 265)

    c. *Pontum* (line 265)
                                 d. *eodem* (line 267)

10. In line 266, the case and number of *exercitus* is

    a. nominative singular
                              b. genitive singular

    c. nominative plural
                                d. accusative plural

11. In line 267, *manu* is translated

    a. hand
                                            b. band

    c. touch
                                          d. valor

12. In line 267, the phrase *non maxima manu* is an example of

    a. hyperbole
                                      b. hendiadys

    c. litotes
                                        d. asyndeton

13. In line 268, *populi Romani laus est* is translated

    a. it is the praise of the Roman people
          b. it is to the credit of the Roman people

    c. there is praise for the Roman people
        d. the Roman people are praised

14. The subject of *ereptam esse* (line 270) is

    a. *laus* (line 268)

    b. *urbem* (line 268)

    c. *eiusdem* (line 269)

    d. *servatam* (line 270)

15. In lines 264–270 (*Populus enim . . . servatam*), we find an example of

    a. hyperbole

    b. hysteron proteron

    c. chiasmus

    d. anaphora

16. In lines 264–268 (*Populus Romanus . . . copias fudit*), we learn that

    a. Lucullus ruled with kingly powers

    b. Pontus was rich in natural resources

    c. the Roman army was outnumbered

    d. the Roman army had vast supplies

17. In lines 268–270 (*populi Romani . . . atque servatam*), we learn that the city of the Cyziceni was

    a. captured by the Romans

    b. friendly to the king

    c. destroyed in the war

    d. saved by Lucullus's plan

18. The case and number of *classis* (line 272) is

    a. nominative singular

    b. genitive singular

    c. dative plural

    d. ablative plural

19. In line 273, *apud* is translated

    a. at the house of

    b. among

    c. in the time of

    d. near

20. In lines 272–273, the verb *depressa . . . est* is translated

    a. was turned aside

    b. is depressed

    c. is destroyed

    d. was sunk

21. In lines 271–274 (*Nostra semper . . . nostri triumphi*), we find an example of

    a. antithesis

    b. anaphora

    c. polysyndeton

    d. hendiadys

22. From lines 271–274 (*Nostra semper . . . nostri triumphi*), we learn that

    a. the Romans won a big naval battle

    b. Lucullus went down with his ship

    c. the enemy leaders were inefficient

    d. many monuments were destroyed

23. In lines 274–275, the phrase *quae . . . efferuntur* is translated

    a. those by whose talents these things are made known

    b. the things which have been carried out by these men

    c. by geniuses, whose deeds are expressed here

    d. lacking the deeds of which these are spoken

24. From lines 274–276 (*Quae . . . celebratur*), we learn that

    a. Lucullus is celebrated for his many talents
    b. the Roman people's reputation is glorified
    c. those who are geniuses are praised
    d. the Roman people are carried away by fame

25. In line 277, *superiori* is translated

    a. elder
    b. taller
    c. higher
    d. smarter

26. In line 278, the case of *Scipionum* is

    a. nominative
    b. genitive
    c. accusative
    d. vocative

27. In line 279, *marmore* is an ablative of

    a. separation
    b. source
    c. place from which
    d. cause

28. In lines 277–279 (*Carus fuit . . . ex marmore*), it is implied that

    a. Ennius is buried with Scipio
    b. a statue of Ennius is in Scipio's tomb
    c. Scipio's tomb is made of marble
    d. Scipio's statue is found in Africa

29. The word *ipse* (line 280) refers to

    a. Archias
    b. Africanus
    c. Ennius
    d. the Roman people

30. The word *huius* (line 281) refers to

    a. Archias
    b. Scipio
    c. Ennius
    d. the Roman people

31. In line 281, *tollitur* is translated

    a. is removed
    b. is lifted up
    c. is destroyed
    d. is made superior

32. The adjective *magnus* (line 281) modifies

    a. *proavus* (line 281)
    b. *Cato* (line 281)
    c. *honos* (line 281)
    d. *rebus* (line 282)

33. In line 283, the words *Maximi, Marcelli, Fulvii* are an example of

    a. hyperbole
    b. asyndeton
    c. chiasmus
    d. litotes

34. In lines 283–284, *omnium nostrum* is

    a. genitive of possession

    b. objective genitive

    c. subjective genitive

    d. genitive of material

35. In lines 281–284 (*In caelum . . . decorantur*), we learn that

    a. Cato praised his great-grandfather highly

    b. the Roman people did not honor Cato

    c. many Roman heroes have been praised

    d. the Maximi, Marcelli and Fulvii were not our men

36. In line 287, *legibus* is

    a. ablative of means

    b. ablative of agent

    c. dative of agent

    d. dative of reference

37. From lines 284–287 (*Ergo illum . . . civitate eiciamus*), we learn that

    a. Ennius was an uncultured man

    b. Archias sought citizenship in many cities

    c. Ennius was accepted as a citizen of Rome

    d. Archias should have stayed in Heraclea

38. In lines 284–287 (*Ergo illum . . . civitate eiciamus*), we find an example of

    a. hendiadys

    b. antithesis

    c. litotes

    d. hyperbole

Translation: *Suggested time: 15 minutes*

> Nostra semper feretur et praedicabitur L. Lucullo dimi-
> cante, cum interfectis ducibus depressa hostium classis
> est, incredibilis apud Tenedum pugna illa navalis, nostra
> sunt tropaea, nostra monumenta, nostri triumphi. Quae
> 5   quorum ingeniis efferuntur, ab eis populi Romani fama
> celebratur.

_____

_____

_____

_____

_____

_____

_____

Short Analysis Questions

Mithridaticum vero bellum magnum
atque difficile et in multa varietate terra marique versatum
totum ab hoc expressum est; qui libri non modo L. Lucul-
lum, fortissimum et clarissimum virum, verum etiam
5   populi Romani nomen inlustrant. Populus enim Romanus
aperuit Lucullo imperante Pontum et regiis quondam opibus
et ipsa natura et regione vallatum, populi Romani exercitus
eodem duce non maxima manu innumerabilis Armeniorum
copias fudit, populi Romani laus est urbem amicissimam
10   Cyzicenorum eiusdem consilio ex omni impetu regio atque
totius belli ore ac faucibus ereptam esse atque servatam.

1.   Describe the subject matter of the poem by Archias to which Cicero refers in lines 1–4.

_____

_____

_____

2.   What or whom does the poem written by Archias make famous (lines 3–5)?

_____

_____

3.   What two factors contributed to the defense of Pontus before the arrival of the Romans? Who was the leader of the Roman forces in Pontus and what did he accomplish?

_____

_____

_____

4.   Which figures of speech does Cicero use to underscore the significance of Rome's defeat of Mithridates (lines 5–9)? Identify at least **two** figures of speech and quote the Latin for each.

_____

_____

_____

_____

Carus fuit Africano superiori noster Ennius,
itaque etiam in sepulcro Scipionum putatur is esse constitutus ex marmore. At eis laudibus certe non solum
ipse qui laudatur sed etiam populi Romani nomen ornatur.
5   In caelum huius proavus Cato tollitur; magnus honos
populi Romani rebus adiungitur. Omnes denique illi
Maximi, Marcelli, Fulvii non sine communi omnium
nostrum laude decorantur. Ergo illum qui haec fecerat,
Rudinum hominem, maiores nostri in civitatem receperunt;
10   nos hunc Heracliensem, multis civitatibus expetitum, in hac
autem legibus constitutum, de nostra civitate eiciamus?

5.   How did the elder Scipio show his respect for Ennius (lines 1–3)?

_____

_____

_____

6.   To whom does *huius* (line 5) refer? _____

_____

7.   What do the *Maximi, Marcelli* and *Fulvii* have in common (lines 6–8)?

_____

_____

8.   To whom does *illum*, line 8, refer and what does the appositive, *Rudinum hominem,* say about
that person in literal terms? How does Cicero use this description to enhance the point he is
making?

_____

_____

_____

_____

9. To whom does *hunc Heracliensem,* line 10, refer? What contrast is set up between *illum* of line 8 and *hunc* of line 10? Quote the Latin that supports your answer and translate or accurately paraphrase.

_____

_____

_____

_____

_____

_____

Essay *Suggested time: 20 minutes*

Mithridaticum vero bellum magnum atque difficile et in multa varietate terra marique versatum totum ab hoc expressum est; qui libri non modo L. Lucul-lum, fortissimum et clarissimum virum, verum etiam

5   populi Romani nomen inlustrant. Populus enim Romanus aperuit Lucullo imperante Pontum et regiis quondam opibus et ipsa natura et regione vallatum, populi Romani exercitus eodem duce non maxima manu innumerabilis Armeniorum copias fudit, populi Romani laus est urbem amicissimam

10   Cyzicenorum eiusdem consilio ex omni impetu regio atque totius belli ore ac faucibus ereptam esse atque servatam.

In this passage Cicero skillfully recounts the accomplishments of L. Lucullus in the Mithridatic War in order to make his case about poetry. In a short essay, discuss the the accomplishments of Lucullus, how they have impacted the Roman people, and how Cicero's recollection of those accomplishments is related to Archias's poetry.

Support your assertions with references to the Latin text throughout the passage above. All Latin words must be copied or their line numbers provided, AND they must be translated or paraphrased closely enough that it is clear you understand the Latin. It is your responsibility to convince the reader that you are basing your conclusions on the Latin text and not merely on a general recollection of the passage. Direct your answer to the question; do not merely summarize the passage. Please write your essay on a separate piece of paper.

CHAPTER 13: LINES 288–309

23 Nam si quis minorem gloriae fructum putat ex
Graecis versibus percipi quam ex Latinis, vehementer errat,
290 propterea quod Graeca leguntur in omnibus fere gentibus,
Latina suis finibus exiguis sane continentur. Quare, si res
eae quas gessimus orbis terrae regionibus definiuntur, cupere debemus, quo hominum nostrorum tela pervenerint,
eodem gloriam famamque penetrare, quod cum ipsis
295 populis de quorum rebus scribitur haec ampla sunt, tum
eis certe qui de vita gloriae causa dimicant hoc maximum
et periculorum incitamentum est et laborum. 24 Quam
multos scriptores rerum suarum magnus ille Alexander
secum habuisse dicitur. Atque is tamen, cum in Sigeo
300 ad Achillis tumulum astitisset: "O fortunate," inquit
"adulescens, qui tuae virtutis Homerum praeconem inveneris!" Et vere: nam nisi Ilias illa exstitisset, idem
tumulus qui corpus eius contexerat nomen etiam obruisset. Quid? Noster hic Magnus qui cum virtute fortunam
305 adaequavit, nonne Theophanem Mytilenaeum, scriptorem
rerum suarum, in contione militum civitate donavit, et
nostri illi fortes viri, sed rustici ac milites, dulcedine quadam gloriae commoti quasi participes eiusdem laudis magno
illud clamore approbaverunt?

Preparatory Questions

Lines 288–89   Identify the type of condition found in these lines. _____

Line 288   What is the case and use of *gloriae*?_____

What is the case and use of *fructum*? _____

Line 289   Identify the form and use of *percipi*. _____

What word must be understood with *Latinis*? _____

Lines 290–91   What word should be understood with *Graeca* (line 290) and *Latina* (line 291)? _____

_____

Line 290   What does *fere* modify?_____

Line 292   What does *eae* modify? _____

Lines 292–93   Identify the form and function of *cupere*. _____

Line 293   What part of speech is *quo?* _____

Line 294   Identify the case and use of *gloriam famamque.* _____

Lines 294–95 Find a correlative construction. _____

       Identify the case and use of *ipsis populis.* _____

Line 295   What is the antecedent of *quorum?* _____

Line 296   What word governs *eis?* _____

       What is the antecedent of *qui?* _____

       What word depends on *causa?* _____

       What is the case and use of *maximum?* _____

Line 297   Identify the subject of *est.* _____

Line 298   Identify the case and use of *scriptores.* _____

Line 299   Identify the form and use of *habuisse.* _____

Line 299   To whom does *is* refer? _____

       Identify the type of *cum* clause. _____

Line 301   What kind of clause does *qui* introduce? _____

Lines 302–3   Identify the type of condition found in these lines. _____

Line 303   What is the case and use of *corpus?* _____

Line 305   What is the function of *nonne?* _____

       Identify the case and use of *scriptorem.* _____

Line 306   To whom does *suarum* refer? _____

       What is the case and use of *civitate?* _____

       Identify the subject of *donavit.* _____

Line 307   What is the case and use of *dulcedine?* _____

Line 308   Identify the form of *commoti.* _____

       Identify the case and use of *laudis.* _____

       What word modifies it? _____

Line 309   To what/whom does *illud* refer? _____

       What is the grammatical subject of *approbaverunt?* _____

Multiple Choice Questions *Suggested time: 36 minutes*

1. In line 288, *quis* is translated

   a. who

   b. anyone

   c. no one

   d. why

2. The subject of *errat* (line 289) has an earlier reference in

   a. *quis* (line 288)

   b. *gloriae* (line 288)

   c. *fructum* (line 288)

   d. *Latinis* (line 289)

3. In line 291, *exiguis* modifies

   a. *Graecis* (line 289)

   b. *Latinis* (line 289)

   c. *gentibus* (line 290)

   d. *finibus* (line 291)

4. From lines 288–291 (*Nam si . . . continentur*), we learn that

   a. Latin poetry has broad appeal

   b. Greek poetry is more widely read than Latin poetry

   c. many people read both Greek and Latin poetry

   d. Greek poetry is seldom read in Rome

5. In line 292, *gessimus* is translated

   a. we have worn

   b. we have accomplished

   c. we have waged

   d. we have motioned

6. In line 292, *regionibus* is ablative of

   a. means

   b. place where

   c. manner

   d. time

7. In line 294, *eodem* is translated

   a. in the same way

   b. to the same place

   c. by the same thing

   d. with the same man

8. In line 294, *cum* is translated

   a. with

   b. since

   c. not only

   d. even so

9. In line 295, *haec* refers to

   a. accomplishments

   b. lands

   c. glory and fame

   d. dangers and labors

10. In line 296, *causa* is translated

    a. for a reason

    b. with cause

    c. in case

    d. for the sake of

11. In line 296, the <u>first</u> *et* is translated

   a. and

   b. but

   c. both

   d. also

12. From lines 291–297 (*Quare, si res . . . est et laborum*), we learn that

   a. desire for glory is a great motivator

   b. fame should come from military victories

   c. the generals should get all the glory

   d. people are not usually interested in fame

13. In line 297, *quam* is translated

   a. as

   b. which

   c. that

   d. how

14. In line 298, *ille* modifies

   a. *scriptores* (line 298)

   b. *rerum* (line 298)

   c. *Alexander* (line 298)

   d. *secum* (line 299)

15. *suarum* (line 298) refers to

   a. *scriptores* (line 298)

   b. *Alexander* (line 298)

   c. *Achillis* (line 300)

   d. *Homerum* (line 301)

16. From lines 297–299 (*Quam multos . . . habuisse dicitur*), we learn that Alexander

   a. was a great writer

   b. was a great general

   c. had writers with him

   d. wrote stories about himself

17. In line 301, *tuae virtutis* is

   a. subjective genitive

   b. objective genitive

   c. dative of reference

   d. dative of indirect object

18. The word *tuae* (line 301) refers to

   a. Alexander

   b. Archias

   c. Homer

   d. Achilles

19. From lines 299–302 (*Atque is . . . inveneris*), we learn that

   a. Achilles and Alexander met at Homer's tomb

   b. Homer and Achilles were buried together

   c. Homer had made Achilles' story well known

   d. Alexander had never heard of Achilles

20. The word *illa* (line 302) modifies

   a. *fortunate* (line 300)

   b. *virtutis* (line 301)

   c. *Ilias* (line 302)

   d. *idem* (line 302)

21. The pronoun *eius* in line 303 refers to
    a. Homer
    b. Archias
    c. Achilles
    d. Alexander

22. From lines 302–303 (*Et vere . . . obruisset*), we learn that
    a. Achilles' fame is celebrated in the *Iliad*
    b. Achilles is buried at Troy
    c. Alexander visited Troy's ruins
    d. Alexander's favorite poem was the *Iliad*

23. In line 304, *quid* is translated
    a. how about it?
    b. why?
    c. what about it?
    d. who?

24. The antecedent of *qui* (line 304) is
    a. *tumulus* (line 303)
    b. *noster* (line 304)
    c. *Magnus* (line 304)
    d. *virtute* (line 304)

25. The object of *donavit* (line 306) is
    a. *fortunam* (line 304)
    b. *Theophanem* (line 305)
    c. *rerum* (line 306)
    d. *militum* (line 306)

26. The word *quadam* (line 307–308) modifies
    a. *civitate* (line 306)
    b. *dulcedine* (line 307)
    c. *gloriae* (line 308)
    d. *commoti* (line 308)

27. The word *participes* (line 308) refers to
    a. poets
    b. enemies
    c. soldiers
    d. generals

28. From lines 304–306 (*Noster hic . . . donavit*), we learn that
    a. Pompey visited Mytilene frequently
    b. Theophanes wrote about his own homeland
    c. Pompey granted Theophanes citizenship
    d. Theophanes was in the Roman army

29. In lines 306–309 (*et nostri . . . approbaverunt*), we find an example of
    a. litotes
    b. antithesis
    c. hendiadys
    d. hyperbole

30. From lines 306–309 (*et nostri . . . approbaverunt*), we learn that the soldiers
    a. recited poetry very loudly
    b. were fond of country life
    c. sought glory above all things
    d. approved of Pompey's action

Translation *Suggested time: 15 minutes*

<blockquote>

Noster hic Magnus qui cum virtute fortunam adaequavit, nonne Theophanem Mytilenaeum, scriptorem rerum suarum, in contione militum civitate donavit, et nostri illi fortes viri, sed rustici ac milites, dulcedine qua-
5   dam gloriae commoti quasi participes eiusdem laudis magno illud clamore approbaverunt?

</blockquote>

_____

_____

_____

_____

_____

_____

_____

Short Analysis Questions

<blockquote>

Quam multos scriptores rerum suarum magnus ille Alexander secum habuisse dicitur. Atque is tamen, cum in Sigeo ad Achillis tumulum astitisset: "O fortunate," inquit
5   "adulescens, qui tuae virtutis Homerum praeconem in- veneris!" Et vere: nam nisi Ilias illa exstitisset, idem tumulus qui corpus eius contexerat nomen etiam obruis- set. Quid? Noster hic Magnus qui cum virtute fortunam adaequavit, nonne Theophanem Mytilenaeum, scriptorem
10   rerum suarum, in contione militum civitate donavit, et nostri illi fortes viri, sed rustici ac milites, dulcedine qua- dam gloriae commoti quasi participes eiusdem laudis magno illud clamore approbaverunt?

</blockquote>

1.   Where was Alexander when he spoke the words quoted in lines 4–7 and to whom did he address them?

_____

_____

_____

2. In what respect did Alexander's observation about Homer and Achilles prove true?

_____

_____

_____

3. To whom does the phrase, *Noster hic Magnus*, line 8, refer? In what respect does it echo the previous reference to Alexander (lines 1–3)?

_____

_____

_____

4. What is the purpose of the *contio militum* mentioned in line 10?

_____

5. In line 11, what point is Cicero making by using the adjectives, *rustici ac milites*, as attributes of *nostri illi fortes viri*?

_____

_____

_____

Essay *Suggested time: 20 minutes*

> Nam si quis minorem gloriae fructum putat ex
> Graecis versibus percipi quam ex Latinis, vehementer errat,
> propterea quod Graeca leguntur in omnibus fere gentibus,
> Latina suis finibus exiguis sane continentur. Quare, si res
> 5   eae quas gessimus orbis terrae regionibus definiuntur, cu-
> pere debemus, quo hominum nostrorum tela pervenerint,
> eodem gloriam famamque penetrare, quod cum ipsis
> populis de quorum rebus scribitur haec ampla sunt, tum
> eis certe qui de vita gloriae causa dimicant hoc maximum
> 10   et periculorum incitamentum est et laborum.

In this passage, Cicero expounds on the nature of fame and glory. In a short essay, discuss his observations about fame and glory and the manner in which he conveys these thoughts.

Support your assertions with references to the Latin text throughout the passage above. All Latin words must be copied or their line numbers provided, AND they must be translated or paraphrased closely enough that it is clear you understand the Latin. It is your responsibility to convince the reader that you are basing your conclusions on the Latin text and not merely on a general recollection of the passage. Direct your answer to the question; do not merely summarize the passage. Please write your essay on a separate piece of paper.

CHAPTER 14: LINES 310–332

CHAPTER 14: LINES 310–332

310   25 Itaque, credo, si civis Romanus Archias legibus
non esset, ut ab aliquo imperatore civitate donaretur perficere non potuit. Sulla cum Hispanos et Gallos donaret,
credo, hunc petentem repudiasset. Quem nos in contione vidimus, cum ei libellum malus poeta de populo
315   subiecisset, quod epigramma in eum fecisset tantum modo
alternis versibus longiusculis, statim ex eis rebus, quas tum
vendebat, iubere ei praemium tribui—sed ea condicione
ne quid postea scriberet. Qui sedulitatem mali poetae
duxerit aliquo tamen praemio dignam, huius ingenium et
320   virtutem in scribendo et copiam non expetisset? 26 Quid? a
Q. Metello Pio, familiarissimo suo, qui civitate multos donavit, neque per se neque per Lucullos impetravisset? qui
praesertim usque eo de suis rebus scribi cuperet ut etiam
Cordubae natis poetis pingue quiddam sonantibus atque
325   peregrinum tamen auris suas dederet. Neque enim est hoc
dissimulandum quod obscurari non potest, sed prae nobis
ferendum; trahimur omnes studio laudis, et optimus
quisque maxime gloria ducitur. Ipsi illi philosophi etiam
in eis libellis quos de contemnenda gloria scribunt nomen
330   suum inscribunt; in eo ipso in quo praedicationem no-
bilitatemque despiciunt praedicari de se ac nominari
volunt.

Preparatory Questions

Line 310   Identify the case and use of *legibus*._____

Line 311   What kind of clause is *ut . . . donaretur?* _____

Line 312   Who/what is understood as the subject of *potuit?* _____

            Identify the type of *cum* clause. _____

Line 313   Identify the form and use of *petentem.* _____

            What is the case and use of *quem?*_____

Lines 314   What is the case and use of *ei?*_____

Line 314–15 Identify the type of *cum* clause. _____

Line 315   To whom/what does *eum* refer? _____

            To whom does the subject of *fecisset* refer?_____

Line 317 Identify the subject of *vendebat*. _____

     Identify the form and use of *iubere*. _____

     To whom does *ei* refer? _____

     Identify the form and use of *tribui*. _____

Line 318 What kind of clause is *ne . . . scriberet*? _____

     Identify the antecedent of *qui*. _____

Line 319 What is the case and use of *praemio?* _____

     To whom/what does *huius* refer? _____

Line 320 Identify the subject of *expetisset*. _____

     Identify the form and use of *expetisset*. _____

Line 321 Identify the antecedent of *qui*. _____

     What is the case and use of *civitate?* _____

Line 322 To whom/what does *se* refer? _____

     Identify the subject of *impetravisset*. _____

     To whom/what does *qui* refer? _____

Line 323 To whom/what does *suis* refer? _____

     Identify the form and use of *scribi*. _____

     Identify the form and use of *cuperet*. _____

     What kind of clause does *ut* introduce? _____

Line 324 What is the case and use of *quiddam?* _____

Line 325 Identify the subject of *dederet*. _____

Lines 325-26 Identify the subject of *est . . . dissimulandum*. _____

Line 326 What is the antecedent of *quod?* _____

Line 327 What is the case and use of *studio?* _____

Line 328 Identify the subject of *ducitur*. _____

Line 329 What is the antecedent of *quos?* _____

     Identify the form of *contemnenda*. _____

Line 330 To whom/what does *suum* refer? _____

Line 331 Identify the form and use of *praedicari*. _____

Multiple Choice Questions *Suggested time: 42 minutes*

1. In line 310, *credo* is translated
   a. believe me
   c. I suppose
   b. on credit
   d. I owe

2. In line 311, the clause *ut . . . donaretur* is dependent on
   a. *credo* (line 310)
   c. *perficere* (line 311–312)
   b. *esset* (line 311)
   d. *potuit* (line 312)

3. In line 311, *aliquo* is translated
   a. another
   c. somewhere
   b. some
   d. anyone

4. The subject of *donaretur* (line 311) is
   a. a Roman citizen
   c. Sulla
   b. Archias
   d. a poet

5. From lines 310–312 (*Itaque . . . potuit*), we learn that
   a. Archias is in fact a Roman citizen
   c. a Roman citizen trusts the laws
   b. any general can be a citizen
   d. citizenship cannot be granted by generals

6. In line 313, *hunc* refers to
   a. a Roman citizen
   c. Archias
   b. Sulla
   d. a Gaul

7. In lines 312–313 (*Sulla . . . repudiasset*), we find an example of
   a. hysteron proteron
   c. irony
   b. hendiadys
   d. litotes

8. The word *quem* (line 313) refers to
   a. *Archias* (line 310)
   c. *Hispanos* (line 312)
   b. *Sulla* (line 312)
   d. *Gallos* (line 312)

9. In line 314, *ei* refers to
   a. Sulla
   c. the poet
   b. Archias
   d. the people

10. In line 315, *quod* is translated
    a. which
    c. because
    b. that
    d. when

11. In line 315, the case of *epigramma* is
    a. nominative
    b. dative
    c. accusative
    d. ablative

12. In line 315, *in eum* is translated
    a. for him
    b. against him
    c. into it
    d. in it

13. In line 315, *tantum modo* is translated
    a. only in this way
    b. in such a manner
    c. merely
    d. just now

14. In line 316, *rebus* is translated
    a. materials
    b. goods
    c. poems
    d. situations

15. In line 317, *ea condicione* is ablative of
    a. means
    b. manner
    c. time
    d. place where

16. In line 318, *quid* is translated
    a. what
    b. why
    c. anything
    d. something

17. From lines 313–316 (*Quem non . . . longiusculis*), we learn that
    a. Sulla preferred epigrams to long poems
    b. only long verses should be written
    c. a bad poet gave his poetry to Sulla
    d. Sulla and the poet were in a writing contest

18. In line 318, the case of *mali poetae* is
    a. nominative
    b. genitive
    c. dative
    d. ablative

19. From lines 316-318 (*statim . . . postea scriberet*), we learn that the poet
    a. was given a reward
    b. was urged to write more
    c. wrote about his own experiences
    d. sold his works for money

20. From lines 318–320 (*Qui . . . expetisset*), we learn that
    a. there is no reward for bad poetry
    b. one must work hard for one's rewards
    c. even bad poets are rewarded sometimes
    d. Archias should get a reward for his writing

21. In line 320, *quid* is translated
    a. What about?
    b. Why?
    c. Since when?
    d. Who?

22. The word *suo* in line 321 refers to
    a. Metellus
    b. Archias
    c. Sulla
    d. Lucullus

23. In line 322, *per se* is translated
    a. of his own accord
    b. through himself
    c. on his own merits
    d. in spite of himself

24. In lines 320–322 (*a Q. Metello . . . impetravisset*), we learn that
    a. Q. Metellus was a good friend of Archias
    b. many people sought citizenship from Metellus
    c. Archias wanted the Luculli to make him a citizen
    d. Metellus thought Archias was already a citizen

25. In line 323, *usque* is translated
    a. as far as
    b. as long as
    c. right up to
    d. to such an extent

26. In line 324, the case of *Cordubae* is
    a. nominative
    b. genitive
    c. dative
    d. locative

27. From lines 322–325 (*qui praesertim . . . dederet*), we learn that
    a. Archias was born in Cordoba
    b. Metellus thought that Spanish poets had talent
    c. Metellus listened to the Spanish poets
    d. Archias wrote poems about Metellus's deeds

28. The subject of *potest* (line 326) is
    a. *hoc* (line 325)
    b. *dissimulandum* (line 326)
    c. *quod* (line 326)
    d. *obscurari* (line 326)

29. In line 327, the word that must be supplied with *ferendum* is
    a. *esse*
    b. *erat*
    c. *fuisse*
    d. *est*

30. In line 327, *laudis* is
    a. subjective genitive
    b. genitive of possession
    c. genitive of source
    d. objective genitive

31. In line 328, the case of *ipsi* is

    a. nominative

    b. genitive

    c. dative

    d. ablative

32. The word *suum* in line 330 refers to

    a. *studio* (line 327)

    b. *quisque* (line 328)

    c. *philosophi* (line 328)

    d. *libellis* (line 329)

33. In line 330, *praedicationem* is translated

    a. public address

    b. pronouncement

    c. publicity

    d. prophecy

34. The pronoun *se* in line 331 refers to

    a. *philosophi* (line 328)

    b. *libellis* (line 329)

    c. *nomen* (line 329)

    d. *ipso* (line 330)

35. From lines 328–332 (*ipsi illi . . . volunt*), we learn that philosophers

    a. seek publicity for their books

    b. dedicate their books to their students

    c. write books condemning glory

    d. wish their books to be considered noble

Translation *Suggested time: 15 minutes*

> . . . trahimur omnes studio laudis, et optimus quisque maxime gloria ducitur. Ipsi illi philosophi etiam in eis libellis quos de contemnenda gloria scribunt nomen suum inscribunt; in eo ipso in quo praedicationem no-
> 5   bilitatemque despiciunt praedicari de se ac nominari volunt.

_____

_____

_____

_____

_____

_____

_____

_____

Short Analysis Questions

> Itaque, credo, si civis Romanus Archias legibus
> non esset, ut ab aliquo imperatore civitate donaretur per-
> ficere non potuit. Sulla cum Hispanos et Gallos donaret,
> credo, hunc petentem repudiasset. Quem nos in con-
> 5   tione vidimus, cum ei libellum malus poeta de populo
> subiecisset, quod epigramma in eum fecisset tantum modo
> alternis versibus longiusculis, statim ex eis rebus, quas tum
> vendebat, iubere ei praemium tribui—sed ea condicione
> ne quid postea scriberet. Qui sedulitatem mali poetae
> 10   duxerit aliquo tamen praemio dignam, huius ingenium et
> virtutem in scribendo et copiam non expetisset?

1.   According to line 3, what has Sulla done for the citizens of Spain and Gaul?

_____

2.   What is the antecedent of *quas*, line 7? _____ To what action taken by Sulla does the relative clause, *quas . . . vendebat* (lines 7–8), refer?

_____

_____

_____

3.   To whom does *qui*, line 9, refer? _____ According to the relative clause introduced by *qui*, what has this person done?

_____

_____

4.   To whom does the demonstrative *huius*, line 10, refer? _____

With what phrase is the word *huius* contrasted? _____

How does the juxtaposition of these words/phrases support the position Cicero is trying to make? Cite the Latin that supports your answer and translate or accurately paraphrase.

_____

_____

_____

_____

_____

Essay *Suggested time: 20 minutes*

Quid? a

Q. Metello Pio, familiarissimo suo, qui civitate multos donavit, neque per se neque per Lucullos impetravisset? qui
praesertim usque eo de suis rebus scribi cuperet ut etiam
5   Cordubae natis poetis pingue quiddam sonantibus atque
peregrinum tamen auris suas dederet. Neque enim est hoc
dissimulandum quod obscurari non potest, sed prae nobis
ferendum; trahimur omnes studio laudis, et optimus
quisque maxime gloria ducitur. Ipsi illi philosophi etiam
10   in eis libellis quos de contemnenda gloria scribunt nomen
suum inscribunt; in eo ipso in quo praedicationem no-
bilitatemque despiciunt praedicari de se ac nominari
volunt.

What is Cicero attempting to prove in this passage? In a short essay, answer this question and show how the details that Cicero provides about Q. Metellus Pius in lines 2–6 support the point that he is making.

Support your assertions with references to the Latin text throughout the passage above. All Latin words must be copied or their line numbers provided, AND they must be translated or paraphrased closely enough that it is clear you understand the Latin. It is your responsibility to convince the reader that you are basing your conclusions on the Latin text and not merely on a general recollection of the passage. Direct your answer to the question; do not merely summarize the passage. Please write your essay on a separate piece of paper.

CHAPTER 15: LINES 332–351

27 Decimus quidem Brutus, summus vir et imperator, Acci, amicissimi sui, carminibus templorum ac monumentorum aditus exornavit suorum. Iam vero ille qui
335   cum Aetolis Ennio comite bellavit Fulvius non dubitavit Martis manubias Musis consecrare. Quare, in qua urbe imperatores prope armati poetarum nomen et Musarum delubra coluerunt, in ea non debent togati iudices a Musarum honore et a poetarum salute abhorrere.
340   28 Atque ut id libentius faciatis, iam me vobis, iudices, indicabo, et de meo quodam amore gloriae nimis acri fortasse, verum tamen honesto vobis confitebor. Nam quas res nos in consulatu nostro vobiscum simul pro salute huius urbis atque imperi et pro vita civium proque universa
345   re publica gessimus, attigit hic versibus atque inchoavit. Quibus auditis, quod mihi magna res et iucunda visa est, hunc ad perficiendum adornavi. Nullam enim virtus aliam mercedem laborum periculorumque desiderat praeter hanc laudis et gloriae. Qua quidem detracta, iudices, quid est
350   quod in hoc tam exiguo vitae curriculo et tam brevi tantis nos in laboribus exerceamus?

Preparatory Questions

Line 333   What is the case and use of *Acci?* _____

            What is the case and use of *carminibus?* _____

Line 334   What is the case and use of *aditus?* _____

            Identify the subject of *exornavit.* _____

            What word does *ille* modify? _____

Line 335   Identify the case and use of *comite.* _____

Line 336   Identify the case and use of *Musis.* _____

            On what word does *consecrare* depend? _____

Line 337   What part of speech is *prope?* _____

Line 338   What word does *togati* modify? _____

Line 339   Identify the case and use of *honore.* _____

Line 340   Identify the type of clause introduced by *ut*._____

               Identify the case of *me*. What kind of pronoun is it? _____

Line 341   What is the case and use of *gloriae?*_____

               With what word does *acri* agree? _____

Line 342   What is the antecedent of *quas?* _____

Line 344   Identify the case and use of *imperi.* _____

Line 345   What is the direct object of *gessimus?* _____

               What is the direct object of *inchoavit?* _____

Line 346   What construction is *quibus auditis?* _____

               What is the antecedent of *quibus?* _____

               Identify the case and use of *mihi.*_____

Line 347   To whom does *hunc* refer? _____

Line 348   Identify the subject of *desiderat.* _____

               To what noun does *hanc* refer?_____

Line 349   What is the antecedent of *qua?*_____

Line 350   What word does *hoc* modify?_____

               Identify the case and use of *brevi.* _____

               What word does *tantis* modify?_____

Line 351   Identify the case and use of *nos.* _____

               Identify the mood and use of *exerceamus.*_____

Multiple Choice Questions *Suggested time: 28 minutes*

1.   The word *sui* in line 333 refers to

    a. Archias
    b. Brutus
    c. Accius
    d. Ennius

2.   In line 334, the case and number of *aditus* is

    a. nominative singular
    b. genitive singular
    c. nominative plural
    d. accusative plural

3. The antecedent of *qui* (line 334) is

   a. *Acci* (line 333)
   b. *Aetolis* (line 335)
   c. *Ennio* (line 335)
   d. *Fulvius* (line 335)

4. The grammatical subject of *bellavit* in line 335 is

   a. *ille* (line 334)
   b. *qui* (line 334)
   c. *Aetolis* (line 335)
   d. *Fulvius* (line 335)

5. From lines 334–336 (*Iam vero . . . consecrare*), we learn that Fulvius dedicated the spoils of war to

   a. the Aeolians
   b. the Muses
   c. Mars
   d. Ennius

6. In lines 334–336 (*Iam vero . . . consecrare*), we find an example of

   a. anaphora
   b. asyndeton
   c. alliteration
   d. antithesis

7. In line 337, *prope* is translated

   a. all but
   b. near
   c. besides
   d. especially

8. In line 338, *ea* refers to

   a. the city
   b. the poet
   c. the shrines
   d. the Muses

9. In line 339, *salute* is ablative of

   a. separation
   b. agent
   c. manner
   d. time

10. In lines 336–339 (*Quare . . . abhorrere*), we find an example of

    a. hendiadys
    b. litotes
    c. antithesis
    d. hyperbole

11. From lines 336–339 (*Quare . . . abhorrere*), we learn that in Rome

    a. generals are sometimes called poets
    b. there are shrines to the Muses
    c. poets enjoy great honor and protection
    d. the Muses are the patrons of poets

12. From lines 340–342 (*Atque ut . . . confitebor*), we learn that Cicero

    a. thinks that glory should not be sought by all
    b. will make a concession to the jury
    c. admits to a love of glory
    d. would prefer that the jurors testify to him

13. In line 343, *nos* refers to
    a. Cicero and the jury
    b. Cicero himself
    c. the Roman people
    d. the poets

14. In line 343, *simul* is translated
    a. together
    b. at once
    c. as soon as
    d. like

15. In lines 343–344, the repetition of *pro* is an example of
    a. hyperbole
    b. alliteration
    c. chiasmus
    d. anaphora

16. In line 345, *hic* refers to
    a. Ennius
    b. Fulvius
    c. Archias
    d. Cicero

17. From lines 342–345 (*Nam quas . . . inchoavit*), we learn that
    a. Archias began a poem about Cicero's consulship
    b. Cicero and the jurors fought for the republic
    c. Cicero defended many clients during his consulship
    d. Archias's poem about Cicero's consulship was famous

18. In line 347, *ad perficiendum* expresses
    a. purpose
    b. result
    c. obligation
    d. anticipation

19. In line 348, *praeter* is translated
    a. especially
    b. moreover
    c. behind
    d. beyond

20. The word *detracta* (line 349) refers to
    a. *res* (line 346)
    b. *virtus* (line 347)
    c. *mercedem* (line 348)
    d. *gloriae* (line 349)

21. From lines 347–349 (*Nullam enim . . . gloriae*), we learn that
    a. praise and glory are desired more than dangers
    b. the desired reward for work and danger is praise
    c. glory is different from praise, but still desirable
    d. no one wants to work without glory and praise

22. The <u>first</u> *tam* in line 350 modifies

    a. *hoc* (line 350)   b. *exiguo* (line 350)

    c. *vitae* (line 350)   d. *curriculo* (line 350)

23. From lines 349–351 (*Qua quidem . . . exerceamus*), we learn that

    a. if there is no reward, people live an unpleasant life   b. life is short and involves many labors

    c. the reason people work is to earn money   d. the distractions of life make it insignificant

Translation *Suggested time: 10 minutes*

                             Nullam enim virtus aliam
     mercedem laborum periculorumque desiderat praeter hanc
     laudis et gloriae. Qua quidem detracta, iudices, quid est
     quod in hoc tam exiguo vitae curriculo et tam brevi tantis
5   **nos in laboribus exerceamus?**

_____

_____

_____

_____

_____

_____

Short Analysis Questions

Atque ut id libentius faciatis, iam me vobis, iudices, indicabo, et de meo quodam amore gloriae nimis acri
fortasse, verum tamen honesto vobis confitebor. Nam quas
res nos in consulatu nostro vobiscum simul pro salute hui-
5   us urbis atque imperi et pro vita civium proque universa
re publica gessimus, attigit hic versibus atque inchoavit.
Quibus auditis, quod mihi magna res et iucunda visa est,
hunc ad perficiendum adornavi. Nullam enim virtus aliam
mercedem laborum periculorumque desiderat praeter hanc
10   laudis et gloriae. Qua quidem detracta, iudices, quid est
quod in hoc tam exiguo vitae curriculo et tam brevi tantis
nos in laboribus exerceamus?

1. What revelation does Cicero make about himself in lines 2–3?

2. To what specific event does the *res* of line 4 refer?

3. How does the tricolon crescens found in lines 3–6 underscore the significance of the *res* in line 4?

4. According to lines 8–12, what keeps men pursuing their goal in the racecourse of life? Quote and translate a Latin phrase that supports your answer.

Essay *Suggested time: 20 minutes*

> Decimus quidem Brutus, summus vir et im-
> perator, Acci, amicissimi sui, carminibus templorum ac
> monumentorum aditus exornavit suorum. Iam vero ille qui
> cum Aetolis Ennio comite bellavit Fulvius non dubitavit
> 5   Martis manubias Musis consecrare. Quare, in qua urbe
> imperatores prope armati poetarum nomen et Mus-
> arum delubra coluerunt, in ea non debent togati iudi-
> ces a Musarum honore et a poetarum salute abhorrere.

In this passage Cicero juxtaposes the *imperatores prope armati* with the *togati iudices* in order to suggest the course of action he would like adopted. In a short essay, discuss how Cicero uses specific historical *exempla* in this passage to suggest what he believes the *togati iudices* should or should not do.

Support your assertions with references to the Latin text throughout the passage above. All Latin words must be copied or their line numbers provided, AND they must be translated or paraphrased closely enough that it is clear you understand the Latin. It is your responsibility to convince the reader that you are basing your conclusions on the Latin text and not merely on a general recollection of the passage. Direct your answer to the question; do not merely summarize the passage. Please write your essay on a separate piece of paper.

CHAPTER 16: LINES 351–375

29 Certe, si nihil animus
praesentiret in posterum, et si, quibus regionibus vitae
spatium circumscriptum est, isdem omnis cogitationes terminaret suas, nec tantis se laboribus frangeret neque tot
355 curis vigiliisque angeretur nec totiens de ipsa vita
dimicaret. Nunc insidet quaedam in optimo quoque virtus,
quae noctes ac dies animum gloriae stimulis concitat
atque admonet non cum vitae tempore esse dimittendam commemorationem nominis nostri, sed cum omni
360 posteritate adaequandam. 30 An vero tam parvi animi
videamur esse omnes qui in re publica atque in his vitae periculis laboribusque versamur ut, cum usque ad
extremum spatium nullum tranquillum atque otiosum
spiritum duxerimus, nobiscum simul moritura omnia
365 arbitremur? An statuas et imagines, non animorum
simulacra, sed corporum, studiose multi summi homines
reliquerunt; consiliorum relinquere ac virtutum nostrarum
effigiem nonne multo malle debemus summis ingeniis expressam et politam? Ego vero omnia quae gerebam iam
370 tum in gerendo spargere me ac disseminare arbitrabar
in orbis terrae memoriam sempiternam. Haec vero sive
a meo sensu post mortem afutura est, sive, ut sapientis-
simi homines putaverunt, ad aliquam animi mei partem
pertinebit, nunc quidem certe cogitatione quadam speque
375 delector.

Preparatory Questions

Lines 351–52 Find the protasis of a conditional sentence. _____

Line 352 Identify the case and use of *regionibus*. _____

Line 353 What word must be understood with *isdem?* _____

What word does *omnis* modify? _____

Lines 354–56 Find the verbs of the apodosis of the condition. _____

Line 354 What word does *suas* modify? _____

To what/whom does *se* refer? _____

What part of speech is *tot?* _____

Line 355   What is the case and use of *curis?* _____

Line 356   Identify the subject of *dimicaret.* _____

           What word does *quaedam* modify? _____

Line 357   Identify the case and use of *noctes.* _____

           Identify the case and use of *stimulis.* _____

Line 358   What is the case and use of *tempore?* _____

           Identify the subject of *esse dimittendam.* _____

Line 360   What word must be understood with *adaequandam?* _____

           Identify the case and use of *animi.* _____

Line 362   What type of clause is introduced by *ut?* _____

Lines 362–64 Identify the type of *cum* clause. _____

Line 363   What does *extremum* modify? _____

Line 364   What word must be understood with *moritura?* _____

           Identify the case and use of *omnia.* _____

Line 366   Identify the case and use of *simulacra.* _____

Line 367   On what word does *relinquere* depend? _____

Line 368   Identify the case and use of *effigiem.* _____

           Identify the form and use of *malle.* _____

Lines 368–69 What do *expressam* and *politam* modify?_____

Line 370   Identify the case and use of *me.* _____

Line 371   To what does *haec* refer? _____

Line 372   Identify the form of *afutura.* _____

Line 373   What is the case and use of *animi?* _____

Line 374   What is the subject of *pertinebit?* _____

           What words does *quadam* modify? _____

Multiple Choice Questions *Suggested time: 29 minutes*

1. In line 352, the object of *praesentiret* is
   a. *nihil* (line 351)
   b. *animus* (line 351)
   c. *posterum* (line 352)
   d. *spatium* (line 353)

2. The antecedent of *quibus* (line 352) is
   a. *animus* (line 351)
   b. *regionibus* (line 352)
   c. *isdem* (line 353)
   d. *omnis* (line 353)

3. In line 352, *regionibus* is translated
   a. regions
   b. boundaries
   c. territories
   d. directions

4. The subject of *terminaret* (lines 353–354) is
   a. *nihil* (line 351)
   b. *animus* (line 351)
   c. *spatium* (line 353)
   d. *omnis* (line 353)

5. The word *suas* (line 354) refers to
   a. *animus* (line 351)
   b. *regionibus* (line 352)
   c. *vitae* (line 352)
   d. *omnis* (line 353)

6. From lines 351–356 (*Certe . . . dimicaret*), we learn that
   a. much labor and anxiety is necessary for life
   b. every life has a specific limit
   c. the soul has some existence after death
   d. it is necessary for the soul to fight death

7. In lines 351–356 (*Certe . . . dimicaret*), we find an example of
   a. antithesis
   b. litotes
   c. asyndeton
   d. tricolon

8. In line 356, *quoque* is translated
   a. indeed
   b. also
   c. certain
   d. each

9. The direct object of *concitat* (line 357) is
   a. *quae* (line 357)
   b. *noctes* (line 357)
   c. *dies* (line 357)
   d. *animum* (line 357)

10. In line 358, *cum* is translated
    a. since
    b. with
    c. when
    d. although

11. The form of *esse dimittendam* (lines 358–359) depends on

    a. *insidet* (line 356)   b. *concitat* (line 357)

    c. *admonet* (line 358)   d. *commemorationem* (line 359)

12. In line 359, *omni* is translated

    a. every   b. each

    c. our   d. all

13. From lines 356–360 (*Nunc insidet . . . adaequandam*), we learn that

    a. it is important that one's name lives on in posterity   b. virtue is required in order for men to be remembered

    c. our lives are most likely to end during the night   d. with enough virtue, anyone can have a glorious soul

14. In line 361, *videamur* is

    a. hortatory   b. consecutive

    c. indicative   d. deliberative

15. The antecedent of *qui* (line 361) is

    a. *animi* (line 360)   b. *omnes* (line 361)

    c. *vitae* (lines 361–362)   d. *periculis laboribusque* (line 362)

16. The word *nullum* (line 363) modifies

    a. *extremum* (line 363)   b. *spatium* (line 363)

    c. *tranquillum* (line 363)   d. *spiritum* (line 364)

17. In lines 360–365 (*An vero . . . arbitremur*), we find an example of

    a. rhetorical question   b. chiasmus

    c. litotes   d. hyperbole

18. In lines 360–365 (*An vero . . . arbitremur*), we may infer that Cicero believes that

    a. people have small minds and little spirit   b. he is continually afraid of dying

    c. poets never have any leisure time   d. everything does not perish at death

19. In line 366, the case of *corporum* is

    a. nominative   b. genitive

    c. dative   d. accusative

20. In lines 365–369 (*An statuas . . . politam*), we find an example of

    a. litotes   b. chiasmus

    c. asyndeton   d. tricolon

21. From lines 365–369 (*An statuas . . . politam*), we learn that Cicero thinks that
    a. too many statues have been set up
    b. statues ought to be highly polished
    c. learned men are too fond of their statues
    d. statues are not images of the soul

22. The object of *spargere* (line 370) is
    a. *omnia* (line 369)
    b. *quae* (line 369)
    c. *me* (line 370)
    d. *memoriam* (line 371)

23. In line 372, *ut* is translated
    a. when
    b. in order to
    c. so that
    d. as

24. From lines 371–375 (*Haec vero . . . delector*), we learn that
    a. some people think that the soul definitely perishes with the body
    b. wise men suppose that the soul lives on in some fashion
    c. Cicero believes that his death is not too far in the future
    d. without hope and expectation, life is not worth living

Translation *Suggested time: 12 minutes*

> An statuas et imagines, non animorum simulacra, sed corporum, studiose multi summi homines reliquerunt; consiliorum relinquere ac virtutum nostrarum effigiem nonne multo malle debemus summis ingeniis ex-
> 5   pressam et politam?

_____

_____

_____

_____

_____

_____

_____

Short Analysis Questions

> Certe, si nihil animus
> praesentiret in posterum, et si, quibus regionibus vitae
> spatium circumscriptum est, isdem omnis cogitationes ter-
> minaret suas, nec tantis se laboribus frangeret neque tot
> 5   curis vigiliisque angeretur nec totiens de ipsa vita
> dimicaret. Nunc insidet quaedam in optimo quoque virtus,
> quae noctes ac dies animum gloriae stimulis concitat
> atque admonet non cum vitae tempore esse dimitten-
> dam commemorationem nominis nostri, sed cum omni
> 10   posteritate adaequandam.

1. What does Cicero suggest (lines 1–6) as evidence that a man's thoughts are not bounded by the finite span of his life? Write out and translate the Latin that answers this question.

_____

_____

_____

_____

_____

2. Cicero uses the parallelism of *cum vitae tempore* and *cum omni posteritate* to surround *commemorationem nominis nostri* (lines 8–9). What point does Cicero wish to make with the construction of this sentence?

_____

_____

_____

An vero tam parvi animi
videamur esse omnes qui in re publica atque in his vitae periculis laboribusque versamur ut, cum usque ad
extremum spatium nullum tranquillum atque otiosum
5   spiritum duxerimus, nobiscum simul moritura omnia
arbitremur? An statuas et imagines, non animorum
simulacra, sed corporum, studiose multi summi homines
reliquerunt; consiliorum relinquere ac virtutum nostrarum
effigiem nonne multo malle debemus summis ingeniis ex-
10   pressam et politam? Ego vero omnia quae gerebam iam
tum in gerendo spargere me ac disseminare arbitrabar
in orbis terrae memoriam sempiternam. Haec vero sive
a meo sensu post mortem afutura est, sive, ut sapientis-
simi homines putaverunt, ad aliquam animi mei partem
15   pertinebit, nunc quidem certe cogitatione quadam speque
delector.

3.   In lines 2–3 (*qui . . . versamur*), what kind of men is Cicero describing?

_____

_____

_____

4.   What metaphor is suggested in line 11 by the use of the words *me spargere ac disseminare*?

_____

_____

5.   What do wise men think happens to an individual's memory after death (lines 12–15)? Quote
and translate a Latin phrase or clause that supports your answer.

_____

_____

_____

Essay *Suggested time: 20 minutes*

An statuas et imagines, non animorum
simulacra, sed corporum, studiose multi summi homines
reliquerunt; consiliorum relinquere ac virtutum nostrarum
effigiem nonne multo malle debemus summis ingeniis ex-
5 pressam et politam? Ego vero omnia quae gerebam iam
tum in gerendo spargere me ac disseminare arbitrabar
in orbis terrae memoriam sempiternam. Haec vero sive
a meo sensu post mortem afutura est, sive, ut sapientis-
simi homines putaverunt, ad aliquam animi mei partem
10 pertinebit, nunc quidem certe cogitatione quadam speque
delector.

In this passage, Cicero elaborates on the legacy that he believes great men should leave for posterity. In a short essay, discuss what many men have chosen to leave, what Cicero believes to be a more suitable alternative and how he personalizes these views.

Support your assertions with references to the Latin text throughout the passage above. All Latin words must be copied or their line numbers provided, AND they must be translated or paraphrased closely enough that it is clear you understand the Latin. It is your responsibility to convince the reader that you are basing your conclusions on the Latin text and not merely on a general recollection of the passage. Direct your answer to the question; do not merely summarize the passage. Please write your essay on a separate piece of paper.

CHAPTER 17: LINES 376–397

31 Quare conservate, iudices, hominem pudore eo
quem amicorum videtis comprobari cum dignitate, tum
etiam vetustate, ingenio autem tanto quantum id convenit
existimari, quod summorum hominum iudiciis expetitum
380 esse videatis, causa vero eius modi quae beneficio legis,
auctoritate municipi, testimonio Luculli, tabulis Metelli
comprobetur. Quae cum ita sint, petimus a vobis, iudices,
si qua non modo humana verum etiam divina in tantis ingeniis commendatio debet esse, ut eum qui vos, qui
385 vestros imperatores, qui populi Romani res gestas semper ornavit, qui etiam his recentibus nostris vestrisque
domesticis periculis aeternum se testimonium laudis daturum esse profitetur, quique est ex eo numero qui
semper apud omnis sancti sunt habiti itaque dicti, sic in
390 vestram accipiatis fidem ut humanitate vestra levatus potius
quam acerbitate violatus esse videatur.

32 Quae de causa pro mea consuetudine breviter
simpliciterque dixi, iudices, ea confido probata esse omnibus; quae a foro aliena iudicialique consuetudine et
395 de hominis ingenio et communiter de ipso studio locutus
sum, ea, iudices, a vobis spero esse in bonam partem accepta, ab eo qui iudicium exercet, certo scio.

Preparatory Questions

Line 376   Identify the case and use of *pudore*. _____

Line 377   What is the antecedent of *quem?* _____

            Identify the form and use of *comprobari.* _____

Line 378   What is the case and use of *vetustate?* _____

            Identify the subject of *convenit.* _____

Line 379   What is the antecedent of *quod?* _____

Lines 379–380 What is the subject of *expetitum esse?* _____

Line 380   Identify the case and use of *causa.* _____

            Identify the case and use of *beneficio.* _____

Line 381   What is the case and use of *municipi?* _____

Line 382   Identify the subject of *comprobetur.* _____

Line 383   Identify the case and use of *qua*. _____

Line 384   Identify the case and use of *eum*. _____

Line 385   Identify the form and use of *gestas*. _____

Line 386   What is the subject of *ornavit*? _____

              What does *recentibus* modify? _____

Line 387   What is the case and use of *periculis*? _____

              To whom does *se* refer? _____

Lines 387–88 Identify the form and use of *daturum esse*. _____

Line 388   What is the antecedent of the <u>second</u> *qui*? _____

Line 389   Identify the case and use of *sancti*. _____

              Who is the subject of *sunt habiti*? _____

Line 390   Identify the case and use of *humanitate*. _____

              With what word does *levatus* agree? _____

Line 391   Identify the form and use of *videatur*. _____

Line 393   What is the object of *dixi*? _____

              Identify the case and use of *ea*. _____

Line 394   What is the antecedent of *quae*? _____

              Identify the case and use of *foro*. _____

              What word does *aliena* modify? _____

              Identify the case and use of *iudiciali(que)*. _____

Lines 395–96 What is the object of *locutus sum*? _____

Line 396   Identify the case and use of *ea*. _____

Multiple Choice Questions Suggested time: 31 minutes

1. In line 377, the case of *quem* is determined by

    a. *conservate* (line 376)   b. *comprobari* (line 377)

    c. *convenit* (line 378)   d. *existimari* (line 379)

2. In line 377, *cum* is translated

    a. with   b. both

    c. when   d. only

3. In line 377, *dignitate* is ablative of

    a. accompaniment

    b. manner

    c. means

    d. description

4. In line 378, *id* refers to

    a. *pudore* (line 376)

    b. *dignitate* (line 377)

    c. *vetustate* (line 378)

    d. *ingenio* (line 378)

5. In line 378, *tanto quantum* is translated

    a. as much as

    b. so great that

    c. much more than

    d. much too great

6. In line 380, *causa* is translated

    a. position

    b. reason

    c. cause

    d. for the sake of

7. The antecedent of *quae* (line 380) is

    a. *causa* (line 380)

    b. *modi* (line 380)

    c. *legis* (line 380)

    d. *auctoritate* (line 381)

8. From lines 376–382 (*Quare . . . comprobetur*), we learn that Archias's

    a. case for citizenship is strong

    b. friends testified in court for him

    c. talent could have been greater

    d. records had all been lost

9. In lines 380–382 (*causa vero . . . comprobetur*), we find an example of

    a. antithesis

    b. litotes

    c. hendiadys

    d. asyndeton

10. In line 383, *qua* is translated

    a. any

    b. some

    c. which

    d. what

11. The antecedent of the <u>second</u> *qui* (line 384) is

    a. *vobis* (line 382)

    b. *ingeniis* (line 384)

    c. *eum* (line 384)

    d. *vos* (line 384)

12. In line 384, *vos* is the object of

    a. *petimus* (line 382)

    b. *debet* (line 384)

    c. *ornavit* (line 386)

    d. *profitetur* (line 388)

13. In line 386, *vestris* refers to

    a. the poets
    c. the Roman people

    b. the jurors
    d. Lucullus and Metellus

14. In lines 384–386 (*ut eum . . . vestrisque*), we find an example of

    a. anaphora
    c. hendiadys

    b. litotes
    d. antithesis

15. In line 388, *quique* is translated

    a. whoever
    c. and who

    b. those who
    d. each

16. In line 389, *apud omnis* is translated

    a. in front of everybody
    c. at everyone's house

    b. with each person
    d. in the eyes of all

17. The clause *ut . . . accipiatis* (lines 384–390) is dependent on

    a. *sint* (line 382)
    c. *debet* (line 384)

    b. *petimus* (line 382)
    d. *profitetur* (line 388)

18. In lines 390–391, the clause *ut . . . videatur* expresses

    a. command
    c. purpose

    b. characteristic
    d. result

19. From lines 382–391 (*Quae cum . . . esse videatur*), we learn that

    a. Archias has written a poem about Cicero's consulship
    c. there is some sort of divine inspiration in Archias

    b. the jury should act humanely in Archias's case
    d. Archias has never written about the deeds of the Romans

20. The antecedent of *quae* (line 392) is

    a. *causa* (line 392)
    c. *ea* (line 393)

    b. *consuetudine* (line 392)
    d. *probata* (line 393)

21. In line 392, *breviter* modifies

    a. *simpliciter* (line 393)
    c. *confido* (line 393)

    b. *dixi* (line 393)
    d. *probata esse* (line 393)

22. In line 394, *aliena* is translated

    a. another's
    c. different

    b. foreign
    d. strange

23. In line 394, –que connects

    a. quae (line 394) and aliena (line 394)
    b. foro (line 394) and aliena (line 394)
    c. foro (line 394) and consuetudine (line 394)
    d. iudiciali (line 394) and consuetudine (line 394)

24. In lines 396–397, esse . . . accepta depends on

    a. locutus sum (lines 395–396)
    b. spero (line 396)
    c. exercet (line 397)
    d. certo (line 397)

25. In lines 392–397 (Quae de . . . certo scio), Cicero tells us that

    a. he usually speaks briefly in a trial
    b. Archias is certain to win his case
    c. the judge has been listening carefully
    d. the court was not located in the forum

26. In lines 392–397 (Quae de . . . certo scio), we find an example of

    a. antithesis
    b. hyperbaton
    c. hendiadys
    d. chiasmus

Translation *Suggested time: 15 minutes*

> Quae de causa pro mea consuetudine breviter
> simpliciterque dixi, iudices, ea confido probata esse om-
> nibus; quae a foro aliena iudicialique consuetudine et
> de hominis ingenio et communiter de ipso studio locutus
> 5   sum, ea, iudices, a vobis spero esse in bonam partem ac-
> cepta, ab eo qui iudicium exercet, certo scio.

_____

_____

_____

_____

_____

_____

_____

_____

Short Analysis Questions

> Quare conservate, iudices, hominem pudore eo
> quem amicorum videtis comprobari cum dignitate, tum
> etiam vetustate, ingenio autem tanto quantum id convenit
> existimari, quod summorum hominum iudiciis expetitum
> 5   esse videatis, causa vero eius modi quae beneficio legis,
> auctoritate municipi, testimonio Luculli, tabulis Metelli
> comprobetur.

1.   According to lines 1–4, what qualities does Archias the man and the poet possess? Quote and translate the Latin that answers this question.

2.   In lines 5–7, Cicero sums up the factors that prove the innocence of his client. Quote and translate the Latin for the four elements that support his case on behalf of Archias.

> Quae cum ita sint, petimus a vobis, iudices,
> si qua non modo humana verum etiam divina in tan-
> tis ingeniis commendatio debet esse, ut eum qui vos, qui
> vestros imperatores, qui populi Romani res gestas sem-
> 5   per ornavit, qui etiam his recentibus nostris vestrisque
> domesticis periculis aeternum se testimonium laudis da-
> turum esse profitetur, quique est ex eo numero qui
> semper apud omnis sancti sunt habiti itaque dicti, sic in
> vestram accipiatis fidem ut humanitate vestra levatus potius
> 10   quam acerbitate violatus esse videatur.

3.   According to lines 4–7 (*qui . . . profitetur*), what service has Archias rendered to the Roman people?

4.   In lines 8–9, with which group does Cicero associate Archias? Quote and translate the Latin he uses to describe this group.

_____

_____

_____

_____

5.   In lines 8–9, what action does Cicero ask the jury to take? Quote and translate the Latin that supports your answer.

_____

_____

_____

Essay *Suggested time: 20 minutes*

> Quae de causa pro mea consuetudine breviter
> simpliciterque dixi, iudices, ea confido probata esse om-
> nibus; quae a foro aliena iudicialique consuetudine et
> de hominis ingenio et communiter de ipso studio locutus
> 5   sum, ea, iudices, a vobis spero esse in bonam partem ac-
> cepta, ab eo qui iudicium exercet, certo scio.

In the passage above, Cicero concludes his defense of Archias. In a short essay, discuss the tactics Cicero uses in this final section of his *peroratio* to win the jury's support.

Support your assertions with references to the Latin text throughout the passage above. All Latin words must be copied or their line numbers provided, AND they must be translated or paraphrased closely enough that it is clear you understand the Latin. It is your responsibility to convince the reader that you are basing your conclusions on the Latin text and not merely on a general recollection of the passage. Direct your answer to the question; do not merely summarize the passage. Please write your essay on a separate piece of paper.

TEXT SELECTIONS
FROM THE
DE AMICITIA
WITH EXERCISES

DE AMICITIA
SECTION 1: LINES 1–20

[V. 17] *Laelius.* Ego vos hortari tantum possum ut
amicitiam omnibus rebus humanis anteponatis;
nihil est enim tam naturae aptum, tam conveniens
ad res vel secundas vel adversas.

5   [18] Sed hoc primum sentio nisi in bonis amicitiam esse non posse; neque id ad vivum reseco, ut illi qui haec subtilius disserunt, fortasse
vere, sed ad communem utilitatem parum; negant
enim quemquam virum bonum esse nisi sapientem.
10 Sit ita sane; sed eam sapientiam interpretantur
quam adhuc mortalis nemo est consecutus. Nos
autem ea quae sunt in usu vitaque communi, non
ea quae finguntur aut optantur, spectare debemus.
Nunquam ego dicam C. Fabricium, M'. Curium, Ti.
15 Coruncanium, quos sapientes nostri maiores iudicabant, ad istorum normam fuisse sapientes. Qua
re sibi habeant sapientiae nomen et invidiosum et
obscurum; concedant ut hi boni viri fuerint. Ne
id quidem facient; negabunt id nisi sapienti posse
20 concedi.

Preparatory Questions

Line 1   Identify the form and use of *hortari*. _____

Lines 1–2   Identify the type of *ut* clause._____

Line 2   Identify the case and use of *rebus*. _____

Line 3   What word modifies *nihil?* _____

                Identify the case and use of *naturae.* _____

Lines 5–6   Identify the main verb in the indirect statement. _____

                Identify the case and use of *amicitiam.* _____

Line 6   Identify the case and use of *id.*_____

Line 7   Identify the case and use of *haec.*_____

	What word does *fortasse* modify? _____
Line 9	Identify the case and use of *sapientem*. _____
Line 11	What is the subject of *est consecutus*? _____
	Of what verb is *nos* the subject? _____
Line 12	Identify the case and use of *quae*._____
Line 13	Identify the form and use of *spectare*. _____
Line 14	For what is *M'* an abbreviation? _____
Line 15	Identify the case and use of *sapientes*. _____
Line 16	Identify the form and use of *fuisse*. _____
Lines 17–18	Find two jussive subjunctives. _____
Line 17	Identify the case and use of *nomen*. _____
Line 19	Identify the case and use of *sapienti*. _____
Line 20	Identify the form and use of *concedi*._____

Multiple Choice Questions *Suggested time: 17 minutes*

1. In line 1, *tantum* is translated
   a. so much
   b. as much as
   c. only
   d. however

2. The direct object of *anteponatis* (line 2) is
   a. *vos* (line 1)
   b. *tantum* (line 1)
   c. *amicitiam* (line 2)
   d. *rebus* (line 2)

3. In line 4, *secundas* is translated
   a. favorable
   b. following
   c. secondary
   d. consequent

4. From lines 1–4 (*Ego . . . adversas*), we learn that friendship is
   a. encouraging
   b. important
   c. natural
   d. humane

5. In line 5, *nisi* is translated
   a. only
   b. except
   c. unless
   d. not if

6.   In line 7, *ut* is translated

    a.   as

    c.   in order that

    b.   so that

    d.   when

7.   The subject of *negant* (line 8) refers to

    a.   *res* (line 4)

    c.   *illi* (line 7)

    b.   *bonis* (line 5)

    d.   *haec* (line 7)

8.   In line 9, *quemquam* is translated

    a.   each one

    c.   everyone

    b.   anyone

    d.   a certain one

9.   From lines 5–9 (*Sed hoc . . . sapientem*), we learn that

    a.   only good men will have good friends

    c.   friendship only exists among good men

    b.   friendship is important for the common good

    d.   wise men do not make good friends

10.   In line 12, *non* must be taken with

    a.   *ea* (line 13)

    c.   *spectare* (line 13)

    b.   *quae* (line 13)

    d.   *debemus* (line 13)

11.   The direct object(s) of *spectare* (line 13) is/are

    a.   *ea* (line 12)

    c.   *ea* (line 13)

    b.   *usu vitaque* (line 12)

    d.   *ea* (line 12) and *ea* (line 13)

12.   In line 14, *dicam* is

    a.   potential

    c.   horatory

    b.   deliberative

    d.   jussive

13.   *nostri* (line 15) modifies

    a.   *Fabricium, Curium* (line 14) and *Coruncanium* (line 15)

    c.   *maiores* (line 15)

    b.   *sapientes* (line 15)

    d.   *sapientes* (line 16)

14.   The word *istorum* (line 16) has an earlier reference in

    a.   *vos* (line 1)

    c.   *nos* (line 11)

    b.   *illi* (line 7)

    d.   *maiores* (line 15)

15.   The pronoun *sibi* in line 17 refers to

    a.   *illi* (line 7)

    c.   *nos* (line 11)

    b.   *nemo* (line 11)

    d.   *quos* (line 15)

16. Lines 16–20 (*Qua re . . . concedi*) tell us that some philosophers believe that

    a. wisdom is popular though rare

    b. wisdom should be granted to the wise men

    c. only a wise man can be considered good

    d. wise men accomplish little that is good

Translation *Suggested time: 15 minutes*

Nunquam ego dicam C. Fabricium, M'. Curium, Ti. Coruncanium, quos sapientes nostri maiores iudicabant, ad istorum normam fuisse sapientes. Qua re sibi habeant sapientiae nomen et invidiosum et
5   obscurum; concedant ut hi boni viri fuerint.

Short Analysis Questions

> Ego vos hortari tantum possum ut
> amicitiam omnibus rebus humanis anteponatis;
> nihil est enim tam naturae aptum, tam conveniens
> ad res vel secundas vel adversas.
>
> 5   Sed hoc primum sentio nisi in bonis amici-
> tiam esse non posse; neque id ad vivum re-
> seco, ut illi qui haec subtilius disserunt, fortasse
> vere, sed ad communem utilitatem parum; negant
> enim quemquam virum bonum esse nisi sapientem.

1. In lines 1–2, what position should friendship hold in men's lives? Quote and translate the Latin that answers this question.

   _____

   _____

2. What point is Laelius making about friendship with his use of the two adjectives, *secundas . . . adversas*, line 4?

   _____

   _____

3. Who are the *illi* of line 7? What claim do they make about good men (lines 8–10)?

   _____

   _____

> Nunquam ego dicam C. Fabricium, M'. Curium, Ti.
> Coruncanium, quos sapientes nostri maiores iudi-
> cabant, ad istorum normam fuisse sapientes. Qua
> re sibi habeant sapientiae nomen et invidiosum et
> 5   obscurum; concedant ut hi boni viri fuerint.

4. How did earlier generations regard the men mentioned in lines 1–2?

   _____

   _____

5. How does Cicero think these men should be regarded? Quote and translate the Latin that supports your answer.

_____

_____

Essay _Suggested time: 20 minutes_

           . . . negant
enim quemquam virum bonum esse nisi sapientem.
Sit ita sane; sed eam sapientiam interpretantur
quam adhuc mortalis nemo est consecutus. Nos
5   autem ea quae sunt in usu vitaque communi, non
ea quae finguntur aut optantur, spectare debemus.
Nunquam ego dicam C. Fabricium, M'. Curium, Ti.
Coruncanium, quos sapientes nostri maiores iudicabant, ad istorum normam fuisse sapientes. Qua
10   re sibi habeant sapientiae nomen et invidiosum et
obscurum; concedant ut hi boni viri fuerint. Ne
id quidem facient; negabunt id nisi sapienti posse
concedi.

In this passage, Laelius both agrees and disagrees with the Stoics' definition of what constitutes a good man. In a short essay, discuss Laelius's disagreement with the Stoics' interpretation and the approach he suggests as an alternative.

Support your assertions with references to the Latin text throughout the passage above. All Latin words must be copied or their line numbers provided, AND they must be translated or paraphrased closely enough that it is clear you understand the Latin. It is your responsibility to convince the reader that you are basing your conclusions on the Latin text and not merely on a general recollection of the passage. Direct your answer to the question; do not merely summarize the passage. Please write your essay on a separate piece of paper.

SECTION 2: LINES 20–43

20   [19] Agamus igitur pingui Minerva, ut aiunt. Qui ita se gerunt, ita vivunt, ut eorum probetur fides, integritas, aequitas, liberalitas, nec sit in eis ulla cupiditas, libido, audacia, sintque magna constantia, ut ei fuerunt modo quos

25 nominavi, hos viros bonos, ut habiti sunt, sic etiam appellandos putemus, quia sequantur quantum homines possunt naturam optimam bene vivendi ducem.

    Sic enim mihi perspicere videor, ita natos esse

30 nos ut inter omnes esset societas quaedam, maior autem, ut quisque proxime accederet. Itaque cives potiores quam peregrini, propinqui quam alieni: cum his enim amicitiam natura ipsa peperit, sed ea non satis habet firmitatis. Namque hoc praestat

35 amicitia propinquitati quod ex propinquitate be- nevolentia tolli potest, ex amicitia non potest: sub- lata enim benevolentia amicitiae nomen tollitur, propinquitatis manet. [20] Quanta autem vis amicitiae sit ex hoc intellegi maxime potest, quod

40 ex infinita societate generis humani, quam conci- liavit ipsa natura, ita contracta res est et adducta in angustum ut omnis caritas aut inter duos aut inter paucos iungeretur.

Preparatory Questions

Line 20   Identify the type of subjunctive represented by *agamus.* _____

               Identify the case and use of *Minerva.* _____

Line 21   What is the subject of *gerunt?*_____

Line 22   What are the subjects of *probetur?* _____

Line 23   Explain the mood of *sit.* _____

               To whom does *eis* refer? _____

Line 24   Identify the case and use of *constantia.* _____

               What is the antecedent of *quos?* _____

Line 25   Identify the case and use of *hos viros*. _____

        Identify the case and use of *bonos*._____

        To what word does the understood subject of *habiti sunt* refer?_____

Line 26   What is the construction of *appellandos?*_____

        Identify the tense, mood, and use of *sequantur.*_____

Line 27   What is the case and use of *naturam?* _____

        What does *optimam* modify?_____

Line 28   Identify the case and use of *ducem.* _____

Line 29   Identify the form and use of *perspicere.*_____

        What is the form and use of *natos esse?* _____

Line 30   What word does *maior* modify?_____

Lines 31–32   What verb must be supplied for *itaque . . . alieni?* _____

Line 32   Identify the case and use of *peregrini.* _____

Line 34   Identify the case and use of *firmitatis.*_____

Line 35   What is the case and use of *propinquitati?* _____

Lines 36–37   Identify the case and use of *sublata . . . benevolentia.* _____

Line 38   What word must be supplied with *propinquitatis?* _____

Line 39   What is the case and use of *amicitiae?* _____

        Identify the use of the subjunctive illustrated by *sit.* _____

        Identify the clause which serves as the subject of *potest.* _____

Lines 40–41   What is the subject of *conciliavit?*_____

Line 41   To what does *res* refer? _____

Line 43   What use of the subjunctive is illustrated by *iungeretur?*_____

Multiple Choice Questions *Suggested time: 25 minutes*

1. In line 20, the case of *pingui* is
    a. nominative
    b. genitive
    c. dative
    d. ablative

2. The clause *ut...probetur* (lines 21–22) is
    a. result
    b. purpose
    c. characteristic
    d. command

3. In line 22, we see an example of
    a. hendiadys
    b. assonance
    c. hyperbole
    d. asyndeton

4. In line 26, *quantum* is translated
    a. how much
    b. how many
    c. as far as
    d. too much

5. From lines 21–28 (*Qui ita . . . ducem*), we learn that good men
    a. follow nature as a guide
    b. are frequently very bold
    c. are only good if they are called good
    d. are few and far between

6. In line 30, the clause *ut . . . quaedam* expresses
    a. purpose
    b. command
    c. result
    d. concession

7. In line 30, *quaedam* is translated
    a. each
    b. some
    c. whichever
    d. certain

8. In line 31, *ut* is translated
    a. when
    b. in order to
    c. as
    d. so that

9. In line 32, *quam* is translated
    a. which
    b. than
    c. where
    d. how

10. In line 33, *cum* is translated
    a. when
    b. since
    c. although
    d. with

11. The word *his* in line 33 refers to

    a. citizens and relatives

    b. foreigners and strangers

    c. citizens and foreigners

    d. relatives and strangers

12. In line 34, *ea* refers to

    a. *cives* (line 31)

    b. *amicitiam* (line 33)

    c. *natura* (line 33)

    d. *firmitatis* (line 34)

13. From lines 31–34 (*Itaque . . . firmitatis*), we learn that

    a. strangers can never become friends

    b. friendship is produced by nature

    c. true friendship is hard to find

    d. powerful citizens have the most friends

14. The subject of *praestat* (line 34) is

    a. *hoc* (line 34)

    b. *amicitia* (line 35)

    c. *propinquitati* (line 35)

    d. *benevolentia* (line 35–36)

15. In line 35, *quod* is translated

    a. which

    b. that

    c. what

    d. because

16. The subject of *potest* (line 36) is

    a. *hoc* (line 34)

    b. *amicitia* (line 35)

    c. *benevolentia* (line 35–36)

    d. *nomen* (line 37)

17. From lines 34–38 (*Namque hoc . . . manet*), we learn that

    a. affection is always a part of true friendship

    b. relationships cannot survive without friendship

    c. affection is not often found in relationships

    d. people who are related are not usually friends

18. The antecedent of *quam* in line 40 is

    a. *vis* (line 38)

    b. *amicitiae* (line 39)

    c. *societate* (line 40)

    d. *natura* (line 41)

19. In line 42, *omnis* modifies

    a. *societate* (line 40)

    b. *natura* (line 41)

    c. *res* (line 41)

    d. *caritas* (line 42)

20. From lines 38–43 (*Quanta . . . iungeretur*), we learn that

    a. intelligent people make friends the most easily

    b. only the most sociable people make friends

    c. nature itself provides friendships for people

    d. friendships do not exist widely for people

Translation *Suggested time: 15 minutes*

Sic enim mihi perspicere videor, ita natos esse
nos ut inter omnes esset societas quaedam, maior
autem, ut quisque proxime accederet. Itaque cives
potiores quam peregrini, propinqui quam alieni:
5   cum his enim amicitiam natura ipsa peperit, sed
ea non satis habet firmitatis.

Short Analysis Questions

Agamus igitur pingui Minerva, ut
aiunt. Qui ita se gerunt, ita vivunt, ut eorum
probetur fides, integritas, aequitas, liberalitas, nec
sit in eis ulla cupiditas, libido, audacia, sintque
5   magna constantia, ut ei fuerunt modo quos
nominavi, hos viros bonos, ut habiti sunt, sic etiam
appellandos putemus, quia sequantur quantum
homines possunt naturam optimam bene vivendi
ducem.

1.   Name the figure of speech that Cicero/Laelius uses in line 1 and discuss its significance in this passage.

---

2. Select and translate five qualities possessed by good men, according to Laelius in lines 2–9 (*qui . . . ducem*).

_____

_____

_____

_____

3. Why does Laelius think that the men he named earlier (*modo quos nominavi*) should be called good men (lines 6–9)?

_____

_____

_____

Essay *Suggested time: 20 minutes*

Itaque cives
potiores quam peregrini, propinqui quam alieni:
cum his enim amicitiam natura ipsa peperit, sed
ea non satis habet firmitatis. Namque hoc praestat
5   amicitia propinquitati quod ex propinquitate benevolentia tolli potest, ex amicitia non potest: sublata enim benevolentia amicitiae nomen tollitur,
propinquitatis manet.

In this passage Laelius uses a series of antitheses to reflect upon friendship. In a short essay, discuss the point he is making and how the antitheses reinforce his position.

Support your assertions with references to the Latin text throughout the passage above. All Latin words must be copied or their line numbers provided, AND they must be translated or paraphrased closely enough that it is clear you understand the Latin. It is your responsibility to convince the reader that you are basing your conclusions on the Latin text and not merely on a general recollection of the passage. Direct your answer to the question; do not merely summarize the passage. Please write your essay on a separate piece of paper.

SECTION 3: LINES 44–65

[VI.] Est autem amicitia nihil aliud nisi omnium
45 divinarum humanarumque rerum cum benevolentia et caritate consensio; qua quidem haud scio
an excepta sapientia nil unquam melius homini
sit a dis immortalibus datum. Divitias alii praeponunt, bonam alii valetudinem, alii potentiam,
50 alii honores, multi etiam voluptates. Beluarum hoc
quidem extremum; illa autem superiora caduca et
incerta, posita non tam in consiliis nostris quam
in fortunae temeritate. Qui autem in virtute summum bonum ponunt, praeclare illi quidem, sed
55 haec ipsa virtus amicitiam et gignit et continet,
nec sine virtute amicitia esse ullo pacto potest.
[21] Iam virtutem ex consuetudine vitae ser-
monisque nostri interpretemur, nec eam, ut
quidam docti, verborum magnificentia metiamur,
60 virosque bonos eos qui habentur numeremus,
Paulos, Catones, Gallos, Scipiones, Philos: his communis vita contenta est: eos autem omittamus qui
omnino nusquam reperiuntur. Tales igitur inter
viros amicitia tantas opportunitates habet quantas
65 vix queo dicere.

Preparatory Questions

Line 44   What is the function of *nihil?* _____

             Identify the case and use of *aliud.* _____

Line 46   Identify the case and use of *consensio.*_____

Line 47   Identify the case and use of *excepta sapientia.*_____

Line 48   Identify the use of the subjunctive illustrated by *sit datum.* _____

Lines 48–49   What are the direct objects of *praeponunt?* _____

Lines 50–51   What word must be understood with the phrase *beluarum . . . extremum?*

             _____

Line 51   To what does *illa* refer? _____

Line 52   What does *posita* modify? _____

Line 53   Identify the case and use of *fortunae*. _____

                  What is the antecedent of *qui?* _____

Line 55   What does *haec* modify? _____

Line 58   What does *nostri* modify? _____

                  To what does *eam* refer? _____

Line 59   Identify the case and use of *magnificentia*. _____

Line 61   Identify the case and use of *Paulos, Catones, Gallos, Scipiones, Philos*.

                  _____

                  What is the case and use of *his?* _____

Line 62   What is the antecedent of *qui?* _____

Line 63   What does *tales* modify? _____

Lines 63–65   Identify the correlative construction. _____

Line 65   What is the use of *dicere?* _____

Multiple Choice Questions *Suggested time: 17 minutes*

1.   In line 45, *cum* is translated

    a. when   b. since

    c. although   d. with

2.   In line 46, *qua* is ablative of

    a. means   b. comparison

    c. time   d. place where

3.   From lines 44–48 (*Est autem . . . datum*), we learn that friendship

    a. is the best gift of the gods to mankind   b. can only exist between men and gods

    c. has nothing to do with goodwill and affection   d. is always strongest among the wisest men

4.   In lines 48–53 (*Divitias . . . temeritate*), we learn that

    a. men depend on chance for acquiring wealth   b. beasts are not interested in pleasures

    c. power and wealth are uncertain and fleeting   d. planning ahead gives better results than luck

5. In line 54, *praeclare* is an

   a. adjective

   b. infinitive

   c. adverb

   d. indicative

6. From lines 53–56 (*Qui autem...potest*), we learn that

   a. virtue is the highest good

   b. friendship can only exist with virtue

   c. friendship gives rise to virtue

   d. only the good can be virtuous

7. In line 58, *interpretemur* is translated

   a. we are understood

   b. we shall be understood

   c. we must interpret

   d. let us interpret

8. In line 58, *ut* is translated

   a. when

   b. as

   c. so that

   d. in order to

9. The antecedent of *qui* (line 60) is

   a. *virtutem* (line 57)

   b. *nostri* (line 58)

   c. *docti* (line 59)

   d. *eos* (line 60)

10. In lines 57–60 (*Iam virtutem . . . numeremus*), we learn that

    a. virtue does not depend on fancy words

    b. good men are considered numerous

    c. all learned men have virtue

    d. learned men use too many words

11. In line 61, these five men are named because Cicero

    a. knows all of these men personally

    b. wants to flatter these men

    c. is emphasizing the number of such men

    d. is name-dropping to impress his readers

12. In lines 60–63 (*virosque . . . reperiuntur*), we find an example of

    a. anaphora

    b. asyndeton

    c. hyperbole

    d. hendiadys

13. In line 60, *qui* refers to

    a. the good men listed in line 61 (*Paulos . . . Philos*)

    b. ideal men who do not exist

    c. philosophers who write about virtue

    d. the close friends of Laelius

14. From lines 63–65 (*Tales igitur . . . dicere*), we learn that

    a. it is not possible to see the opportunities of friendship

    b. for some men, friendship has many opportunities

    c. only certain men can evaluate the opportunities of friendship

    d. the opportunities of friendship are too numerous to count

Translation *Suggested time: 15 minutes*

Iam virtutem ex consuetudine vitae ser-
monisque nostri interpretemur, nec eam, ut
quidam docti, verborum magnificentia metiamur,
virosque bonos eos qui habentur numeremus,
5   Paulos, Catones, Gallos, Scipiones, Philos: his communis vita contenta est:

_____

_____

_____

_____

_____

_____

_____

Short Analysis Questions

Divitias alii prae-
ponunt, bonam alii valetudinem, alii potentiam,
alii honores, multi etiam voluptates. Beluarum hoc
quidem extremum; illa autem superiora caduca et
5   incerta, posita non tam in consiliis nostris quam
in fortunae temeritate. Qui autem in virtute summum bonum ponunt, praeclare illi quidem, sed
haec ipsa virtus amicitiam et gignit et continet,
nec sine virtute amicitia esse ullo pacto potest.

1.   In lines 1–3 (*divitias . . . voluptates*), Laelius employs anaphora, asyndeton, and chiasmus to
make his point. What is the effect of using these particular figures?

_____

_____

_____

2. In lines 1–3, quote and translate the Latin for four qualities that others esteem more than friendship.

_____

_____

_____

3. In lines 3–6, what drawback does Laelius see to the gifts that others prefer? Quote the Latin that answers this question and translate or accurately paraphrase.

_____

_____

_____

4. What is the *sine qua non* for the existence of friendship (lines 8–9)?

_____

_____

Essay *Suggested time: 20 minutes*

                                                  sed

      haec ipsa virtus amicitiam et gignit et continet,
      nec sine virtute amicitia esse ullo pacto potest.
      Iam virtutem ex consuetudine vitae ser-
5   monisque nostri interpretemur, nec eam, ut
      quidam docti, verborum magnificentia metiamur,
      virosque bonos eos qui habentur numeremus,
      Paulos, Catones, Gallos, Scipiones, Philos: his com-
      munis vita contenta est: eos autem omittamus qui
10   omnino nusquam reperiuntur. Tales igitur inter
      viros amicitia tantas opportunitates habet quantas
      vix queo dicere.

In this passage, what point is Cicero making about friendship? What do the men Cicero mentions by name have to do with the point he is making? In a short essay, discuss Cicero's assertion about friendship and how the inclusion of these men supports his ideas.

Support your assertions with references to the Latin text throughout the passage above. All Latin words must be copied or their line numbers provided, AND they must be translated or paraphrased closely enough that it is clear you understand the Latin. It is your responsibility to convince the reader that you are basing your conclusions on the Latin text and not merely on a general recollection of the passage. Direct your answer to the question; do not merely summarize the passage. Please write your essay on a separate piece of paper.

SECTION 4: LINES 66–87

[22] Principio, qui potest esse vita vitalis, ut ait
Ennius, quae non in amici mutua benevolentia
conquiescat? Quid dulcius quam habere quicum
omnia audeas sic loqui ut tecum? Qui esset tantus
70   fructus in prosperis rebus, nisi haberes qui illis
aeque ac tu ipse gauderet? Adversas vero ferre difficile esset sine eo qui illas gravius etiam quam
tu ferret. Denique ceterae res quae expetuntur
opportunae sunt singulae rebus fere singulis;
75   divitiae ut utare; opes ut colare; honores ut laudere; voluptates ut gaudeas; valetudo ut dolore
careas et muneribus fungare corporis: amicitia
res plurimas continet. Quoquo te verteris praesto
est: nullo loco excluditur: nunquam intempestiva,
80   nunquam molesta est. Itaque non aqua, non igni,
ut aiunt, locis pluribus utimur quam amicitia.
Neque ego nunc de vulgari aut de mediocri, quae
tamen ipsa et delectat et prodest, sed de vera et
perfecta loquor, qualis eorum qui pauci nominantur
85   fuit. Nam et secundas res splendidiores facit
amicitia, et adversas partiens communicansque
leviores.

Preparatory Questions

Line 66   What is the case and use of *vitalis?* _____

Line 67   What is the antecedent of *quae?* _____

Line 68   Identify the form and use of *quid.* _____

              What verb must be supplied with *quid?* _____

              Identify the form of *dulcius.* _____

Line 69   Identify the form and use of *loqui.* _____

              What part of speech is *qui?* _____

Lines 70–71 Identify the type of condition. _____

Line 70   To what does *illis* refer? _____

Line 71   What word must be understood with *adversas?* _____

Line 72   What is the subject of *esset?* _____

To what does *illas* refer? _____

Line 73   Identify the form and use of *ferret.* _____

Line 74   What is the case and use of *rebus?* _____

Line 75   Identify the tense and mood of *utare.* _____

Lines 75–76   Identify the form and use of *laudere.* _____

Line 76   What is the case and use of *dolore?* _____

Line 79   Identify the case and use of *loco.* _____

Line 80   What is the case and use of *igni?* _____

Line 82   What word must be understood with *vulgari* and with *mediocri?* _____

Line 83   Identify the case and use of *vera.* _____

Line 84   What does *qualis* modify? _____

Line 85   Identify the subject of *fuit.* _____

What is the form and use of *splendidiores?* _____

Line 86   What word must be understood with *adversas?* _____

What does *communicans(que)* modify? _____

Multiple Choice Questions *Suggested time: 31 minutes*

1.   In line 66, *principio* is translated
    a. to the chief
    c. in the first place
    b. I begin
    d. having begun

2.   In line 66, *qui* is translated
    a. which
    c. who
    b. what
    d. how

3.   In line 68, *quicum* is translated
    a. whomever
    c. with whom
    b. with each
    d. whenever

4.   In lines 66–68 (*Principio . . . conquiescat*), we learn that friendship offers
    a. leadership
    c. goodwill
    b. vitality
    d. peace

5. The case of *omnia* (line 69) is determined by

   a. *dulcius* (line 68)   b. *habere* (line 68)

   c. *audeas* (line 69)   d. *loqui* (line 69)

6. From lines 68–71 (*Quid dulcius . . . gauderet*), we learn that one of the pleasures of friendship is

   a. talking to yourself   b. sharing in prosperous things

   c. taking dares together   d. eating lots of fruit

7. In lines 69–71, the phrase *Qui . . . gauderet* is a clause of

   a. characteristic   b. purpose

   c. indirect question   d. indirect command

8. In lines 66–71 (*Principio . . . gauderet*), we find an example of

   a. hyperbole   b. anaphora

   c. litotes   d. rhetorical question

9. In line 72, *gravius* is

   a. an adjective   b. a noun

   c. an adverb   d. a preposition

10. In line 72, *etiam* is translated

   a. even   b. also

   c. too   d. indeed

11. From lines 71–73 (*Adversas . . . ferret*), we may infer that friends are

   a. sometimes hard to take   b. occasionally too serious

   c. supportive in adverse times d. always truthful with you

12. The subject of *expetuntur* (line 73) is

   a. *ceterae* (line 73)   b. *res* (line 73)

   c. *quae* (line 73)   d. *singulae* (line 74)

13. In line 75, the case of *divitiae* is

   a. nominative   b. genitive

   c. dative   d. ablative

14. In line 75, *colare* is a(n)

   a. indicative   b. subjunctive

   c. infinitive   d. imperative

15. In lines 73–78 (*Denique . . . continet*), we find an example of
    a. litotes
    b. anaphora
    c. hendiadys
    d. apostrophe

16. From lines 73–78 (*Denique . . . continent*), we learn that
    a. other things besides friendship are more important
    b. friendship embraces wealth, honors, praise, etc.
    c. healthy friendships are good for a person
    d. it is best to have a lot of friends

17. In line 78, *quoquo* is translated
    a. also
    b. wherever
    c. whomever
    d. someone

18. The tense and mood of *verteris* (line 78) is
    a. present indicative
    b. perfect subjunctive
    c. present subjunctive
    d. future perfect indicative

19. The understood subject of *est, excluditur,* and *est* (lines 79–80) is
    a. *valetudo* (line 76)
    b. *corporis* (line 77)
    c. *amicitia* (line 77)
    d. *res* (line 78)

20. From lines 78–81 (*Quoquo . . . amicitia*), we learn that friendship
    a. is sometimes stormy
    b. is everywhere
    c. is better than fire and water
    d. is always useful

21. The antecedent of *quae* (line 82) is
    a. *amicitia* (line 81)
    b. *ego* (line 82)
    c. *vulgari* (line 82)
    d. *ipsa* (line 83)

22. In line 83, *prodest* is translated
    a. is present
    b. is in favor
    c. benefits
    d. transmits

23. From lines 82–85 (*Neque ego . . . fuit*), we learn that
    a. only true friendship can give pleasure
    b. friendship is never common or ordinary
    c. perfect friendship belongs only to a few people
    d. there is no such thing as perfect friendship

24. In line 85, *et* is translated
    a. but
    b. and
    c. both
    d. too

25. In line 86, *partiens* is translated
    a. sharing
    b. departing
    c. obeying
    d. sparing

26. From lines 85–87 (*Nam et . . . leviores*), we may infer that
    a. good things happen to friendly people
    b. trivial things can be harsh
    c. good things are better with friendship
    d. trivial things are easily communicated

Translation *Suggested time: 15 minutes*

> Quid dulcius quam habere quicum omnia audeas sic loqui ut tecum? Qui esset tantus fructus in prosperis rebus, nisi haberes qui illis aeque ac tu ipse gauderet? Adversas vero ferre dif-
> 5 ficile esset sine eo qui illas gravius etiam quam tu ferret.

_____

_____

_____

_____

_____

_____

_____

_____

Short Analysis Questions

Quoquo te verteris praesto
est: nullo loco excluditur: nunquam intempestiva,
nunquam molesta est. Itaque non aqua, non igni,
ut aiunt, locis pluribus utimur quam amicitia.
5   Neque ego nunc de vulgari aut de mediocri, quae
tamen ipsa et delectat et prodest, sed de vera et
perfecta loquor, qualis eorum qui pauci nominantur
fuit. Nam et secundas res splendidiores facit
amicitia, et adversas partiens communicansque
10   leviores.

1. Identify one figure of speech used in lines 2–3? What point is Laelius making in using this figure in this place?

_____

_____

_____

2. For what purpose does Laelius mention *aqua* and *igni,* line 3?

_____

_____

_____

3. About what kinds of friendship does Laelius not intend to speak (lines 5–7) and about what kinds will he speak? Quote and translate the Latin that supports your answer.

_____

_____

_____

_____

Essay *Suggested time: 20 minutes*

Principio, qui potest esse vita vitalis, ut ait
Ennius, quae non in amici mutua benevolentia
conquiescat? Quid dulcius quam habere quicum
omnia audeas sic loqui ut tecum? Qui esset tantus
5   fructus in prosperis rebus, nisi haberes qui illis
aeque ac tu ipse gauderet? Adversas vero ferre difficile esset sine eo qui illas gravius etiam quam
tu ferret. Denique ceterae res quae expetuntur
opportunae sunt singulae rebus fere singulis;
10 divitiae ut utare; opes ut colare; honores ut laudere; voluptates ut gaudeas; valetudo ut dolore
careas et muneribus fungare corporis: amicitia
res plurimas continet.

In this passage, Cicero, through the person of Laelius, expounds on the advantages of friendship. In a short essay, discuss how he uses language, rhetorical devices, syntax and sentence structure to highlight these advantages.

Support your assertions with references to the Latin text throughout the passage above. All Latin words must be copied or their line numbers provided, AND they must be translated or paraphrased closely enough that it is clear you understand the Latin. It is your responsibility to convince the reader that you are basing your conclusions on the Latin text and not merely on a general recollection of the passage. Direct your answer to the question; do not merely summarize the passage. Please write your essay on a separate piece of paper.

SECTION 5: LINES 88–107

[VII. 23] Cumque plurimas et maximas com-
moditates amicitia contineat, tum illa nimirum
90 praestat omnibus, quod bonam spem praelucet in posterum nec debilitari animos aut cadere patitur. Verum enim amicum qui intuetur,
tamquam exemplar aliquod intuetur sui. Quocirca
et absentes adsunt et egentes abundant et imbecilli
95 valent, et, quod difficilius dictu est, mortui
vivunt; tantus eos honos, memoria, desiderium prosequitur amicorum, ex quo illorum beata mors videtur, horum vita laudabilis. Quod si exemeris ex
rerum natura benevolentiae coniunctionem, nec
100 domus ulla nec urbs stare poterit; ne agri quidem
cultus permanebit. Id si minus intellegitur, quanta vis amicitiae concordiaeque sit ex dissensioni-
bus atque discordiis percipi potest. Quae enim
domus tam stabilis, quae tam firma civitas est,
105 quae non odiis atque discidiis funditus possit
everti? ex quo quantum boni sit in amicitia iudicari
potest.

Preparatory Questions

Line 88–89   Identify the type of *cum* clause. _____

Line 89   To what does *illa* refer? _____

Lines 90–91 Identify the subject of *praelucet.* _____

Line 91   What is the case and use of *animos?* _____

Line 92   What is the antecedent of *qui?* _____

Line 93   Identify the case and use of *exemplar.* _____

             Identify the case and use of *sui.* _____

             To whom does *sui* refer? _____

             What part of speech is *quocirca?* _____

Line 95   What does *difficilius* modify? _____

             Identify the case and use of *mortui.* _____

Line 96   To whom/what does *eos* refer? _____

Lines 96–97   What is the subject of *prosequitur?* _____

Line 97   What is the antecedent of *quo?* _____

                     Identify the case and use of *beata.* _____

Line 98   What word must be understood with *vita?* _____

Lines 98–100 Identify the type of condition. _____

Line 100   What two nouns does *ulla* modify? _____

Line 101   Identify the subject of *permanebit.* _____

Line 101   What part of speech is *minus?* _____

Line 103   What part of speech is *quae?* _____

Line 105   What is the antecedent of *quae?* _____

Line 106   To what does *quo* refer? _____

Line 107   What is the subject of *potest?* _____

Multiple Choice Questions *Suggested time: 29 minutes*

1.   In line 89, *nimirum* is translated
     a.   too much   b.   certainly
     c.   not at all   d.   excessively

2.   In line 90, *omnibus* is
     a.   dative of indirect object   b.   dative with *praestat* (line 90)
     c.   ablative with *praestat* (line 90)   d.   ablative of means

3.   In line 90, *quod* is translated
     a.   which   b.   that
     c.   because   d.   what

4.   The verb form *debilitari* (line 91) is dependent on
     a.   *praelucet* (lines 90–91)   b.   *animos* (line 91)
     c.   *cadere* (lines 91–92)   d.   *patitur* (line 92)

5.   From lines 88–92 (*Cumque . . . patitur*), we learn that friendship
     a.   is worth a lot of money   b.   is preferable to hope in the future
     c.   maintains people's spirits   d.   excels in many ways

6. In line 93, *tamquam* is translated

    a. although
    b. so great
    c. as though
    d. finally

7. The word *aliquod* (line 93) modifies

    a. *verum* (line 92)
    b. *amicum* (line 92)
    c. *exemplar* (line 93)
    d. *intuetur* (line 93)

8. The subject of *intuetur,* to which *sui* refers, has an earlier reference in

    a. *spem* (line 90)
    b. *posterum* (line 91)
    c. *amicum* (line 92)
    d. *qui* (line 92)

9. From lines 92–93 (*Verum . . . sui*), we learn that a true friend

    a. is hard to find
    b. is like a second self
    c. offers an example to everyone
    d. never thinks of himself

10. In line 95, *dictu* is translated

    a. in a word
    b. to say
    c. by a speech
    d. having been said

11. In lines 93–96 (*Quocirca . . . vivunt*), we find an example of

    a. oxymoron
    b. asyndeton
    c. litotes
    d. hendiadys

12. In lines 97–98, the words *illorum . . . horum* are translated

    a. the former . . . the latter
    b. those . . . these
    c. theirs . . . ours
    d. the living . . . the dead

13. In lines 96–98 (*tantus eos . . . laudabilis*), we find an example of

    a. litotes
    b. hendiadys
    c. asyndeton
    d. anaphora

14. From lines 93–98 (*Quocirca . . . laudabilis*), we learn that

    a. people forget their absent friends
    b. friendships survive after death
    c. a praiseworthy life is a happy life
    d. it is difficult to speak about the dead

15. In line 100, the case of *agri* is

    a. nominative
    b. genitive
    c. dative
    d. ablative

16. From lines 98–101 (*Quod si . . . permanebit*), we learn that

    a. without kindness, civilization would perish

    b. many things in nature are joined by kindness

    c. cities are especially dependent on farms

    d. cultivation of fields is necessary for mankind

17. In lines 101–102, the clause *quanta . . . sit* is

    a. a relative clause of characteristic

    b. an indirect command

    c. the apodosis of a condition

    d. an indirect question

18. In line 103, *percipi* is translated

    a. to perceive

    b. to be observed

    c. to be completed

    d. to receive

19. In line 105, the words *odiis atque discidiis* are

    a. dative of reference

    b. dative of indirect object

    c. ablative of time

    d. ablative of means

20. In line 105, *funditus* is

    a. a noun

    b. an adverb

    c. an adjective

    d. a participle

21. In line 105, *possit* indicates

    a. a result clause

    b. a purpose clause

    c. an indirect question

    d. an indirect command

22. In line 106, *boni* is a _____ genitive

    a. descriptive

    b. possessive

    c. partitive

    d. qualitative

23. In lines 103–107 (*Quae enim . . . iudicari potest*), we find an example of

    a. hyperbole

    b. litotes

    c. alliteration

    d. chiasmus

24. From 103–107 (*Quae enim . . . iudicari potest*), we learn that

    a. stability is only possible in some cities

    b. friendship is necessary for civilization

    c. good friends are able to be considered happy

    d. a home without discord is a stable one

Translation *Suggested time: 15 minutes*

> Id si minus intellegitur, quan-
> ta vis amicitiae concordiaeque sit ex dissensioni-
> bus atque discordiis percipi potest. Quae enim
> domus tam stabilis, quae tam firma civitas est,
> 5 quae non odiis atque discidiis funditus possit
> everti?

_____

_____

_____

_____

_____

_____

_____

_____

Short Analysis Questions

> Cumque plurimas et maximas com-
> moditates amicitia contineat, tum illa nimirum
> praestat omnibus, quod bonam spem praelu-
> cet in posterum nec debilitari animos aut ca-
> 5 dere patitur. Verum enim amicum qui intuetur,
> tamquam exemplar aliquod intuetur sui. Quocirca
> et absentes adsunt et egentes abundant et imbecilli
> valent, et, quod difficilius dictu est, mortui
> vivunt; tantus eos honos, memoria, desiderium pro-
> 10 sequitur amicorum, ex quo illorum beata mors vi-
> detur, horum vita laudabilis.

1. According to lines 1–5 (*cumque . . . patitur*), in what respects does friendship surpass all other virtues?

_____

_____

_____

2. In lines 5–6, who is the antecedent of *qui*? According to these lines, what will that person find in the presence of a friend?

_____

_____

_____

3. What two figures of speech does Cicero/Laelius use in lines 6–8 (*quocirca . . . vivunt*)? Quote the Latin which illustrates these figures and discuss their significance in underscoring the point being made about friendship.

_____

_____

_____

_____

_____

4. To whom does the *illorum* of line 10 refer? To whom does the *horum* (line 11) refer? Explain the connection established between these two groups in lines 8–11.

_____

_____

_____

_____

Essay *Suggested time: 20 minutes*

> Quod si exemeris ex
> rerum natura benevolentiae coniunctionem, nec
> domus ulla nec urbs stare poterit; ne agri quidem
> cultus permanebit. Id si minus intellegitur, quan-
> 5   ta vis amicitiae concordiaeque sit ex dissensioni-
> bus atque discordiis percipi potest. Quae enim
> domus tam stabilis, quae tam firma civitas est,
> quae non odiis atque discidiis funditus possit
> everti? ex quo quantum boni sit in amicitia iudicari
> 10   potest.

In this passage, Laelius expands his vision of friendship beyond that of personal friendship and views its significance within a broader social context. In a short essay, discuss how he views goodwill in society as a whole and how he argues his views on this matter.

Support your assertions with references to the Latin text throughout the passage above. All Latin words must be copied or their line numbers provided, AND they must be translated or paraphrased closely enough that it is clear you understand the Latin. It is your responsibility to convince the reader that you are basing your conclusions on the Latin text and not merely on a general recollection of the passage. Direct your answer to the question; do not merely summarize the passage. Please write your essay on a separate piece of paper.

SECTION 6: LINES 1–30

[100] [XXVII.]Virtus, virtus, inquam, C. Fanni et
tu, Q. Muci, et conciliat amicitias et conservat. In
ea est enim convenientia rerum, in ea stabilitas, in
ea constantia, quae cum se extulit et ostendit lumen
5   suum et idem adspexit agnovitque in alio, ad id se
admovet vicissimque accipit illud quod in altero est,
ex quo exardescit sive amor sive amicitia. Utrumque
enim dictum est ab amando; amare autem nihil aliud est nisi eum ipsum diligere quem ames,
10   nulla indigentia, nulla utilitate quaesita; quae tamen
ipsa efflorescit ex amicitia, etiam si tu eam minus
secutus sis. [101] Hac nos adulescentes benevolentia senes illos L. Paulum, M. Catonem, C. Gal-
lum, P. Nasicam, Ti. Gracchum Scipionis nostri
15   socerum, dileximus. Haec etiam magis elucet
inter aequales ut inter me et Scipionem, L. Furium,
P. Rupilium, Sp. Mummium. Vicissim autem senes
in adolescentium caritate acquiescimus, ut in vestra,
ut in Q. Tuberonis: equidem etiam admodum
20   adulescentis P. Rutilii, A. Verginii familiaritate
delector. Quoniamque ita ratio comparata est vitae
naturaeque nostrae ut alia aetas oriatur, maxime
quidem optandum est ut cum aequalibus possis,
quibuscum tamquam e carceribus emissus sis, cum
25   isdem ad calcem, ut dicitur, pervenire.

[102] Sed quoniam res humanae fragiles
caducaeque sunt, semper aliqui anquirendi sunt
quos diligamus et a quibus diligamur: caritate enim
benevolentiaque sublata omnis est a vita sublata
30   iucunditas.

Preparatory Questions

Line 3   To what/whom does the <u>first</u> *ea* refer? _____

Line 4   Identify the antecedent of *quae.* _____

                What is the subject of *ostendit?*_____

Line 5   What is the case and use of *idem?* _____

Line 6   What is the object of *accipit?*_____

Line 7   What is the antecedent of *quo?* _____

             Identify the subject of *exardescit.* _____

             What is the case and use of *utrumque?* _____

Line 8   What part of speech is *amando?* _____

Line 9   What is the subject of *est?* _____

             Identify the form and use of *diligere.* _____

Line 10   Identify the case and use of *quaesita.* _____

             What two words must be translated with *quaesita?* _____

Line 11   To what does *eam* refer? _____

Lines 12–13   Identify the case and use of *benevolentia.* _____

Line 15   Identify the case and use of *socerum.* _____

             What word must be understood with *haec?* _____

Line 17   Identify the case and use of *senes.* _____

Line 18   What does *vestra* modify? _____

Line 20   Identify the case and use of *adulescentis.* _____

Lines 21–23   Identify the type of clause found in these lines (*Quoniamque . . . possis*). _____

Line 23   What is the construction of *optandum est?* _____

Line 24   What is the antecedent of *quibus(cum)?* _____

             Identify the form and syntax of *emissus sis.* _____

Line 25   What is the meaning of *isdem?* _____

             To what earlier word does *isdem* refer? _____

Line 28   What is the antecedent of *quos?* _____

             Identify the form and syntax of *diligamur.* _____

Line 29   Identify the use of *sublata.* _____

             What does *omnis* modify? _____

Line 30   Identify the case and use of *iucunditas.* _____

Multiple Choice Questions *Suggested time: 34 minutes*

1. In line 1, the case of *Fanni* is
    a. nominative
    b. genitive
    c. dative
    d. vocative

2. In line 4, *cum* is translated
    a. when
    b. since
    c. although
    d. with

3. The word *se* (line 4) refers to
    a. *virtus* (line 1)
    b. *amicitias* (line 2)
    c. *stabilitas* (line 3)
    d. *constantia* (line 4)

4. The word *id* (line 5) refers to
    a. friendship
    b. virtue
    c. light
    d. concord

5. In line 6, *–que* connects
    a. *in alio* (line 5) and *in altero* (line 6)
    b. *id* (line 5) and *illud* (line 6)
    c. *admovet* (line 6) and *accipit* (line 6)
    d. *vicissim* (line 6) and *accipit* (line 6)

6. In line 6, *quod* is translated
    a. what
    b. which
    c. because
    d. where

7. In lines 2–7 (*In ea . . . amicitia*), we find an example of
    a. alliteration
    b. hyperbole
    c. anaphora
    d. litotes

8. From lines 2–7 (*In ea . . . amicitia*), we learn that virtue
    a. is necessary for strong friendships
    b. exists mainly in stable conditions
    c. recognizes vice in others
    d. shines its light for all to see

9. The antecedent of *quem* (line 9) is
    a. *utrumque* (line 7)
    b. *nihil* (lines 8–9)
    c. *aliud* (line 9)
    d. *eum* (line 9)

10. *quae* (line 10) refers to
    a. friendship
    b. love
    c. nothing
    d. advantage

11. From lines 7–12 (*Utrumque . . . secutus sis*), we learn that

    a. "love" and "friendship" come from the same word

    b. love brings with it certain demands and requirements

    c. friendship cannot exist without love, and vice versa

    d. only friends will ever fall in love with each other

12. In lines 12–15 (*Hac nos . . . dileximus*), we find an example of

    a. anaphora and asyndeton

    b. antithesis and alliteration

    c. chiasmus and antithesis

    d. chiasmus and alliteration

13. In line 16, *ut* is translated

    a. in order that

    b. as

    c. when

    d. as a result

14. In line 18, the case of *adulescentium* is

    a. nominative

    b. genitive

    c. accusative

    d. ablative

15. *admodum* (line 19) modifies

    a. *acquiescimus* (line 18)

    b. *equidem* (line 19)

    c. *etiam* (line 19)

    d. *delector* (line 21)

16. In line 20, *familiaritate* is ablative of

    a. manner

    b. means

    c. cause

    d. comparison

17. From lines 17–21 (*Vicissim . . . delector*), we learn that

    a. Tubero, Rutilius and Verginius are friends

    b. it is good for people to have lots of friends

    c. old men can be friends with young men

    d. friends offer peacefulness and delight

18. In line 23, *ut* is translated

    a. as

    b. when

    c. that

    d. in order to

19. In line 24, *tamquam* is translated

    a. although

    b. as it were

    c. finally

    d. however

20. The word *isdem* (line 25) refers to

    a. *vitae naturaeque* (lines 21–22)

    b. *aequalibus* (line 23)

    c. *quibuscum* (line 24)

    d. *carceribus* (line 24)

21. *pervenire* (line 25) depends on

   a. *optandum est* (line 23)

   b. *possis* (line 23)

   c. *emissus sis* (line 24)

   d. *dicitur* (line 25)

22. From lines 21–25 (*Quoniamque . . . pervenire*), we learn that

   a. everybody's life should have a plan

   b. it is good to go through life with friends

   c. friends often go to the races together

   d. life brings people of all ages together

23. In lines 21–25 (*Quoniamque . . . pervenire*), we find an example of

   a. synchysis

   b. hyperbole

   c. litotes

   d. metaphor

24. In line 27, *–que* connects

   a. *humanae* and *fragiles* (line 26)

   b. *quoniam* and *semper* (lines 26–27)

   c. *res* and *caducae* (lines 26–27)

   d. *fragiles* and *caducae* (lines 26–27)

25. In line 28, *a quibus* is ablative of

   a. manner

   b. agent

   c. separation

   d. means

26. In line 29, *a vita* is ablative of

   a. manner

   b. agent

   c. separation

   d. means

27. From lines 26–30 (*Sed quoniam . . . iucunditas*), we learn that

   a. kindness comes from affection

   b. everybody needs to love and be loved

   c. human beings are very fragile

   d. life should be full of pleasure

Translation *Suggested time: 15 minutes*

Sed quoniam res humanae fragiles
caducaeque sunt, semper aliqui anquirendi sunt
quos diligamus et a quibus diligamur: caritate enim
benevolentiaque sublata omnis est a vita sublata
5 iucunditas.

_____

_____

_____

_____

_____

_____

_____

_____

Short Analysis Questions

Virtus, virtus, inquam, C. Fanni et
tu, Q. Muci, et conciliat amicitias et conservat. In
ea est enim convenientia rerum, in ea stabilitas, in
ea constantia, quae cum se extulit et ostendit lumen
5 suum et idem adspexit agnovitque in alio, ad id se
admovet vicissimque accipit illud quod in altero est,
ex quo exardescit sive amor sive amicitia. Utrumque
enim dictum est ab amando; amare autem nihil aliud est nisi eum ipsum diligere quem ames,
10 nulla indigentia, nulla utilitate quaesita; quae tamen
ipsa efflorescit ex amicitia, etiam si tu eam minus
secutus sis.

1. In lines 4–7 (*quae . . . amicitia*), what power does Laelius ascribe to *virtus*? Quote the Latin and translate or accurately paraphrase.

_____

_____

2. In etymological terms, what do the words, *amor* and *amicitia*, have in common (line 7)?

    _____

    _____

3. In lines 8–10, how does Laelius define love between friends?

    _____

    _____

    _____

Essay *Suggested time: 20 minutes*

Hac nos adulescentes benevo-
lentia senes illos L. Paulum, M. Catonem, C. Gal-
lum, P. Nasicam, Ti. Gracchum Scipionis nostri
socerum, dileximus. Haec etiam magis elucet
5   inter aequales ut inter me et Scipionem, L. Furium,
P. Rupilium, Sp. Mummium. Vicissim autem senes
in adolescentium caritate acquiescimus, ut in vestra,
ut in Q. Tuberonis: equidem etiam admodum
adulescentis P. Rutilii, A. Verginii familiaritate
10   delector. Quoniamque ita ratio comparata est vitae
naturaeque nostrae ut alia aetas oriatur, maxime
quidem optandum est ut cum aequalibus possis,
quibuscum tamquam e carceribus emissus sis, cum
isdem ad calcem, ut dicitur, pervenire.

In this passage Laelius speaks of friendship among peers and about intergenerational friendship. In a short essay, discuss the different configurations that friendship may take and the merits of each kind of relationship.

Support your assertions with references to the Latin text throughout the passage above. All Latin words must be copied or their line numbers provided, AND they must be translated or paraphrased closely enough that it is clear you understand the Latin. It is your responsibility to convince the reader that you are basing your conclusions on the Latin text and not merely on a general recollection of the passage. Direct your answer to the question; do not merely summarize the passage. Please write your essay on a separate piece of paper.

SECTION 7: LINES 30–63

30   Mihi quidem Scipio, quamquam est subito ereptus, vivit tamen semperque vivet; virtutem enim amavi illius viri quae exstincta non est. Nec mihi soli versatur ante oculos, qui illam semper in manibus habui, sed etiam posteris erit

35   clara et insignis. Nemo unquam animo aut spe maiora suscipiet qui sibi non illius memoriam atque imaginem proponendam putet.

    [103] Equidem ex omnibus rebus quas mihi aut fortuna aut natura tribuit, nihil habeo quod cum

40   amicitia Scipionis possim comparare. In hac mihi de re publica consensus, in hac rerum privatarum consilium, in eadem requies plena oblectationis fuit. Nunquam illum ne minima quidem re offendi quod quidem senserim; nihil

45   audivi ex eo ipse quod nollem. Una domus erat, idem victus isque communis; neque militia solum sed etiam peregrinationes rusticationesque communes. [104] Nam quid ego de studiis dicam cognoscendi semper aliquid atque discendi, in

50   quibus remoti ab oculis populi omne otiosum tempus contrivimus? Quarum rerum recordatio et memoria si una cum illo occidisset, desiderium coniunctissimi atque amantissimi viri ferre nullo modo possem. Sed nec illa exstincta sunt

55   alunturque potius et augentur cogitatione et memoria; et si illis plane orbatus essem, magnum tamen adfert mihi aetas ipsa solacium, diutius enim iam in hoc desiderio esse non possum; omnia autem brevia tolerabilia esse debent, etiam si magna sunt.

60   Haec habui de amicitia quae dicerem. Vos autem hortor ut ita virtutem locetis, sine qua amicitia esse non potest, ut ea excepta nihil amicitia praestabilius putetis.

Preparatory Questions

Line 30   What is the case and use of *mihi*? _____

Line 31   Identify the subject of *vivit* and *vivet*. _____

Line 32   What is the case and use of *illius viri*? _____

                 Identify the antecedent of *quae*. _____

Line 33   To what does *illam* refer? _____

Line 34   Identify the case and use of *posteris*. _____

Line 35   Identify the case and use of *clara et insignis*. _____

                 What does *unquam* modify? _____

Line 36   What is the case and use of *maiora*? _____

                 Identify the subject of *suscipiet*. _____

                 What tense is *suscipiet*? _____

                 To whom does *sibi* refer? _____

Lines 36–37   What are the subject(s) of the indirect statement? _____

Line 37   What word must be understood with *proponendam*? _____

Line 38   What is the antecedent of *quas*? _____

Line 40   Identify the form and syntax of *possim*. _____

                 What noun must be understood with *hac*? _____

Line 41   Identify the case and use of *mihi*. _____

Line 42   Identify the case and use of *consilium*. _____

Line 43   What does *minima* modify? _____

Line 44   Identify the form and use of *offendi*. _____

                 What is the tense and mood of *senserim*? _____

Line 45   To whom does *eo* refer? _____

                 What is the antecedent of *quod*? _____

Line 46   What does *idem* modify? _____

Lines 46–47   Identify the correlative construction. _____

                 What verb needs to be supplied for *idem . . . rusticationesque*? _____

Line 49   Identify the form and use of *aliquid*. _____

Line 50   What is the antecedent of *quibus?* _____

Line 51   What is the case and use of *tempus?* _____

Lines 52–54   Identify the type of condition illustrated in this sentence. _____

Line 53   What is the object of *ferre?* _____

                 Identify the use of *ferre.* _____

Lines 54–55   What is the subject of all three verbs in these lines? _____

Line 56   Identify the use of *orbatus essem.* _____

                 What does *magnum* modify? _____

Line 57   Identify the subject of *adfert.* _____

Line 59   What does *brevia* modify? _____

                 Identify the case and use of *tolerabilia.* _____

Line 60   What is the antecedent of *quae?* _____

Line 61   What kind of clause is *ut . . . locetis?* _____

Line 62   What is the case and use of *ea?* _____

                 To what does *ea* refer? _____

                 Identify the form and use of *amicitia.* _____

Multiple Choice Questions *Suggested time: 41 minutes*

1.   In line 30, *quamquam* is translated
     a.   and how
     b.   however
     c.   although
     d.   certain

2.   In line 31, *–que* connects
     a.   *mihi* (line 30) and *Scipio* (line 30)
     b.   *subito* (line 31) and *semper* (line 31)
     c.   *vivit* (line 31) and *vivet* (line 31)
     d.   *tamen* (line 31) and *semper* (line 31)

3.   From lines 30–33 (*Mihi . . . non est*), we learn that
     a.   Scipio and Laelius were friends
     b.   Scipio's death was unexpected
     c.   Laelius was older than Scipio
     d.   Laelius admired Scipio's life

4.   The subject of *versatur* (line 33) refers to
     a.   *mihi* (line 30)
     b.   *Scipio* (line 30)
     c.   *virtutem* (line 32)
     d.   *illius viri* (line 32)

5. In line 33, *mihi* is dative of

    a. agent   b. indirect object

    c. reference   d. possession

6. The antecedent of *qui* (line 33) is

    a. *mihi* (line 33)   b. *soli* (line 33)

    c. *oculos* (line 33)   d. *manibus* (line 34)

7. In line 34, *in manibus* is translated

    a. in my hands   b. by hand

    c. within reach   d. in my mind

8. In line 36, *maiora* is translated

    a. the ancestors   b. the majors

    c. greater things   d. most things

9. The antecedent of *qui* (line 36) is

    a. *nemo* (line 35)   b. *animo* (line 35)

    c. *spe* (line 35)   d. *maiora* (line 36)

10. The word *illius* (line 36) refers to

    a. Scipio   b. Laelius

    c. friendship   d. virtue

11. In lines 36–37, *qui. . . putet* is a clause of

    a. purpose   b. result

    c. characteristic   d. doubt

12. From lines 33–37 (*Nec mihi . . . putet*), we learn that

    a. Cicero is well known for his vivid imagination   b. Scipio's example should be an inspiration to posterity

    c. it takes a lot of courage and hope to do important things   d. memory provides people with a lasting image of virtue

13. In line 38, *mihi* is dative of

    a. reference   b. respect

    c. agent   d. indirect object

14. In line 39, *quod* is translated

    a. when   b. as far as

    c. which   d. because

15. From lines 38–40 (*Equidem . . . comparare*), we learn that

    a. Scipio's friendship was incomparable

    b. Laelius gave his fortune to Scipio

    c. Scipio had no other friends besides Laelius

    d. Laelius and Scipio had similar natures

16. *eadem* (line 42) refers to

    a. money

    b. advice

    c. agreement

    d. friendship

17. In line 43, *oblectationis* is

    a. partitive genitive

    b. genitive with *plena*

    c. possessive genitive

    d. genitive of the source

18. In lines 40–43 (*In hac . . . fuit*), we find an example of

    a. hendiadys

    b. litotes

    c. tricolon

    d. alliteration

19. The word *illum* (line 43) refers to

    a. *Scipionis* (line 40)

    b. *consensus* (line 41)

    c. *consilium* (line 42)

    d. *oblectationis* (line 43)

20. In line 45, *ipse* refers to

    a. Scipio

    b. Laelius

    c. friendship

    d. hearing

21. From lines 43–45 (*Nunquam . . . nollem*), we may infer that Laelius and Scipio

    a. never disagreed about virtue

    b. thought little things unimportant

    c. got along very well together

    d. sometimes had arguments

22. From lines 45–48 (*Una domus . . . communes*), we learn that one thing that Laelius and Scipio did NOT share was

    a. a victory

    b. a house

    c. travels

    d. vacations

23. The mood of *dicam* (line 48) indicates

    a. purpose

    b. wish

    c. deliberation

    d. characteristic

24. The word *remoti* (line 50) modifies

    a. *studiis* (line 48)

    b. *oculis* (line 50)

    c. *populi* (line 50)

    d. the subject of *contrivimus* (line 51)

25. From lines 48–51 (*Nam quid . . . contrivimus*), we learn that
    a. Laelius likes to talk about learning
    b. people think studying is a waste of time
    c. Laelius spent his free time in studies
    d. people don't have enough vacations

26. In line 52, *cum* is translated
    a. although
    b. since
    c. when
    d. with

27. The pronoun *illo* (line 52) refers to
    a. memory
    b. Scipio
    c. time
    d. the people

28. In line 53, *viri* is
    a. genitive of possession
    b. objective genitive
    c. genitive of quality
    d. partitive genitive

29. From lines 51–54 (*Quarum rerum . . . possem*), we learn that Laelius
    a. misses his dead friend
    b. wishes he were dead
    c. has lost his best friend
    d. has trouble remembering things

30. In line 54, *illa* refers to
    a. past times
    b. recollection and memory
    c. friends who have died
    d. study and learning

31. In line 56, *illis* is ablative of
    a. separation
    b. cause
    c. means
    d. source

32. In line 56, *plane* is translated
    a. utterly
    b. flatly
    c. clearly
    d. easily

33. From lines 54–59 (*Sed nec . . . magna sunt*), we learn that
    a. memories of deceased friends eventually fade away
    b. comfort for one's sorrows comes with increasing age
    c. one can only tolerate sorrows for a short time
    d. longing for deceased friends lasts longer than one thinks

34. From lines 60–63 (*Vos autem . . . putetis*), we learn that
    a. virtue should be always be encouraged
    b. friendship and virtue are the same thing
    c. friendship is more excellent than virtue
    d. virtue cannot exist without friendship

Translation *Suggested time: 15 minutes*

Quarum rerum recordatio et
memoria si una cum illo occidisset, desiderium
coniunctissimi atque amantissimi viri ferre nullo
modo possem. Sed nec illa exstincta sunt
5   alunturque potius et augentur cogitatione et
memoria;

Short Analysis Questions

Mihi quidem Scipio, quamquam est
subito ereptus, vivit tamen semperque vivet;
virtutem enim amavi illius viri quae exstincta non
est. Nec mihi soli versatur ante oculos, qui illam
5   semper in manibus habui, sed etiam posteris erit
clara et insignis. Nemo unquam animo aut spe
maiora suscipiet qui sibi non illius memoriam atque
imaginem proponendam putet.

1. Discuss Laelius's use of verb tenses in speaking about Scipio in lines 1–2.

---

2. In lines 6–8, how does Scipio inspire future generations? Quote the Latin and translate or accurately paraphrase.

_____

_____

_____

_____

<blockquote>

Quarum rerum recordatio et
memoria si una cum illo occidisset, desiderium
coniunctissimi atque amantissimi viri ferre nullo
modo possem. Sed nec illa exstincta sunt

5 alunturque potius et augentur cogitatione et
memoria; et si illis plane orbatus essem, magnum
tamen adfert mihi aetas ipsa solacium, diutius enim
iam in hoc desiderio esse non possum; omnia autem
brevia tolerabilia esse debent, etiam si magna sunt.
</blockquote>

3. In lines 1–5, what two things help Laelius to endure the loss of his friend, Scipio? Quote the Latin and translate.

_____

_____

4. What other observation does Laelius make in lines 5–9 about how he finds solace in the midst of his sadness? Quote and translate the Latin that supports the answer.

_____

_____

_____

Essay *Suggested time: 20 minutes*

Equidem ex omnibus rebus quas mihi aut
fortuna aut natura tribuit, nihil habeo quod cum
amicitia Scipionis possim comparare. In hac
mihi de re publica consensus, in hac rerum
5   privatarum consilium, in eadem requies plena
oblectationis fuit. Nunquam illum ne minima
quidem re offendi quod quidem senserim; nihil
audivi ex eo ipse quod nollem. Una domus erat,
idem victus isque communis; neque militia solum sed etiam peregrinationes rusticationesque
10   communes.

In this passage Laelius characterizes his friendship with Scipio as an incomparable gift in his life. In a short essay, discuss some of the techniques Laelius/Cicero uses to depict the special nature of this friendship.

Support your assertions with references to the Latin text throughout the passage above. All Latin words must be copied or their line numbers provided, AND they must be translated or paraphrased closely enough that it is clear you understand the Latin. It is your responsibility to convince the reader that you are basing your conclusions on the Latin text and not merely on a general recollection of the passage. Direct your answer to the question; do not merely summarize the passage. Please write your essay on a separate piece of paper.

VOCABULARY*

Vocabulary notes

The guiding principle in compiling this lexicon was clarity and ease of use. For this reason, abbreviations are used only for those nouns, adjectives, and verbs whose paradigms present no possibility for ambiguity or confusion. Generally, all words included in this vocabulary are given in the standard dictionary format, with the following exceptions:

1) VERBS: for regular verbs of the first conjugation, the last three principal parts appear in standard abbreviated form (e.g., **amo, -are, -avi, -atus**); for verbs of the second, third, and fourth conjugations, and all irregular verbs, principal parts are given in full (e.g., **teneo, tenere, tenui, tentus**).

2) NOUNS: for regular nouns of the first, second, and fourth declensions, the genitive is supplied in abbreviated form (e.g., **adulescentia, -ae; ingenium, -i,** etc.); genitives of third and fifth declension nouns, on the other hand, appear in full, unabbreviated form (e.g., **facultas, facultatis; effigies, effigiei,** etc.).

3) ADJECTIVES: two- and three-termination adjectives appear in abbreviated form to reflect the morphology of the three genders (e.g., **carus, -a, -um; fortis, -e**); for single-termination adjectives, the nominative and genitive are given in full, unabbreviated form (e.g., **excellens, excellentis**).

The following abbreviations have been used in the vocabulary:

abl. = ablative
acc. = accusative
adj. = adjective
comp. = comparative
conj. = conjunction
dat. = dative
f. = feminine
impers. = impersonal
indef. = indefinite

infin. = infinitive
leg. = legal, of law
m. = masculine
n. = neuter
pl. = plural
prep. = preposition
refl. = reflexive
subst. = substantive

* The vocabulary of the present work is a compilation with some slight variations of the glossaries published in *Cicero De Amicitia Selections*, by Patsy Rodden Ricks and Sheila K. Dickison, Bolchazy-Carducci Publishers (2006): 65–73, © 2006 Bolchazy-Carducci Publishers and *M. Tulli Ciceronis Pro Archia Poeta Oratio* 2ⁿᵈ Edition by Steven M. Cerutti, Bolchazy-Carducci Publishers (2006): 105–128, © 2006 Bolchazy-Carducci Publishers.

A

a, ab (*prep. w. abl.*), from, away from; (*of time*), from, after, since; (*expressing agency with passive verbs*), by.

abdo, abdere, abdidi, abditus, to put away; to bury; (*refl.*), to devote oneself completely (*to someone, something, etc.*).

abhorreo, abhorrere, abhorrui, to avoid, be adverse to.

absens, absentis, not present, absent; *esp.* despite being absent (*i.e., without benefit of meeting the other party*).

abstraho, abstrahere, abstraxi, abstractus, to distract, divert.

absum, abesse, afui, afuturus (*w.* **a/ab** + *abl.*), to be absent, away (*from*).

abundo, -are, -avi, -atus, to be rich, live in abundance.

ac (atque) (*conj.*), and, and also.

accedo, accedere, accessi, accessus, to draw near, approach; to be added (*to something, a group, etc.*).

accipio, accipere, accepi, acceptus, to take, receive; (*w. acc.* + *infin.*), to understand, learn, hear, be told.

accommodo, -are, -avi, -atus, to suit, accommodate, be appropriate (*to someone, something, etc.*).

accurate (*adv.*), with attention to detail; meticulously, carefully.

acer, acris, acre, sharp, harsh, keen.

acerbitas, acerbitatis, *f.*, harshness, severity, cruelty; suffering, distress.

acquiesco, acquiescere, acquievi, acquietus, to rest in, find comfort in, find pleasure in.

acroama, acroamatis, *n.*, an act; any form of entertainment.

acuo, acuere, acui, acutus, to stir up, arouse, incite; (*of the senses*), to sharpen, make keen.

ad (*prep. w. acc.*), to, toward; at, near; among, by.

adaequo, -are, -avi, -atus, to equate, make (*someone, something*) equal (*to someone, something else*).

adduco, adducere, adduxi, adductus, to draw, draw together.

adeo, adire, adii, aditus, to enter, come into; accept the duties or responsibilities (*of a certain position*).

adfero, adferre, attuli, adlatus, to bring (*as a contribution, etc.*).

adficio, adficere, adfeci, adfectus, to affect, influence; (*pass.*), to be treated (*by others*).

adfluo, adfluere, adfluxi, adfluctus (*w. abl.*), to be rich.

adhibeo, adhibere, adhibui, adhibitus, to offer, furnish, provide.

adhuc (*adv.*), still, yet.

aditus, -us, *m.*, a means of approach, access; an entryway.

adiungo, adiungere, adiunxi, adiunctus, to add, attribute; to mention in addition.

adiuvo, -are, -avi, -atus, to help, aid; (*w. dat.*), to give aid (*to someone, something, etc.*); (*w.* **ad** *or* **in** + *acc.*), to facilitate progress towards, contribute to (*a goal, end, cause, etc.*).

administro, -are, -avi, -atus, to manage, perform the duties of, administer.

admiratio, admirationis, *f.*, admiration, veneration.

admiror, -ari, -atus, to admire, hold in high esteem or regard.

admodum (*adv.*), quite.

admoneo, admonere, admonui, admonitus (*w. acc. of person, abl. or gen. of thing*), to warn, caution, admonish; (*w. acc.* + *infin.*), to remind.

admoveo, admovere, admovi, admotus, to move toward, approach.

adorno, -are, -avi, -atus, to decorate, adorn, praise.

adservo, -are, -avi, -atus, to keep safe, guard, protect.

adspicio, adspicere, adspexi, adspectus, to see; look at; behold.

adsum, adesse, afui, afuturus, to be present, at hand.

adulescens, adulescentis, young, youthful; (*as substant.*), young man, youth.

adulescentia, -ae, *f.*, youth, young manhood; adolescence.

adventus, -us, *m.*, arrival, visit, appearance.

adversus, -a, -um, adverse, unfavorable, hostile.

aequales, aequalium, *m./f., pl.*, people of the same age; friends.

aeque (*adv.*), equally.

aequitas, aequitatis, *f.*, fairness, justice, reasonableness, patience.

aequus, -a, -um (*of actions, laws, etc.*), fair, just, reasonable.

aerarium, -i, *n.*, the treasury.

aetas, aetatis, *f.*, one's life or lifetime; the span of a life; old age.

aeternus, -a, -um, eternal, lasting through all time; timeless.

ager, agri, *m.*, field.

agnosco, agnoscere, agnovi, agnitus, to recognize.

ago, agere, egi, actus, to do, act; to be actively engaged (*in something*); to be involved, take part (*in an action or activity, etc.*).

agrestis, -e, boorish, coarse, unrefined, unsophisticated.

aio (*defective verb*); **ait**, he says; **aiunt**, they say.

alienus, -a, -um, of or belonging to another; foreign, of another country.

alienus, -i, *m.*, a stranger.

aliquando (*adv.*), from time to time, occasionally.

aliquis, aliquid (*indef. pron., adj.*), someone, anyone; some, any; **aliquo** (*adv.*), to somewhere; somewhere.

alius, -a, -ud, another, other, else; **alius . . . alius**, one . . . another; **alii . . . alii**, some . . . others.

alo, alere, alui, al(i)tus, to nourish.

alter, -tera, -terum, one of two; the other; another; **alter . . . alter**, the one . . . the other.

alternus, -a, -um, occurring in alternation with something else; (*of poetry, w.* **versus**, *etc.*), a reference to the alternating metrics of elegiac verse.

alveolus, -i, *m.*, a gaming board.

amatus, -a, -um, loved, beloved, esteemed.

amicitia, -ae, *f.*, friendship.

amicus, -a, -um, friendly, well-disposed.

amicus, -i, *m.*, a friend.

amo, -are, -avi, -atus, to love, esteem.

amor, amoris, *m.*, love, affection; the object of love or desire.

amplius (*comp. adv. <* **amplus**), more, further; in addition; besides.

amplus, -a, -um (*of things*), large, spacious, extensive; (*of persons, status, etc.*), magnificent, distinguished, great.

an (*conj.*), whether.

ango, angere, anxi, anctus, to cause mental pain or distress; to vex, irk, afflict; (*pass.*), to be distressed, feel anxious.

angustum, -i, *n.*, narrow limit.

animus, -i, *m.*, the mind, spirit, soul, heart, courage.

annus, -i, *m.*, year.

anquiro, anquirere, anquisivi, anquisitus, to search.

ante (*prep. with acc.*), before; (*adv.*), before, earlier.

antecello, antecellere (*w. dat.*), to excel, surpass.

antepono, anteponere, anteposui, antepositus, to place before, prefer.

aperio, aperire, aperui, apertus, to open up (*a territory*); to make available, place at one's disposal.

appello, -are, -avi, -atus, to name, call; (*w. spec. titles, epithets, etc.*), to address, recognize (*as*).

approbo, -are, -avi, -atus, to approve, express approval.

aptus, -a, -um (*w. dat.*), fitting, suitable, suited (*to*).

apud (*prep. w. acc. denoting position or relationship*), at (*the house of*); in (*the army of*); before, in the presence of (*a magistrate, etc.*).

aqua, -ae, *f.*, water.

arbitror, -ari, -atus, to think, suppose.

argumentum, -i, *n.*, evidence; the basis for a charge.

armatus, -a, -um, armed; (*subst.*), an armed man, soldier.

ars, artis, *f.*, cultural pursuits, liberal studies.

artifex, artificis, *m.*, an artisan; (*w.* **scaenicus**), an actor.

ascisco, asciscere, ascivi, ascitus, to admit (*someone*) to the citizenship.

ascribo, ascribere, ascripsi, ascriptus, to enroll as a citizen.

aspectus, -us, *m.*, the range of vision, sight, view.

asto, astare, astiti (*w.* **ad** + *acc.*), to stand at or on (*a place, etc.*).

at (*conj.*), but; yet; at least.

atque (ac) (*conj.*), and, and also.

attendo, attendere, attendi, attentus (*w. acc.*), to listen to, pay attention to.

attingo, attingere, attigi, attactus, to touch, make physical contact with; to touch upon, treat, address (*a subject, issue, etc.*).

auctoritas, auctoritatis, *f.*, the quality of leadership, authority; personal influence; prestige.

audacia, -ae, *f.*, insolence, daring, audacity.

audeo, audere, ausus sum (*semi-deponent*), to dare.

audio, audire, audivi, auditus, to hear, listen to.

augeo, augere, auxi, auctus, to increase.

auris, auris, *f.*, ear.

aut (*conj.*), or; **aut . . . aut**, either . . . or.

autem (*conj.*), but, however; on the other hand.

aversus, -a, -um (*w.* **a/ab** + *abl.*), estranged (*from*), averse (*to*), at variance (*with*).

avoco, -are, -avi, -atus, to call away one's attention, distract, divert.

B

barbaria, -ae, *f.*, lack of civilization, brutality, barbarism.

beatus, -a, -um, happy, blessed.

bello, -are, -avi, -atus, to wage war, take part in battle.

bellum, -i, *n.*, war.

belua, beluae, *f.*, beast; animal.

bene (*adv.*), well.

beneficium, -i, *n.*, favor, formal thanks; a reward.

benevolentia, -ae, *f.*, good will, kindness, affection.

benignitas, benignitatis, *f.*, kindness, indulgence.

bestia, -ae, *f.*, a beast, animal, creature (*distinct from man*).

boni, bonorum, *m. pl.*, conservatives, constitutionalists; men of substance and social standing; good men/people.

bonus, -a, -um, good, kind, kindhearted.

brevis, -e, brief, short.

breviter (*adv.*), briefly.

C

cado, cadere, cecidi, casus, to fall, sink.

caducus, -a, -um, frail, transitory, perishable.

caelum, -i, *n.*, sky; heaven.

calamitas, calamitatis, *f.*, misfortune, disaster, ruin, calamity.

calx, calcis, *f.*, goal line.

cantus, -us, *m.*, singing, a song.

carcer, carceris, *m.*, starting gates.

careo, carere, carui, cariturus (+ *abl.*), to be without, lack; be free from.

caritas, caritatis, *f.*, regard; love, affection.

carmen, carminis, *n.*, a song or poem.

carus, -a, -um, dear, valued, beloved (*w. dat.*).

causa, -ae, *f.*, cause, reason, pretext; (*leg.*), a case, trial; (*abl. w. preceding gen.*), for the sake of.

celeber, -bris, -bre, busy, frequented, populous.

celebritas, celebritatis, *f.*, renown, notoriety.

celebro, -are, -avi, -atus, to throng, attend in large numbers, honor with ceremonies; to praise, extol, celebrate (*in speech, song, poetry, etc.*).

celeritas, celeritatis, *f.*, swiftness, speed.

celeriter (*adv.*), swiftly.

censeo, censere, censui, census, to think, assess; to express an opinion, recommend; (*spec.*), to register or enroll at a census.

censor, censoris, *m.*, one of two magistrates whose duties included the taking of the census (*i.e., registering citizens according to their property*).

census, -us, *m.*, the registration of Roman citizens and their property (*usu. every five years*); the written records of the census; the census roll; census returns.

certe (*adv.* < **certus**), certainly, surely; at least, at any rate.

certus, -a, -um, fixed, definite, certain; (*of individuals*), resolute, trusty, faithful.

ceterus, -a, -um, other, the rest or the remaining.

circumscribo, -scribere, -scripsi, -scriptus, to define, mark the bounds of, delimit.

civis, civis, *m. or f.*, citizen, fellow countryman.

civitas, civitatis, *f.*, citizenship, state, community, city.

clamor, clamoris, *m.*, shout, outcry; protest; applause.

clarissimus, -a, -um (*superl. adj.* < **clarus**) most distinguished (*an honorific expression used espec. to designate men of senatorial rank*).

clarus, -a, -um (*adj.*), clear; famous.

classis, -is, *f.*, a naval force, fleet.

coepi, coepisse, coeptus (*defective verb, only in perfect; w. infin.*), I began.

cogitate (*adv.*), with thought; carefully.

cogitatio, cogitationis, *f.*, the act of thinking, thought; reflection; acknowledgement; recognition.

cognatio, cognationis, *f.*, blood relationship, kinship.

cognitio, cognitionis, *f.*, recognition.

cognosco, cognoscere, cognovi, cognitus, to learn, discover.

colo, colere, colui, cultus, to cultivate, develop, honor.

comes, comitis, *m.*, a friend, companion, comrade.

commemoratio, commemorationis, *f.*, a recollection, memory.

commendatio, commendationis, *f.*, a recommendation; the act of entrusting or committing (*something, someone*) to the care of another.

commendo, -are, -avi, -atus, to give, entrust for safekeeping; to recommend (*someone for something, etc.*).

commoditas, commoditatis, *f.*, comfort, advantage.

commodum, -i, *n.*, advantage, interest.

commoveo, commovere, commovi, commotus, to stir the emotions of; to disturb, trouble, make anxious.

communico, -are, -avi, -atus, to share, have in common.

communis, -e, common, shared jointly by two parties.

communiter (*adv.*), both or all alike, indiscriminately; jointly, in common, together.

commuto, -are, -avi, -atus, to change, exchange one for another.

comparo, -are, -avi, -atus, to join, arrange, put together, order.

comprobo, -are, -avi, -atus, to approve, sanction, ratify.

concedo, concedere, concessi, concessus, to concede, grant.

concilio, -are, -avi, -atus, to procure, get; to win over, obtain, unite.

concito, -are, -avi, -atus, to excite, stir up; to rouse, incite.

concordia, -ae, *f.*, concord, unity, harmony.

concursus, -us, *m.*, a crowd, assembly.

condicio, condicionis, *f.*, a condition, term, stipulation.

confero, conferre, contuli, collatus, to devote, bestow, apply; to bring together; (*refl. w.* **se**), to betake oneself, go.

confido, confidere, confisus sum (*semi-deponent*), to trust, be confident.

confirmo, -are, -avi, -atus, to establish, confirm; to assure, reassure.

confiteor, confiteri, confessus, to confess, admit.

conformatio, conformationis, *f.*, training through formal instruction; education.

conformo, -are, -avi, -atus, to train, shape, mold; (*w.* **animus, mens**, *etc.*), to educate oneself.

coniunctio, coniunctionis, *f.*, union, connection, relationship.

coniunctus, -a, -um, close, intimate.

conlegium, -i, *n.*, a board or body of magistrates.

conloco, -are, -avi, -atus, to settle, establish, set up.

conquiesco, conquiescere, conquievi, conquietus, to rest, take repose; to relax, take a break.

consecro, -are, -avi, -atus, to vow, consecrate, devote (*i.e., as an offering to a god, etc.*).

consensio, consensionis, *f.*, agreement, harmony, unanimity.

consensus, -us, *m.*, agreement.

consequor, consequi, consecutus, to follow.

conservo, -are, -avi, -atus, to save, preserve, rescue.

consilium, -i, *n.*, deliberation; counsel; advice; an advisory body.

consisto, consistere, constiti, to come to a stop, stand still.

constantia, -ae, *f.*, firmness, steadiness, constancy.

constituo, constituere, constitui, constitutus (*of people*), to set up, place, establish (*in a position, etc.*); (*of objects, statues, etc.*), to erect.

consto, -are, constiti, -atus (*w.* **e/ex** + *abl.*), to consist (*of*).

consuetudo, consuetudinis, *f.*, custom, habit; a convention of society; friendship.

consul, consulis, *m.*, consul, the highest magistrate in the Roman republican government.

consulatus, -us, *m.*, consulship, the office of consul.

contego, contegere, contexi, contectus, to cover; to entomb, bury.

contemno, contemnere, contempsi, contemptus, to treat with contempt, regard of little value.

contendo, contendere, contendi, contentus, to assert, allege, maintain; to argue (*a point, an issue, etc.*); to take issue (*over something*).

contentio, contentionis, *f.*, conflict, contention; a disagreement, quarrel.

contentus, -a, -um, content, satisfied.

contero, conterere, contrivi, contritus, to spend (*w.* **tempus**).

continens, continentis, self-restrained, temperate.

contineo, continere, continui, contentus, to hold together (*e.g., by bonds of relationship or common interest*); to contain, hold, keep; preserve.

contio, contionis, *f.*, a public assembly, rally.

contraho, contrahere, contraxi, contractus, to draw together, unite.

conveniens, convenientis, suitable, fitting.

convenientia, -ae, *f.*, harmony.

convenio, convenire, conveni, conventus, to come together; (*impers.*), to be fitting, proper.

conventus, -us, *m.*, an assembly, a court of law.

convicium, -i, *n.*, noise, clamor, shouts (*usu. angry*).

convivium, -i, *n.*, a dinner party, banquet, feast.

copia, -ae, *f.* (*sing.*), abundance, plenty; (*pl.*), troops, forces.

copiosus, -a, -um, rich, well-supplied.

corpus, corporis, *n.*, body.

corrumpo, corrumpere, corrupi, corruptus, to tamper with, corrupt.

cotidianus, -a, -um, daily, everyday.

cotidie (*adv.*), every day, daily, day by day.

credo, credere, credidi, creditus (*w. acc. and infin.*), to believe, suppose (*often used sarcastically as an aside*).

cresco, crescere, crevi, cretus, to grow; (*w.* **ab** *or* **de**), to arise from.

criminor, -ari, -atus, to accuse, make an allegation.

cruciatus, -us, *m.*, pain, anguish, agony; the act of physical torture.

cultus, -a, -um, cultivated.

cum (*conj.*), when, since, although.

cum (*prep. w. abl.*), with, together with.

cum . . . tum (*correlatives*) in general . . . and in particular; both . . . and (*w. indicative*).

cunctus, -a, -um, whole, entire, all together; the whole of, all.

cupiditas, cupiditatis, *f.*, longing, desire, passion, lust.

cupio, cupere, cupivi (-ii), cupitus (*w. infin.*), to desire, want.

cur (*interrog. adv.*), why?

cura, -ae, *f.*, care, anxiety, distress, trouble.

curriculum, -i, *n.*, a course, track, race; (*w.* **vitae**), the course or race of life.

D

damnatio, damnationis, *f.*, condemnation in a court of law.

de (*prep. w. abl.*), from, about, concerning.

debeo, debere, debui, debitus (*w. infin.*), to be under obligation to do something; ought, must.

debilito, -are, -avi, -atus, to weaken, disable.

decedo, decedere, decessi, decessurus, to go away, depart, leave.

decoro, -are, -avi, -atus, to decorate (*with honors, etc.*), embellish, praise, extol.

dedico, -are, -avi, -atus, to dedicate.

dedo, dedere, dedidi, deditus, to devote oneself to.

defendo, defendere, defendi, defensus, to defend (*in court*).

defero, deferre, detuli, delatus, to confer, recommend (*for an award, etc.*).

defetiscor, defetisci, defessus, to be worn out, suffer exhaustion.

definio, definire, definivi (-ii), definitus, to define the limits, bound; to define.

delectatio, delectationis, *f.*, the gaining of pleasure or delight; a source of enjoyment.

delecto, -are, -avi, -atus, to delight, charm; (*pass. w. abl.*), to take pleasure (*in*), be delighted (*by someone, something*).

delubrum, -i, *n.*, a shrine, temple.

denique (*adv.*), finally, at length, at last.

depravo, -are, -avi, -atus, to corrupt, deprave.

deprimo, deprimere, depressi, depressus, to press or force down; (*of ships*) to sink.

desiderium, -ii (*or* -i), *n.*, desire, longing for; grief.

desidero, -are, -avi, -atus, to desire, want.

despicio, despicere, despexi, despectus, to despise, look down on, view with contempt.

desum, deesse, defui (*w. dat. of person, situation, etc.*), to fail (*in respect of*), be neglectful in one's duty (*to*) or support (*of someone, something*); to be lacking, not forthcoming.

detraho, detrahere, detraxi, detractus, to take away, remove, deprive; to cause the loss (*of something*).

deus, -i, *m.*, god, deity.

devincio, devincere, devinxi, devinctus, to hold, bind (*under obligation*).

dico, dicere, dixi, dictus, to say, speak; to speak of, tell; to speak publicly, make a speech; **ut dicitur**, as it is said.

dies, diei, *m. or f.*, day; the appointed time.

difficilis, -e, not easy, difficult; hard, painful; dangerous.

dignitas, dignitatis, *f.*, rank, status, professional or public standing or position.

dignus, -a, -um (*w. abl.*), worthy or deserving (*of*).

diligenter (*adv.*), diligently, with care.

diligentia, -ae, *f.*, carefulness, attentiveness, diligence.

diligo, diligere, dilexi, dilectus, to love, cherish; (*perf. pass. part.*), beloved.

dimicatio, dimicationis, *f.*, struggle.

dimico, -are, -avi, -atus, to struggle, contend, fight.

dimitto, dimittere, dimisi, dimissus, to give up, let go; to pass away (*into obscurity, etc.*).

discidium, -i, *n.*, alienation.

disciplina, -ae, *f.*, formal instruction, training.

disco, discere, didici, to examine, learn.

discordia, -ae, *f.*, discord, disagreement.

dissemino, -are, -avi, -atus, to scatter, disseminate; to broadcast.

dissensio, dissensionis, *f.*, disagreement, dissension, violent division.

dissero, dissere, disserui, dissertus, to discuss, argue.

dissimulo, -are, -avi, -atus, to hide, conceal.

diu (*adv.*), long, for a long time.

divinus, -a, -um, divine, sacred, god-like.

divitiae, -arum, *f. pl.*, riches.

do, dare, dedi, datus, to give, grant, endow.

doctrina, -ae, *f.*, formal teaching, instruction; a branch or area of learning.

doctus, -a, -um, educated, learned.

doctus, -i, *m.*, wise man, learned man.

dolor, doloris, *m.*, pain, ache; sorrow.

domesticus, -a, -um, internal, domestic, civil.

domicilium, -i, *n.*, a permanent residence, domicile.

domus, -us, *f.*, house, home; household.

dono, -are, -avi, -atus, to award, endow (*w. abl. of thing given*).

donum, -i, *n.*, gift, award.

dubito, -are, -avi, -atus (*w. acc.*), to doubt, question; (*w.* **de**) to be in doubt about; to hesitate.

duco, ducere, duxi, ductus, to lead, guide; to consider, believe.

dulcedo, dulcedinis, *f.*, pleasantness (*to the mind, etc.*); an object causing agreeable sensations or emotions.

dulcis, -e, sweet, pleasant, delightful.

duo, duae, duo (*adj.*), two.

durus, -a, -um (*of people*), dull, slow, obtuse; insensitive, unresponsive.

dux, ducis, *m.*, military leader, commander; guide.

E

e, ex (*prep. with abl.*), out of, from; after; according to.

effero, efferre, extuli, elatus, to lift up, raise; to carry off, remove.

effigies, effigiei, *f.*, an image, representation, likeness.

effloresco, efflorescere, efflorescui, to blossom, bloom, flourish.

egeo, egere, egui, to be needy, be in want; **egentes**, needy.

ego, mei, mihi, me, me (*pers. pron.*), I, me; **egomet** (*intensive*), I myself.

eicio, eicere, eieci, eiectus, to throw out, drive away, banish.

eluceo, elucere, eluxi, to shine forth, shine out.

emitto, emittere, emisi, emissus, to send out.

enim (*conj.*), for; indeed; in truth.

epigramma, epigrammatis, *n.*, a short poem, epigram.

equidem (*adv.*), truly, indeed, of course, for my part.

ergo (*adv.*), therefore, accordingly.

eripio, eripere, eripui, ereptus, to snatch away.

erro, -are, -avi, -atus, to err, be wrong, make a mistake.

erudio, erudire, erudivi (-ii), eruditus, to instruct, train, educate.

eruditus, -a, -um (< **erudio**), learned, educated; accomplished.

et (*conj.*), and; **et . . . et**, both . . . and; (*adv.*) also, too.

etenim (*conj.*), for, and indeed, the fact is.

etiam (*adv.*), also, even, too.

everto, evertere, everti, eversus, to overturn, turn upside down.

exardesco, exardescere, exarsi, exarsus, to burn, catch fire.

excedo, excedere, excessi, excessus, to grow out of; to leave, go out.

excellens, excellentis, outstanding, excellent.

excipio, excipere, excepi, exceptus, to except, set aside.

excito, -are, -avi, -atus, to rouse, stir (*the senses*), to stimulate (*the spirit*), to inspire.

excludo, excludere, exclusi, exclusus, to shut out, exclude.

excolo, excolere, excolui, excultus, to improve, develop; to cultivate.

exemplar, exemplaris, *n.*, likeness, copy, image, model.

exemplum, -i, *n.*, example; (*leg.*) precedent.

exerceo, exercere, exercui, exercitus, to carry on, perform, execute; (*w.* **iudicium**), to preside over (*a trial*).

exercitatio, exercitationis, *f.*, practice, experience.

exercitus, -us, *m.*, a military force, an army.

exiguus, -a, -um, small, scanty, slight, insignificant.

eximie (*adv.*), especially, exceptionally, outstandingly.

eximius, -a, -um, special, remarkable, outstanding, exceptional.

eximo, eximere, exemi, exemptus, to take away.

existimo, -are, -avi, -atus, to judge, consider, hold an opinion.

exorno, -are, -avi, -atus (*of things*), to adorn, decorate, beautify; (*of people*), to enhance, embellish, decorate (*w. honors, offices, etc.*).

expeto, expetere, expetivi (-ii), expetitus, to seek after, desire; to try to obtain.

exprimo, exprimere, expressi, expressus, to make, produce; to express, portray (*in painting, sculpture, etc.*).

exsilium, -i, *n.*, the condition of banishment, exile.

exsisto, exsistere, exstiti, to come into being, emerge, arise.

exspectatio, expectationis, *f.*, expectation, anticipation.

exstinguo, exstinguere, exstinxi, exstinctus, to destroy; (*pass.*), die out.

exsto, exstare, exstiti, to emerge, stand out, exist (*in a given manner or capacity*).

extremum, -i, *n.*, final goal; prime desire.

extremus, -a, -um, occurring at the end, last, final.

F

facilis, -e, easy; ready at hand.

facio, facere, feci, factus, to make, do, execute, offer.

facultas, facultatis, *f.*, ability, skill.

fama, -ae, *f.*, reputation, public opinion.

familiaris, -e, intimate, close, closely associated (*by bonds of kinship or friendship*); (*w. dat.*), congenial, welcome, intimate, familiar (*to someone, something, etc.*).

familiaritas, familiaritatis, *f.*, friendship, intimacy.

fateor, fateri, fassus, to confess, acknowledge; to admit, declare.

fauces, faucium, *f.* (*usu. pl.*), throat, jaws; (*of a house*), the entryway; (*of a mountain, etc.*), a pass, an approach.

faveo, favere, favi, fautus (*w. dat.*), to show favor, give support (*to*).

fere (*adv.*), nearly, almost, virtually, usually.

fero, ferre, tuli, latus, to carry, bear, convey, bestow; to endure; (*esp. in pass.*), to mention, spread abroad, cite; to speak of, refer to (*someone, something*) as (*someone, something else*).

festus, -a, -um, festal, taking place on a holiday.

fides, fidei, *f.*, faith, confidence; a trust or agreement; honesty.

filius, -i, *m.*, son.

fingo, fingere, finxi, fictus, to pretend, invent.

finis, finis, *m.*, end, limit; (*of countries, territories, etc.*), the boundary, border; (*pl.*), territory.

firmitas, firmitatis, *f.*, constancy, steadfastness, strength.

firmus, -a, -um, firm, stable, secure.

flagito, -are, -avi, -atus, to ask for, demand.

flecto, flectere, flexi, flectus, to bend, turn, prevail upon, influence.

foederatus, -a, -um, federated, bound by treaty to Rome.

foedus, foederis, *n.*, a formal agreement between states, peoples, or cities; a treaty.

fons, fontis, *m.*, the source (*usu. of a river*); origin.

forensis, -e, of, or connected to, the law courts.

foris (*adv.*), abroad; outside; away from home.

fortasse (*adv.*), perhaps, possibly.

forte (*adv.*), perhaps, by chance.

fortis, -e, brave, fearless.

fortuna, -ae, *f.*, fortune, chance, fate, luck (*either good or bad*); (*pl.*), wealth, property.

fortunatus, -a, -um, fortunate, lucky, successful.

forum, -i, *n.*, a marketplace, public square; the **Forum Romanum**.

fragilis, -e, weak, frail, perishable.

frango, frangere, fregi, fractus, to break, crush, destroy.

frequentia, -ae, *f.*, a crowd, large attendance.

fructus, -us, *m.*, advantage, gain, profit; enjoyment, gratification, pleasure.

funditus (*adv.*), entirely, completely.

fundo, fundere, fudi, fusus, to pour out, scatter; to rout, put to flight, defeat utterly.

fungor, fungi, functus (*with abl.*), to use, exercise, perform, function, enjoy.

G

gaudeo, gaudere, gavisus sum (*semi-deponent*), to rejoice.

gens, gentis, *f.*, family, race, clan.

genus, generis, *n.*, type, class, race, family.

gero, gerere, gessi, gestus, to carry on, perform, wear, accomplish, achieve; **res gestae**, deeds, exploits, achievements.

gigno, gignere, genui, genitus, to give birth to, produce, give rise to.

gloria, -ae, *f.*, fame, renown, glory, pride.

gratia, -ae, *f.*, popularity, influence, esteem or the influence derived thereof.

gratuito (*adv. <* **gratuitus**), without payment, for nothing.

gravis, -e, heavy, ponderous; (*of people*), venerable, serious, severe, distinguished.

gusto, -are, -avi, -atus, to taste.

H

habeo, habere, habui, habitus, to have, hold, possess; regard, consider, treat.

habitus, -us, *m.*, quality, character.

haud (*adv.*), not, not at all.

haurio, haurire, hausi, haustus, to draw (*usu. water*); to take in; to derive.

hereditas, hereditatis, *f.*, inheritance, hereditary possession.

hic, haec, hoc, this, this one; **hic . . . hic**, this . . . that, the one . . . the other; **hic** (*adv.*), here, in this place, at this point.

homo, hominis, *m. or f.*, man, mankind, human being, person.

honestas, honestatis, *f.*, moral rectitude, decency; honor or honorableness.

honos (honor), honoris, *m.*, respect, esteem; public office.

hortatus, -us, *m.*, encouragement.

hortor, hortari, hortatus, to urge, persuade, advise.

hospitium, -i, *n.*, a formal relationship existing between host and guest.

hostis, hostis, *m. or f.*, enemy, foe.

humanitas, humanitatis, *f.*, civilization, culture.

humanus, -a, -um, human, of man or mankind.

humilis, -e, suitable to humble persons or situation, lowly, insignificant.

I

iaceo, iacere, iacui, iaciturus, to lie, lie dead; be situated.

iam (*adv.*), now, at length; (*to denote the completion of an action or state of affairs prior to the time indicated*), by this time, by now, already.

ibi (*adv.*), in that place, there.

idem, eadem, idem (*pron. and adj. usu. referring to a person or thing previously mentioned*), the same man (*woman, thing*).

igitur (*conj.*), therefore, then.

ignis, ignis, *m.*, fire.

ille, -a, -ud, that one; he, she, it; (*with proper names*), the famous, that well-known (*man, woman, thing, etc.*).

imago, imaginis, *f.*, image, likeness; the death-masks of their ancestors that Romans displayed in the atria of their houses and carried in funeral processions.

imbecillis, -e, weak.

imitor, -ari, -atus, to copy the conduct of, imitate.

immanis, -e, huge, vast; monstrous, dreadful.

immo (*adv. implying complete denial of the preceding statement*), on the contrary.

immortalis, -e, immortal.

impedio, impedire, impedivi (-ii), impeditus, to obstruct, impede.

imperator, imperatoris, *m.*, commander, general.

imperium, -i, *n.*, dominion, the power of government; military command.

impero, -are, -avi, -atus, to order, command; to lead an army.

impertio, impertire, impertivi (-ii), impertitus, to present, offer.

impetro, -are, -avi, -atus, to obtain by request or application (*w.* **a** *or* **ab** *+ the person or source*).

impetus, -us, *m.*, attack, assault; violence or violent behavior.

in (*prep.*) 1) (*w. acc.*), into, to; upon, on; against, toward; for, among; 2) (*w. abl.*), in, on, upon; among; in case of.

incendio, incendere, incensi, incensus, to burn.

incertus, -a, -um, uncertain.

incitamentum, -i, *n.*, that which urges or incites; a stimulus, incentive.

incoho (inchoo), -are, -avi, -atus, to start, begin work on (*a task, topic, etc.*).

incolumis, -e, safe, unharmed, intact.

incredibilis, -e, incredible, beyond belief.

inde (*adv.*), from that time or place; thence; then, next.

indico, -are, -avi, -atus, to make known, show, point out, indicate.

indigentia, -ae, *f.*, material need, personal need.

infinitus,-a, -um, countless, infinite.

infirmo, -are, -avi, -atus, to weaken, invalidate; void, annul.

infitior, infitiari, infitiatus, to deny.

inflo, -are, -avi, -atus, to blow into, fill with breath; to inspire.

informo, -are, -avi, -atus, to mold, shape.

ingenium, -i, *n.*, natural ability or talent.

ingredior, ingredi, ingressus, to begin, embark; enter.

inlustris, -e, illustrious, famous, distinguished.

inlustro, -are, -avi, -atus, to give glory to, embellish, make famous.

innumerabilis, -e, countless, endless.

inquam, inquis, inquit, to say (*defective verb, cf.* **aiunt**).

inrepo, inrepere, inrepsi, to slip in; to insinuate oneself (*into a position, etc.*).

inscribo, inscribere, inscripsi, inscriptus, to write, inscribe (*a name, title, etc., on something*).

insideo, insidere, insedi, insessus (*w.* **in** + *abl.*), to be present (*in a situation, with an individual*).

insignis, -e, outstanding, remarkable, extraordinary, excellent.

instituo, instituere, institui, institutus, to form, set in order; to instruct, teach.

integer, integra, integrum (*of places*), in an undiminished state, not affected by war.

integritas, integritatis, *f.*, honesty, integrity.

intellego, intellegere, intellexi, intellectus, to understand, comprehend.

intempestivus, -a, -um, out of season.

inter (*prep. w. acc.*), between, among.

intereo, interire, interii, interitus (*of things*), to be destroyed; (*of persons*), to die, perish.

interficio, interficere, interfeci, interfectus, to kill, murder.

interim (*adv.*), meanwhile.

interpretor, interpretari, interpretatus, to explain, interpret, understand, call.

intersum, interesse, interfui, interfuturus, to be among, attend; be present (*as an onlooker*).

intervallum, -i, *n.*, an intervening period of time, an interval.

intueor, intueri, intuitus, to watch, gaze at; to examine, consider, reflect upon (*as an example*).

inusitatus, -a, -um, unusual, unfamiliar.

invenio, invenire, inveni, inventus, to come upon, find, discover.

invidiosus, -a, -um, hated, unacceptable.

ipse, -a, -um (*intensive pron.*) himself, herself, itself; ourselves, etc.; the very (*person, thing, etc.*).

is, ea, id (*pron.*) he, she, it; (*adj.*) that, this.

iste, ista, istud (*pron. and adj.*), that, that one, that of yours.

ita (*adv.*), so, thus, in this way; as follows.

Italia, -ae, *f.*, Italy.

Italicus, -a, -um, Italian; (*subst.*), an inhabitant of Italy.

itaque (*conj.*), and so, therefore; (*adv.*), accordingly.

item (*adv.*), in addition, as well; in the same manner, likewise.

iubeo, iubere, iussi, iussus, to order, command.

iucunditas, iucunditatis, *f.*, pleasantness, cheerfulness, joy.

iucundus, -a, -um (*w. dat.*), congenial, agreeable, pleasing (*to*).

iudex, iudicis, *m.*, one appointed to decide a case, juror, judge.

iudicialis, -e, of or relating to the law courts or their administration; judicial, forensic.

iudicium, -i, *n.*, a legal proceeding, a trial.

iudico, -are, -avi, -atus, to judge, appraise.

iungo, iungere, iunxi, iunctus, to join, unite, connect.

iure (*adv.* < **ius**), according to the law; with good reason, rightly.

iuro, -are, -avi, -atus, to take an oath, swear.

ius, iuris, *n.*, that which is sanctioned, law; (*of cities, communities*), privileges of citizenship; (*of individuals*), one's right, what one is entitled to; (*w. defining gen.*), a legal code, system, or its branches.

L

labor, laboris, *m.*, labor, task; effort, struggle; trial, hardship.

largior, largiri, largitus, to bestow, confer, grant.

Latina, -ae, *f.*, the Latin language.

laudabilis, -e, praiseworthy.

laudo, -are, -avi, -atus, to praise, commend, extol.

laus, laudis, *f.*, praise, glory, renown, distinction.

lectus, -a, -um, excellent, special, worthy of choice.

legatus, -i, *m.*, an ambassador, envoy, delegate.

legitimus, -a, -um, of or concerned with the law.

lego, legere, legi, lectus, to read.

levis, -e, unimportant, of little consequence; insignificant; trivial; slight.

levitas, levitatis, *f.*, unreliability, frivolity.

levo, -are, -avi, -atus, to relieve; (*w. abl.*), to free (*someone from something, etc*).

lex, legis, *f.*, law; legal reasoning or argument.

libellus, -i, *m.*, small book, pamphlet.

libenter (*adv.*), gladly, willingly, of one's own free will.

liber, libri, *m.*, book; a written account.

liberalis, -e, gentlemanly, decent; liberal; characteristic of a liberal arts education; (*w.* **studium**), the liberal arts.

liberalitas, liberalitatis, *f.*, generosity, nobility of character.

libere (*adv.*), freely, at will.

libido, libidinis, *f.*, desire, pleasure, lust.

littera, -ae, *f.*, (*usu. pl.*) literature; what is learned from books or formal education; erudition or culture.

litteratus, -a, -um, well-read, cultured.

litura, -ae, *f.*, a rubbing out; an erasure, correction.

loco, -are, -avi, -atus, to place, rank.

locus, -i, *m.*, place, spot, region; site, position; situation.

longe (*adv.*), far, by far, a far way off.

longiusculus, -a, -um, a little longer (*in length, duration, extent, etc.*).

longus, -a, -um, long, prolonged, lengthy.

loquor, loqui, locutus, to speak, say.

ludus, -i, *m.* (*pl.*), public games, festivals, holidays.

lumen, luminis, *n.*, light; brilliance, excellence.

lux, lucis, *f.*, light, daylight; (*of individuals*), glory, brilliance.

M

magis (*adv.*), more; (*w.* **quam** *or abl. of comparison*), rather.

magnificentia, -ae, *f.*, splendor, greatness, magnificence.

magnus, -a, -um, big, large, great.

maior, maioris (*comp. adj.* < **magnus**), greater, larger; (*pl. as subst.*) **maiores**, one's ancestors.

malo, malle, malui, to prefer.

malus, -a,-um, bad, evil.

mandatum, -i, *n.*, a commission, charge; a directive; official orders (*usu. conveyed by* **legati**).

mando, -are, -avi, -atus, to hand over, entrust; to order, command.

maneo, manere, mansi, mansurus, to stay, remain.

manubiae, -arum, *f. pl.*, booty, spoils.

manus, -us, *f.*, military force, an army; hand.

mare, maris, *n.*, sea.

marmor, marmoris, *n.*, marble; something made of marble, a statue.

maxime (*superl. adv.* < **magis**), most, very much, especially.

maximus, -a, -um (*superl. adj.* < **magnus**), greatest, largest; most outstanding.

mediocris, -e, ordinary, average, common, undistinguished.

mediocriter (*adv.*), somewhat, to a moderate extent, moderately.

melior, melius (*comp. adj.* < **bonus**), better.

memoria, -ae, *f.*, memory.

mens, mentis, *f.*, the mind, intellect.

merces, mercedis, *f.*, reward, prize; fee.

-met (*enclitic particle*), attached for emphasis to pronouns.

metior, metiri, mensus, to measure, estimate, value.

meus, -a, -um, my, mine.

miles, militis, *m.* (*sing.*), a soldier; (*pl.*), soldiers, the army.

militia, -ae, *f.*, military service.

minime (*adv.*), hardly, not really, not at all.

minimus, -a, -um (*superl. adj.* < **parvus**), least, smallest.

minor, minus (*comp. adj.* < **parvus**), smaller (*in size, qualtiy, value, etc.*); less, less important; (*of people*), younger.

minus (*adv.*) (*after* **si**), not quite, not exactly.

miror, mirari, miratus, to wonder.

mirus, -a, -um, extraordinary, remarkable, strange.

moderatus, -a, -um, temperate, restrained, moderate.

modestus, -a, -um, restrained, temperate, mild.

modo (*adv.*), but; just now; only, merely; **non modo**, not only.

modus, -i, *m.*, manner, mode, way; a kind, form, type.

molestus, -a, -um, annoying, tiresome.

monumentum, -i, *n.*, memento, monument; a remembrance, token.

morior, mori, mortuus, to die, be killed.

mors, mortis, *f.*, death.

mortalis, -e, mortal.

mortuus, -a, -um, dead.

motus, -us, *m.*, motion, movement.

moveo, movere, movi, motus, to move, remove; arouse, excite; (*pass.*), to be moved, affected (*esp. emotionally*).

multus, -a, -um, much; (*pl.*) many.

munus, muneris, *n.*, duty; gift, tribute, offering; prize, reward.

municipium, -i, *n.*, a self-governing community or township of Italy awarded the rights of Roman citizenship without the right to vote (**civitas sine suffragio**).

Musae, -arum, *f. pl.*, the Muses.

mutuus, -a, -um, mutual, reciprocal.

N

nam (*explanatory particle*), for.

namque (*conj.*), for.

nanciscor, nancisci, nactus, to obtain; establish a relationship or connection with someone (*i.e., as an ally or supporter*).

nascor, nati, natus, to be born.

natura, -ae, *f.*, inborn abilities; natural endowments; nature.

navalis, -e, of or pertaining to ships or the sea, naval.

ne (*adv.*), not; (*conj.*), that . . . not; in order that . . . not; lest.

ne . . . quidem, not even.

nec (*conj., shortened form of* **neque**), nor; and . . . not.

neglegentius (*comp. adv.* < **neglegens**), somewhat carelessly, without due caution.

neglego, neglegere, neglexi, neglectus, to neglect, fail to observe or respect.

nego, -are, -avi, -atus, to deny, say . . . not.

nemo, nullius, no one.

nescioquid, *n.* (*indecl.*), something or other (< **nescio, nescire, nescivi (-ii), nescitus** [to not know, be ignorant] + **quid** [something] (*often used to describe something ineffable or inscrutable*).

neque or **nec** (*conj.*), nor, and...not; **neque (nec) . . . neque (nec)**, neither . . . nor.

neque solum . . . sed etiam, not only . . . but also.

nescio, nescire, nescivi (-ii), nescitus, to not know, be ignorant.

nihil (nil), *n.* (*indecl.*), nothing; (*adv.*) not, not at all.

nimirum (*adv.*), without doubt, certainly, to be sure.

nimis (*adv.*), very much, too much, exceedingly.

nisi (*conj.*), if not, unless.

nobilis, -e, noble; well-mannered; high-born, well-known, famous.

nobilitas, nobilitatis, *f.*, renown, celebrity.

nolo, nolle, nolui (*w. infin.*) to be unwilling, not to want.

nomen, nominis, *n.*, name; reputation.

nomino, -are, -avi, -atus, to name, call by name.

non (*adv.*), not, no.

nonne (*interrog. particle introducing a question that expects a positive answer*), Is it not the case that . . . ?

norma, -ae, *f.*, a carpenter's square.

nos, nostrum (*pers. pron.*), we, us.

noster, nostra, nostrum, our, our own, of us.

notus, -a, -um, well-known, noted.

novus, -a, -um, new, strange.

nox, noctis, *f.*, night; darkness.

nullus, -a, -um, no, none, not any.

numero, -are, -avi, -atus, to number, count.

numerus, -i, *m.*, number; **in numero**, in the company (*of*).

numquam (nunquam) (*adv.*), never.

nunc (*adv.*), now.

nuper (*adv.*), recently, lately; (*adj.*), recent.

nusquam (*adv.*), nowhere.

O

obeo, obire, obivi (-ii), obitus, to take on, deal with, carry out.

obicio, obicere, obieci, obiectus, to throw, hurl, cast; (*refl.*), to offer, expose oneself.

oblectatio, oblectationis, *f.*, pleasure, enjoyment.

oblecto, -are, -avi, -atus, to delight, amuse, entertain.

obruo, obruere, obrui, obrutus, to bury, hide, conceal (*i.e., in obscurity*).

obscuro, -are, -avi, -atus, to cover up, conceal; to obscure, make unclear.

obscurus, -a, -um, not clear, uncertain, doubtful; not widely known, obscure.

obtineo, obtinere, obtinui, obtentus, to have, possess.

occido, occidere, occidi, occasus, to die, perish.

oculus, -i, *m.,* eye.

odium, -i, *n.,* hatred, enmity.

offendo, offendere, offendi, offensus, to offend, annoy, bother.

olim (*adv.*), for a long time past, since long ago, formerly.

omitto, omittere, omisi, omissus, to omit, to pass over, pass by.

omnino (*adv.*), altogether, wholly, entirely.

omnis, -e (*sing.*), each, every; (*pl.*), all.

opinor, -ari, -atus, to hold as an opinion; to suppose, believe.

opitulor, opitulari, opitulatus (*w. dat.*), to give help (*to*).

oppidum, -i, *n.,* town.

opportunitas, opportunitatis, *f.,* advantage, convenience, opportunity.

opportunus, -a, -um, fit, suited, appropriate.

ops, opis, *f.,* power, resource; (*usu. pl.*), wealth.

optime (*superl. adv. <* **bene**), most satisfactorily, competently.

optimus, -a, -um (*superl. adj. <* **bonus**), best; (*of persons*), most excellent, virtuous; (*of ideas*), highest, most noble-minded; (*of studies*), most liberal.

opto, -are, -avi, -atus, to wish, hope for.

opus, operis, *n.,* work, task, labor; **opus est** (*w. abl.*), there is need of.

oratio, orationis, *f.,* a speech, oration.

orbis, orbis, *m.,* circle, circuit, course; **orbis terrarum** (*or* **terrae**), the world.

orbo, -are, -avi, -atus (*w. abl.*), to deprive.

orior, oriri, ortus, to rise, rise up, arise.

orno, -are, -avi, -atus, to adorn, decorate.

os, oris, *n.,* mouth, lips; face; (*pl.*), expression.

ostendo, ostendere, ostendi, ostentus, to show, reveal; (*pass.*), be evident.

otiosus, -a, -um, at leisure, idle.

otium, -i, *n.,* leisure (*esp. as devoted to cultural pursuits*).

P

pactum, -i, *n.,* agreement; manner; **nullo pacto,** in no way; not at all.

pario, parere, peperi, partus, to give birth to, produce, create.

pars, partis, *f.,* part, portion.

particeps, participis, *m.,* participant, member (*of a group, office, etc.*).

partior, -iri, -itus (*and* **partio, partire, partivi, partitus**), to divide, share.

parum (*adv.*), too little, not enough, not sufficiently.

parvus, -a, -um, small in size, amount, quantity; of little worth; insignificant, of no consequence.

pater, patris, *m.,* father.

patior, pati, passus (*w. infin.*), to allow; to suffer, endure.

pauci, -orum, *m. pl.,* a few.

paulo (*adv.*), by a little, somewhat.

paulus, -a, -um, small, little.

penetro, -are, -avi, -atus, to work a way, make one's way (*to or into a place, etc.*); to reach, enter, penetrate.

penitus (*adv.*), completely, thoroughly.

per (*prep. w. acc.*), through; over; among; throughout; during.

percipio, percipere, percepi, perceptus, to perceive, take in or grasp with the mind; to take possession of, acquire, derive.

peregrinatio, peregrinationis, *f.,* foreign travel.

peregrinor, -ari, -atus, to go or travel abroad.

peregrinus, -a, -um, foreign, alien.

peregrinus, -i, *m.,* foreigner, stranger.

perfectus, -a, -um, perfect, faultless.

perficio, perficere, perfeci, perfectus, to effect, bring about; to finish, bring to completion, complete.

perfugium, -i, *n.*, a place of refuge, shelter; a means of safety; a sanctuary.

periculum, -i, *n.*, danger, hazard; (*usu. pl.*), legal liability; the risks or hazards of litigation.

permaneo, permanere, permansi, permansus, to remain, stay, abide.

permultus, -a, -um, a great many, very many.

pernocto, -are, -avi, -atus, to spend the night.

persequor, persequi, persecutus, to seek to obtain; to strive to accomplish.

persona, -ae, *f.*, role, part, position (*assumed or adopted*).

perspicio, perspicere, perspexi, perspectus, to understand, perceive.

pertineo, pertinere, pertinui, to pertain, relate to.

pervenio, pervenire, perveni, perventus, to arrive (*at a place, situation, station, etc.*); to attain (*a position*).

peto, petere, petivi (-ii), petitus, to seek; to aim for, attack.

philosophus, -i, *m.*, a philosopher.

pila, -ae, *f.*, a ball (*for play or exercise, etc.*).

pinguis, -e, slow-witted, dull, obtuse; (*of literary works, style, etc.*), clumsy, unrefined, coarse.

plane (*adv.*), entirely.

plenus, -a, -um (*w. gen.*), full, stocked.

plurimus, -a, -um (*superl. adj.* < **multus**), most.

plus, pluris, *n.* (*w. gen.*), more.

poeta, -ae, *m.*, poet.

politus, -a, -um, refined, elegant.

pono, ponere, posui, positus, to place, put.

populus, -i, *m.*, the Roman people.

possum, posse, potui, to be able (*w. infin.*).

post (*prep. w. acc.*) after; behind; (*adv.*), afterwards.

postea (*adv.*), later on, thereafter, afterwards.

posteri, -orum, *m. pl.*, posterity, those who come after.

posteritas, posteritatis, *f.*, the future; future generations.

posterus, -a, -um, next, following; (*of time*), in the future; (*m. pl.*), posterity.

potentia,-ae, *f.*, power, influence.

potius (*adv.*), preferably, rather; **potius...quam**, rather...than.

prae (*prep. w. abl.*), before, in front of.

praebeo, praebere, praebui, praebitus, to offer, supply, present.

praeceptum, -i, *n.*, instruction, precept.

praeclare (*adv.*), especially well; nobly; very well.

praeclarus, -a, -um, illustrious, glorious, distinguished.

praeco, praeconis, *m.*, one who makes public announcements; an auctioneer.

praeconium, -i, *n.*, the action of announcing or proclaiming in public, a declaration.

praedicatio, praedicationis, *f.*, announcement, public address.

praedico, -are, -avi, -atus, to announce, proclaim, declare publicly.

praeditus, -a, -um (*w. abl.*), endowed (*with*).

praeluceo, praelucere, praeluxi, to shine, light up.

praemium, -i, *n.*, reward, prize, legal benefit.

praepono, praeponere, praeposui, praepositus, to put before, put ahead, put first, prefer.

praesentio, praesentire, praesensi, praesensus, to apprehend beforehand; to predict, have a presentiment of.

praesertim (*adv. emphasizing single words or subordinate clauses*), especially; (*w.* **cum**), especially since; (*w.* **si**), especially if.

praestabilis, -e, excellent, outstanding, superior.

praesto (*adv.*), ready; at hand; present.

praesto, praestare, praestiti, praestitus (*w. dat.*), to excel, stand above.

praeter (*prep. w. acc.*), by; beyond; before.

praeterea (*adv.*); moreover; besides; after that.

praeteritus, -a, -um, past, bygone, former.

praetextatus, -a, -um, wearing the **toga praetexta** (*worn by boys up to the official age of manhood, about 16 or 17*).

praetor, praetoris, *m.*, Roman magistrate, second only to the consul; often presided over a public court.

primum (*adv.*), first, at first.

primus, -a, -um (*superl. adj.* < **prior**), first; (*w. gen.*), the first part (*of something*); **in primis**, especially; first and foremost.

princeps, principis, first in time, earliest.

principio (*adv.*), in the beginning, in the first place.

privatus, -a, -um, private.

pro (*prep. w. abl.*), for; in return for; before; on account of; in place of; instead of.

proavus, -i, *m.*, a great-grandfather; any distant ancestor.

probo, -are, -avi, -atus, to approve, commend.

prodo, prodere, prodidi, proditus, to hand down, transmit.

profecto (*adv.*), surely, certainly; without doubt.

profero, proferre, protuli, prolatus, to produce, bring before the public.

professio, professionis, *f.*, a formal declaration before a magistrate.

proficiscor, proficisci, profectus, to start a journey, set out, depart; (*of things*), to derive (*from*).

profiteor, profiteri, professus, to state openly, declare publicly; (**apud praetorem**), to submit one's name, register, enroll.

profligatus, -a, -um, ruined; desperate.

prope (*adv.*), almost, nearly, all but.

propinquitas, propinquitatis, *f.*, kinship, relationship by birth.

propinquus, -i, *m.*, a relative, kinsman.

propono, proponere, proposui, propositus (*refl. w. dat.*), to hold up to oneself (*as a model or example*).

propter (*prep. w. acc.*), because of, on account of.

propterea (*adv.*), for this reason, because of this, therefore.

prosequor, prosequi, prosecutus, to follow, accompany, attend upon.

prosperus, -a, -um, fortunate, favorable, prosperous.

prosum, prodesse, profui (*w. dat.*), to benefit, be of benefit to.

provincia, -ae, *f.*, a province; the provincial assignment of a pro-magistrate.

proxime (*superl. adv. < prope*), nearest.

proximus, -a, -um (*of place*), nearest, next; (*of periods of time*), immediately preceding, last.

publicus, -a, -um, public; (*subst.*) public official.

pudet, pudere, puduit and **puditum est** (*impers.*), to fill with shame, make ashamed, shame.

pudor, pudoris, *m.*, shame; modesty; honor.

puer, -i, *m.*, boy.

puerilis, -e, of a boy or boyhood; youthful.

pueritia, -ae, *f.*, boyhood, childhood.

pugna, -ae, *f.*, fight, battle.

pugno, -are, -avi, -atus, to fight, contend.

puto, -are, -avi, -atus, to think, suppose, consider.

Q

qua re (*adv.*), therefore, wherefore.

quaero, quaerere, quaesivi (-ii), quaesitus, to search for, hunt, seek; to try to obtain; to ask for.

quaestio, quaestionis, *f.*, a judicial investigation, trial.

quaestor, quaestoris, *m.*, the lowest-ranking elected magistrate in the Roman government, often assigned as a deputy to a higher magistrate.

qualis, -e, such as, as; **talis . . . qualis**, such . . . as.

quam (*conj. w. adj. and adv.*), how; (*w. comp. adj. or adv. introducing a comparison*), than; (*w. superl. adj. or adv.*), as . . . as possible.

quamquam (*conj.*), although.

quantum (*interrog. and rel. adv.*) to what extent?, to the extent to which; as much as, as far as.

quantus, -a, -um, how much? how great?; (*correlative*) **tantus . . . quantus**, as much . . . as.

quantuscumque, -acumque, -umcumque (*rel. adj.*), of whatever size; however great (*or small*).

quare (*interrog. and rel. adv.*), for what reason?, wherefore.

quasi (*adv.*), as it were, in a manner of speaking.

-que (*enclitic*), and.

quemadmodum (= **ad quem modum**; *interrog. and rel. adv.*), how?; as, in the manner in which.

queo, quire, quivi (quii), quitus, to be able.

qui (*adv.*; = *archaic abl. used as an adverb*), how.

qui, quae, quod (*rel. pron.*), who, which, what, that (*man, woman, thing, etc.*); (*interrog. adj.*), which? what? (*man, woman, thing, etc.*).

quia (*conj.*), because.

quidam, quaedam, quoddam (quiddam) (*indef. pron. and adj.*), some or a certain (*man, woman, thing*).

quidem (*particle*), indeed, certainly, to be sure (*usu. emphasizes the word it immediately follows*); **ne . . . quidem**, not even (*always brackets the word or phrase it emphasizes*).

quis, quid (*interrog. pron.*) who? what?; **quid** (*adv.*), why?

quispiam, quaepiam, quippiam (quidpiam), an unspecified person or thing; someone, something; anyone, anything.

quisquam, quicquam (*indef. pron.*), anyone, anything.

quisque, quidque (*pron. and adj.*), each, every.

quo (*interrog. and rel. adv.*), to what place? where ?; (*abl. sing. of rel. pron. used as conj.*), whereby, in order that.

quoad (*conj.*), as far as, as long as.

quocirca (*adv.*), therefore, and so.

quod (*conj.*), because.

quod si (*conj.*), but if.

quondam (*adv.*), formerly, once upon a time.

quoniam (*conj.*), since, because.

quoque (*adv. emphasizing the word it follows*), also, even, too.

quoquo (*adv.*), wherever.

quotiens (*interrog. and rel. adv.*), how many times? how often? (*rel.*), as often as; whenever.

R

ratio, rationis, *f.* (*w. gen.*), methodology, strategy, or system; a professional ethic directing one's actions.

recens, recentis, fresh, recent.

recipio, recipere, recepi, receptus, to receive, admit.

recolo, recolere, recolui, recultus, to resume a practice, pursuit, etc.

recordatio, recordationis, *f.*, remembrance, recollection.

recordor, recordari, recordatus, to call to mind, recall.

reficio, reficere, refeci, refectus, to restore, refresh, revive.

regio, regionis, *f.*, the geographical position or situation of a territory; a region.

regius, -a, -um, kingly, characteristic of a king; royal, on a regal scale.

reicio, reicere, reieci, reiectus, to refuse to admit, reject; to exclude.

relaxo, -are, -avi, -atus, to relieve the tension (*of someone, something, etc.*); to relax, unbend.

religio, religionis, *f.*, reverence for what is divine; the quality of evoking awe or respect.

relinquo, relinquere, reliqui, relictus, to leave, leave behind.

remissio, remissionis, *f.*, the act of relaxing; (*w. animi*), the relaxation of the mind.

removeo, removere, removi, remotus, to remove, withdraw.

reperio, reperire, repperi, repertus, to find.

repeto, repetere, repetivi (-ii), repetitus, to seek in return, to trace, search for.

reprehendo, reprehendere, reprehensi, reprehensus, to find fault with, rebuke; to mark with disapproval.

repudio, -are, -avi, -atus, to refuse, reject; to disregard as false or invalid.

requies, requietis, *f.*, rest, repose, relaxation.

requiro, requirere, requisivi (-ii), requisitus, to ask for, inquire about; to try to obtain; to demand.

res, rei, *f.*, thing, affair, occurrence, incident, event, matter, issue; (*leg.*), a case, trial; any point of law or legal issue; (*pl.*), achievements (*cf.* **res gestae**), exploits.

reseco, resecare, resecui, resectus, to cut back.

resigno, -are, -avi, -atus (*w.* **fidem**), to break an agreement.

respicio, respicere, respexi, respectus, to look back on.

respondeo, respondere, respondi, responsus, to answer, respond.

retardo, -are, -avi, -atus, to hold back, inhibit, discourage.

reus, -i, *m.*, the accused, a defendant.

revinco, revincere, revici, revictus, to convict of a falsehood; to rebut a charge.

revoco, -are, -avi, -atus, to call back, recall (*esp. for an encore*).

ridiculus, -a, -um, absurd, ridiculous.

Romanus, -a, -um, Roman, of Rome.

Rudinus, -a, -um, of or belonging to Rudiae, the birthplace of Ennius.

rusticatio, rusticationis, *f.*, country living.

rusticor, -ari, -atus, to live or stay in the country.

rusticus, -a, -um, of or belonging to the country; rustic, uncultured, unrefined.

S

saepe (*adv.*), often, continuously.

salus, salutis, *f.*, a means of (*judicial*) deliverance, security.

sanctus, -a, -um, holy, blessed, inviolate; scrupulous, upright, virtuous; secured by religious sanctions.

sane (*adv.*), certainly, truly, absolutely.

sapiens, sapientis, wise, learned, educated; (*subst.*), a wise man, philosopher.

sapientia, -ae, *f.,* wisdom, philosophy.

satis (*indecl. noun*), enough, sufficient; (*adv.*), sufficiently.

saxum, -i, *n.,* stone, rock, boulder.

scaenicus, -a, -um, of or connected with the stage; (*of persons*), of actors, stage performers.

scilicet (*exclamatory particle affirming an obvious fact*), to be sure! obviously! (*often w. sarcastic overtone*), of course! certainly!

scio, scire, scivi (-ii), scitus, to know (*as fact*); to have certain knowledge of.

scribo, scribere, scripsi, scriptus, to write.

scriptor, scriptoris, *m.,* writer, author.

se, see **sui.**

secundus, -a, -um, favorable, advantageous.

sed (*conj.*) but, on the other hand; (*conj. introducing a qualification of a previous idea*), but at the same time; (*with concessive force*), albeit, although.

sedes, sedis, *f.,* where an individual lives, a dwelling place, home.

sedulitas, sedulitatis, *f.,* assiduity, attention to detail.

segrego, -are, -avi, -atus, to separate, exclude.

semper (*adv.*), always.

sempiternus, -a, -um, lasting forever, perpetual, eternal.

senectus, senectutis, *f.,* the period of old age.

senex, senis, *m.,* old man (*a term of distinction usu. applied to historical figures with allusion to their venerability*).

sensus, -us, *m.,* the faculties of perception; any of the five senses.

sententia, -ae, *f.,* thought, opinion; (*leg.*), a vote, ballot.

sentio, sentire, sensi, sensus, to realize, perceive; to feel (*with the senses*).

sepulcrum, -i, *n.,* tomb.

sequor, sequi, secutus, to follow, pursue.

sermo, sermonis, *m.,* speech, conversation; a style of speaking.

servo, -are, -avi, -atus, to defend (*e.g., in court*); to save, keep safe.

severus, -a, -um, strict, old-fashioned.

sexaginta (*indecl. adj.*), sixty.

si (*conj.*) if.

sibi, see **sui.**

sic (*adv.*), so, thus, to such an extent.

simpliciter (*adv.*), easily, simply.

simul (*adv.*), at the same time, at once; **simul atque** (*conj.*), as soon as.

simulacrum, -i, *n.,* an image, statue, representation.

simulo, -are, -avi, -atus (*w. infin.*), to pretend.

sine (*prep. w. abl.*), without.

singularis, -e, singular, remarkable, unusual.

singuli, -ae, -a, one each.

situs, -a, -um, placed or lying in one's control or power.

sive (seu) (*conj.*), or if (*usu. following a conditional clause and introducing an alternate condition*); **sive . . . sive,** whether...or (*introducing each of two or more conditions*).

socer, soceri, *m.,* father-in-law.

societas, societatis, *f.,* tie, bond, society, connection.

solacium, -i, *n.,* relief in sorrow, solace; consolation or compensation (*spiritual, emotional, etc.*) for a loss.

soleo, solere, solui, solitus (*w. infin.*), to be accustomed.

solitudo, solitudinis, *f.,* solitude, the state of being alone; (*of places*), a deserted place, uninhabited country.

solus, -a, -um, alone, only.

somnus, -i, *m.,* sleep.

sono, -are, -avi, -atus, to give out a sound, utterance (*usu. of a particular nature or quality*).

spargo, spargere, sparsi, sparsus, to scatter, sprinkle.

spatium, -i, *n.,* a period, interval.

specto, -are, -avi, -atus, to see, look at.

spero, -are, -avi, -atus, to hope.

spes, spei, *f.,* hope.

spiritus, -us, *m.,* divine inspiration.

splendidus, -a, -um, splendid, magnificent.

stabilis, -e, stable, firm, secure.

stabilitas, stabilitatis, *f.,* stability, security.

statim (*adv.*), immediately, at once.

statua, -ae, *f.,* statue.

stimulus, -i, *m.,* something that rouses to fury, passion, or action; spur, goad.

sto, -are, steti, status, to stand.

strepitus, -us, *m.,* excessive sound; noise, noisy talking; clamour, uproar (*of a crowd, etc.*); din, turmoil (*of business, etc.*).

studeo, studere, studui (*w. infin.*), to devote oneself, be eager.

studiose (*adv.*), earnestly, assiduously; with serious application.

studium, -i, *n.* (*w. gen.*), the study (*of*).

suadeo, suadere, suasi, suasus (*w. dat. of person*), to persuade, give advice (*to*); to advise; to urge.

subicio, subicere, subieci, subiectus (*w. acc.* object, *dat. of person*), to furnish, supply (*something to someone*).

subito (*adv.*), suddenly, unexpectedly.

sublatus, past participle of **tollo**.

subtiliter (*adv.*), precisely, exactly, accurately, in too much detail.

sui, sibi, se, se (*reflex. pron.*), himself, herself, itself; (*pl.*), themselves.

sum, esse, fui, futurus, to be.

summus, -a, -um (*superl. adj.* < **superior**), the highest, greatest, supreme.

sumo, sumere, sumpsi, sumptus, to undertake (*an activity, etc.*); to take on, assume (*a duty, responsibility, etc.*).

superior, superioris (*comp. adj.* < **superus**), preceding in time, earlier, previous; (*w. proper names*), the elder.

supero, -are, -avi, -atus, to excell, surpass, outdo.

suppedito, are, -avi, -atus, to supply, make available.

suppeto, suppetere, suppetivi (-ii) (*of people*), to be available; (*of something*), to present itself when needed or required.

suscenseo, suscensere, suscensui, to be angry (*with*).

suscipio, suscipere, suscepi, susceptus, to undertake; (*w. infin.*) to attempt.

suus, -a, -um (*reflex. adj.*) his own, her own, its own; (*pl.*), their own.

T

tabula, -ae, *f.*, a written document; (*pl.*), public records.

tabularium, -i, *n.*, the record-office; public registry.

taceo, tacere, tacui, tacitus, to keep silent; be quiet.

talis, -e, such, of such a kind.

tam (*adv.*), so, so much; **tam . . . quam** (*correlative conj.*) so much . . . as.

tamen (*adv.*), still, nevertheless, however.

tamquam (*adv.*), as if, just as if, as though.

tandem (*adv.*), at length, at last.

tantus, -a, -um, so great, such great; **tantus . . . quantus**, of such a size . . . as, so great . . . as; **tantum** (*adv.*), only.

telum, -i, *n.*, weapon (*usu. defined in context, e.g., a dagger, knife, spear, etc.*).

temeritas, temeritatis, *f.*, whim; caprice; rashness.

tempestivus, -a, -um, timely, occurring at the right time; (*w.* **convivium**), a dinner party starting at an early hour (*i.e., an elaborate banquet*).

templum, -i, *n.*, temple; the inaugurated site of a temple; any inaugurated location.

tempus, temporis, *n.*, time, a moment or period, etc.; (*spec.*), conditions or circumstances surrounding or affecting a particular person, group, etc.

tenebrae, -arum, *f. pl.*, darkness, shadows; obscurity.

teneo, tenere, tenui, tentus, to hold, maintain, keep.

termino, -are, -avi, -atus, to set the limits of; to define; to mark the boundaries.

terra, -ae, *f.*, land, the earth; a country.

testamentum, -i, *n.*, a will.

testimonium, -i, *n.*, evidence given by a witness in a court of law.

togatus, -a, -um, wearing a toga; living as a citizen (*i.e., Roman*).

tolerabilis, -e, tolerable, able to be endured.

tollo, tollere, sustuli, sublatus, to remove, take away; to raise, lift up; to elevate to a position of superiority.

tot (*indecl. adj.*), so many.

totiens (*adv.*), so many times.

totus, -a, -um (*usu. w. defining gen.*), the whole of, all; whole, complete.

tracto, -are, -avi, -atus, to have to do (*w. something*), be experienced.

traho, trahere, traxi, tractus, to drag, draw, pull.

tranquillitas, tranquillitatis, *f.*, a peaceful condition.

tranquillus, -a, -um, calm, undisturbed, tranquil.

tribuo, tribuere, tribui, tributus, to grant, bestow.

triumphus, -i, *m.*, a triumphal procession, the highest award granted by the senate to a victorious general; the victory itself.

tropaeum, -i, *n.*, trophy commemorating a military victory; victory itself.

tu, tui, tibi, te, te (*pers. pron.*), you (*singular*).

tum (*adv.*), then, at that time (*in the past*).

tumulus, -i, *m.*, a burial-mound, grave, tomb.

tuus, -a, -um, yours, of you (*sing.*).

U

ubi (*interrog. adv.*), where?; (*rel. adv.*), where, when, as soon as.

ullo pacto, at all.

ullus, -a, -um, any.

ultimus, -a, -um, remotest in time, earliest.

umquam (unquam) (*adv.*), at any time, ever.

una (*adv.*), together with, at the same time.

universus, -a, -um, whole, altogether.

unus, -a, -um, one; only; alone.

urbs, urbis, *f.*, city.

usque (*adv.*), as far as; ever; continually.

usus, -us, *m.*, use, practice, experience.

ut (uti) (*conj. w. indicative*), as, when; (*w. subjunctive*), in order that, so that, that.

ut dicitur, as it is said; as people say.

uterque, utraque, utrumque, each, both.

utilitas, utilitatis, *f.*, material gain, personal advantage.

utor, uti, usus (*w. abl.*); to use, enjoy, possess; exploit.

V

valeo, valere, valui, valiturus, to be strong, be in good health; to have power, influence.

valetudo, valetudinis, *f.*, health.

vallo, -are, -avi, -atus, to surround (*i.e., to deny access*), hem in; to fortify (*w. a rampart, palisade, etc.*).

varietas, varietatis, *f.*, variety; the quality of being many different things, (*i.e., forms, aspects, natures, etc.*).

vehementer (*adv.*), aggressively, vehemently; seriously, gravely.

vel (*conj.*), or; **vel...vel**, either . . . or; (*adv.*), even.

vendo, vendere, vendidi, venditus, to sell, offer for sale.

venia, -ae, *f.*, indulgence, favor.

venio, venire, veni, venturus, to come.

venustas, venustatis, *f.*, the quality of being charming or delightful.

verbum, -i, *n.*, word, utterance; **verbum facere**, to say something, make a statement.

vere (*adv.*), truly, in truth.

vero (*adv.*), truly; (*particle with adversative force*), however, on the other hand (*often w.* **immo**).

verso, -are, -avi, -atus, to turn; (*pass.*), to be engaged in.

versor, versari, versatus, to live, stay.

versus, -us, *m.*, a line of verse, poetry.

verto, vertere, verti, versus, to turn.

verum (*conj.*), but, but yet.

verus, -a, -um, true, real, genuine; (*as noun*), **verum, -i**, *n.*, truth.

vester, vestra, vestrum, your, yours (*pl.*).

vetus, veteris, long-standing, well-established; veteran.

vetustas, vetustatis, *f.*, the people, customs, or institutions of the distant past; antiquity.

vicissim (*adv.*), in turn.

victus, -us, *m.*, food.

video, videre, vidi, visus, to see; (*pass.*), to appear, seem (*w. infin.*).

vigilia, -ae, *f.*, (*usu. pl.*) the action or fact of keeping watch; watchful attention; vigilance.

vinculum, -i, *n.*, bond.

vindico, -are, -avi, -atus, to lay claim, assert one's title (*to something*).

violo, -are, -avi, -atus, to violate.

vir, -i, *m.*, man; hero; husband.

virtus, virtutis, *f.*, moral excellence, character.

vis, vis, *f.* (*sing.*), force, power, violence; (*pl.*), physical strength, resources; (*of intellect, w.* **animus, mens**, *etc.*), capabilities, the ability or faculty (*of*).

vita, -ae, *f.*, life.

vitalis, -e, vital.

vivo, vivere, vixi, victus, to live, be alive.

vivum, -i, *n.*, the quick; the heart.

vivus, -a, -um, alive, living.

vix (*adv.*), scarcely, barely.

volo, velle, volui, to want, wish, desire (*w. infin.*).

voluntas, voluntatis, *f.*, free will, choice; personal inclination.

voluptas, voluptatis, *f.*, pleasure; organized formal entertainment.

vos (*pers. pron.*), you (*pl.*).

vox, vocis, *f.*, voice.

vulgaris, -e, common, ordinary.

CICERO'S PRO ARCHIA

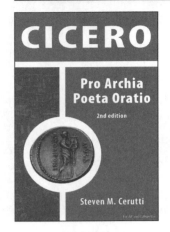

CICERO: Pro Archia Poeta Oratio, 2nd Ed.
Student Text by Steven M. Cerutti; Teacher's Guide by Linda A. Fabrizio

Cicero's Pro Archia Poeta Oratio is one of the best defenses of literature and the humanities. Cerutti's edition provides a comprehensive treatment of grammatical issues with a keen analysis of the rhetorical devices Cicero wove into the fabric of the oration.

This edition combines:
- the Latin text
- running vocabulary and commentary
- a brief bibliography
- glossary of proper names and places
- glossary of terms
- general vocabulary

The new *Pro Archia Poeta Oratio* Teacher's Guide by Linda A. Fabrizio is designed to meet the needs of the busy AP* teacher.

It includes:
- the oration in large print suitable for photocopying
- a literal translation of the oration
- a select bibliography
- a set of assessments/questions with sample answers.

Student Text: xxviii + 132 pp (2006) Paperback 6" x 9" ISBN 978-0-86516-642-4
Teacher's Guide: (2006) Paperback 8.5" x 11" ISBN 978-0-86516-616-5

A Must for Every Teacher. A Desideratum for Each Student.

CICERO PRO ARCHIA POETA ORATIO
A Structural Analysis of the Speech and Companion to the Commentary
Steven Cerutti

The "COMPANION" was written to accompany *Cicero: Pro Archia Poeta Oratio*, but makes an excellent independent resource for all *Pro Archia* texts.

Comprehensive diagrams and detailed sentence-by-sentence analysis provide the student with a reliable road map through the periodic structure of the Ciceronian sentence.

Features:
- Introduction, "Reading the Diagrams"
- Latin text with same-page and facing
  - Translation
  - Notes & Discussion
  - Latin text in sentence diagrams

xii + 118 pp (1999) Paperback 6" x 9" ISBN 978-0-86516-439-0

 BOLCHAZY-CARDUCCI PUBLISHERS, INC.
WWW.BOLCHAZY.COM

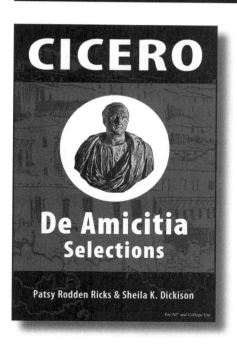

Cicero:
De Amicitia Selections
Patsy Rodden Ricks & Sheila K. Dickison

for AP and College Courses*

In *de Amicitia* Cicero gives insights on the relationship between two historical persons, Laelius *sapiens* and Scipio Aemilianus, as well as on the meaning of true friendship. He bases his positions on readings in Greek philosophy as well as on his own personal relationships. His writing is thought-provoking and his reasoning at times seems startlingly modern.

The two passages in this edition were chosen for the Advanced Placement Cicero syllabus and are also appropriate as a high-school or college-level introduction to Cicero's essays.

Features of this edition include:
- Introduction to Cicero and the historical setting of *de Amicitia*
- Latin text of selected passages: V.17–VII.23 and XXVII.100b–104
- English summary of all other passages in *de Amicitia*
- Grammatical, literary, historical, and vocabulary notes on facing pages
- Glossary of Figures of Speech
- Bibliography
- Full Vocabulary

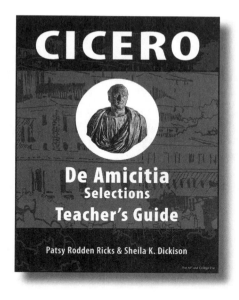

The *De Amicitia: Selections* Teacher's Guide by Patsy Rodden Ricks and Sheila K. Dickison features:
- Large size text for reproduction on transparencies
- Literal Translations
- Answers to Student Edition's Points to Ponder
- Sample assessments that include:
  - "spot" questions
  - translation passages
  - essay questions
  - vocabulary and grammar identifications
- Discussion questions to complement Points to Ponder
- Annotated Bibliography

Student Text: vi + 82 (2006) 6" x 9" Paperback ISBN 978-0-86516-639-4
Teacher's Guide: vi + 34 pp (2006) 8.5" x 11" Paperback ISBN 978-0-86516-641-7

*AP is a registered trademark of the College Entrance Examination Board, which was not involved in the production of, and does not endorse, this product.

Bolchazy-Carducci Publishers, Inc.
www.BOLCHAZY.com

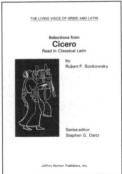
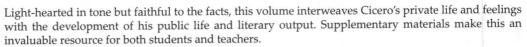

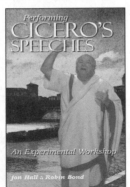
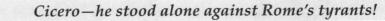

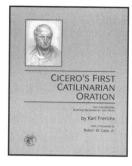
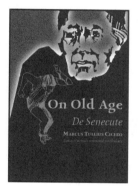
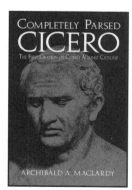

WORKBOOKS THAT WORK

WRITINGS OF FIVE SIGNIFICANT ANCIENT AUTHORS
Now Accessible to High School and College Students

Catullus • Cicero • Horace • Ovid • Vergil

The *Latin Literature Workbook Series* has been designed to reinforce a set of practical approaches to reading classical authors in the original.

These varying approaches appear as a set of exercises that enables the student to quickly reach a higher degree of comprehension on sight or prepared passages. These approaches include:

- Short analysis questions
- Translation passages
- Short and long essay questions on literary interpretation
- Lines for scansion
- Short answer questions and multiple choice questions on
  - The grammatical underpinnings of the passage
  - Figures of speech and rhetorical devices
  - Identification of characters, events, places, historical and mythical allusions

By working through passages provided in the books, the student will develop the habit of using these approaches and thereby develop a greater facility in reading and appreciating the ancient authors.

Each workbook was written by a team of authors—one, a university scholar with special expertise in the Latin literary text, and the other, a high school Advanced Placement Latin teacher. Because of the double focus of these experts, the series is sensitive to the needs of both college and high school students at the intermediate level. College professors will discover in this pedagogy a viable transition between introductory courses and intermediate level author courses.

The Latin text in each workbook consists of the AP* syllabus passages. These are representative samplings of the ancient authors' work—**small** enough perhaps to allow the professor to cover several authors in one course, yet **comprehensive** enough to be significant to the student.

A TEACHER'S MANUAL—not only a key or a set of answers—is planned for each workbook. These manuals will identify not just one answer but the salient points necessary for complete answers to the short analysis

questions. The "chunking" method of evaluating a translation is included for each translation passage. The topics essential to answer the essay question fully and instructions on how to use the six to one grading rubric are given. In addition, selected lines show the scansion marks according to the meter.

Use this series as a mini-textbook or as a part of training your students to read Latin authors with greater ease and pleasure, to comprehend and analyze content, and to develop skills and interest in literary analysis.

A HORACE WORKBOOK
David Murphy & Ronnie Ancona

Student Text: xii + 204 pp. (2005) 8½" x 11" Paperback
ISBN 978-0-86516-574-8
Teacher's Manual: xvi + 274 pp. (2006) 6" x 9" Paperback
ISBN 978-0-86516-649-3

A VERGIL WORKBOOK
Katherine Bradley & Barbara Weiden Boyd

Student Text: x + 262 pp. (2006) 8½" x 11" Paperback
ISBN 978-0-86516-614-1
Teacher's Manual: (Forthcoming) 6" x 9" Paperback
ISBN 978-0-86516-651-6

AN OVID WORKBOOK
Charbra Adams Jestin & Phyllis B. Katz

Student Text: (2006) 8½" x 11" Paperback
ISBN 978-0-86516-625-7
Teacher Manual: (Forthcoming) 6" x 9" Paperback
ISBN 978-0-86516-626-4

A CATULLUS WORKBOOK
Helena Dettmer & LeaAnn A. Osburn

Student Text: (2006) 8½" x 11" Paperback
ISBN 978-0-86516-623-3
Teacher Manual: (Forthcoming) 6" x 9" Paperback
ISBN 978-0-86516-624-0

A CICERO WORKBOOK
Jane W. Crawford & Judith A. Hayes

Student Text: (2006) 8½" x 11" Paperback
ISBN 978-0-86516-643-1
Teacher Manual: (Forthcoming) 6" x 9" Paperback
ISBN 978-0-86516-626-4

 BOLCHAZY-CARDUCCI PUBLISHERS, INC.
WWW.BOLCHAZY.COM